The
BikeBook

4th Edition

The BikeBook

4th Edition

Haynes ®

Complete bicycle maintenance

Contents

Written and edited by: Fred Milson
Technical editor: Paul Smith
Studio photography: Steve Behr
Tim Ridley
Polly Wreford
Paul Buckland
Illustrations: Ian Bott
Page make-up: Jeremy Phillips
James Robertson
Project manager: Louise McIntyre

Fred Milson has asserted his right to be identified as the author of this work.

First published 1994
Second edition published 1995
Third edition published 1999
Reprinted 2000 (with minor amendments)
Reprinted 2002
Fourth revised and updated edition, 2003
Reprinted 2003, 2004 and 2005

© Fred Milson 2003

Published by: Haynes Publishing
Sparkford, Yeovil, Somerset BA22 7JJ, UK

British Library Cataloguing-in-Publication Data:
A catalogue record for this book is available from the British Library.

ISBN 1 84425 000 8

Printed and bound in Great Britain by
J.H. Haynes & Co. Ltd, Sparkford.

While every effort is taken to ensure the accuracy of the information given in this book, no liability can be accepted by the author or the publishers for any loss, damage or injury caused by errors in, or omissions from, the information given.

CHAPTER 1

KNOW YOUR BIKE

This book has been written using as little cycling jargon as possible, but there are a few essential words you need to know.

Name that part

OTHER STYLES OF SADDLE

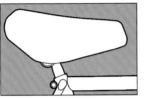

WOMEN'S SADDLE
Specially designed saddle, can be fitted to almost any bike.

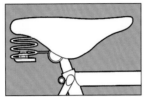

MATTRESS SADDLE
For utility bikes only.

SADDLE

SEAT POST

WHEEL NUTS

REAR BRAKE

CABLE S

MULTIPLE FREEWHEEL
OR CASSETTE

SEAT T

FRONT M

PE

ALTERNATIVE
GEARING SYSTEMS

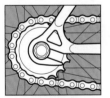

**SINGLE SPEED
FREEWHEEL**
Mainly used on kids' bikes and BMX.

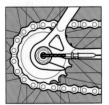

HUB GEARS,
As used on most utility bikes.

GEAR CABLE

REAR MECH

CHAIN STAYS

BOTTOM
BRACKET

CHAIN

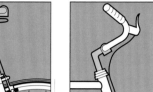

ALTERNATIVE HANDLEBARS

DROP HANDLEBARS
For racing, sports and touring bikes.

FLATS
For hybrids, utilities and Fast Road bikes.

RISER BARS
Used on utility bikes and MTBs.

BAR ENDS

HANDLEBARS

STEM

BRAKE LEVER

HEADSET

HEAD TUBE

TOP TUBE

FRONT BRAKE

DOWN TUBE

FRONT WHEEL

SPOKE

TYRE

CRANKS

FORKS

RIM

HUB

CHAINRINGS

QUICK RELEASE

TYRE VALVE

VARIOUS TYPES OF TYRE

KNOBBLY TYRES
For off-road mountain bikes.

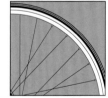

MOUNTAIN BIKE SLICKS
For use on the road.

700C and 27in.
Tyres for racers, tourers, hybrids and Fast Road bikes.

Adult bikes

Mountain bikes outsell every other type of bike because they are fun, fashionable and fine for use in town and country. But there are plenty of other types that might suit you better.

More than two millions bikes are sold every year in the Unitied Kingdom. Most of them are mountain bikes (MTBs), but other designs are slowly becoming more popular. Although when you look at hybrid or leisure bikes, it is obvious that they are a development of the MTB. Hybrids are particularly popular with regular commuters, thanks to their comfortable upright riding position and wide range of gears. Most hybrids also have sprung forks. But unlike mountain bikes, they have large, lightweight wheels and narrow tyres, so it takes much less effort to reach a reasonable speed on the road.

Folding bikes, usually with small wheels, are also popular with commuters. Some owners even bike to their local station, put their folded bike on the luggage rack and then ride the last lap to work at the other end. The best designs are fitted with a pair of skate wheels so that the bike can be pulled along like a suitcase when it is folded.

Evolution has also been at work on the sports bike in recent years, resulting in the Fast Road bike. Also known as the roadster and the flat handlebar road bike. Their main feature is flat, straight handlebars that are fitted with MTB-style gear changers. These enable the rider to sit comfortably upright, with a better view of the traffic than when riding a classic drop handlebar sports bike. The rest of the components are taken from good-quality racers, so Fast Road bikes are light, fast and responsive. As a result, they are usually more expensive than an MTB or hybrid, but are well worth the extra.

MOUNTAIN BIKES

The key to mountain bike (MTB) popularity is their versatility. The small frames and 26in wheels with well-cushioned tyres originated in California among riders who built them for plummeting down mountain sides. By coincidence, the same features suit city riders who need to bump up and down kerbs and ride through potholes. The bike shown is one variation on the Y-frame design, and has full suspension for cross-country use. This design is now very popular in the budget price range and for children's bikes. But hard tail MTBs with round or egg-shaped tubes, a sloping top tube and suspension at the front end only are the best all-rounders. And much lighter as well.

FOLDING BIKES

Nearly all folding bikes have small wheels so they can be folded down into the minimum package size. But small wheels fall int potholes and are harder to push along as well. So good quality folding bikes have some sort of suspension and high quality tyres to minimise these problems. When buying, bear in mind that the designs range from the clever to the crude. And that while the clever ones are fun to ride, the crude ones are very uncomfortable and often have a cramped riding position.

RACING BIKE

Welded aluminium frames have replaced steel ones on most sports and racing bikes. On the road, racers are much faster than MTBs but not so comfortable, although carbon forks and gel saddles can take the worst out of the bumps. Touring and Audax bikes are closely related to racers, although the frames and wheels are more heavily-built. They usually have triple chainsets giving 24 or 27 gears, including very low ratios for climbing steep slopes.

UTILITY BIKE

For city use, the upright riding position allows you to wear formal clothes but still cycle to work. Various components specially designed for utility bikes, including the Shimano C600 range, are fitted. Battery-powered electrical assistance is now available but at a price.

WOMAN'S BIKE

An open frame bike allows you the option of riding in a skirt but a mountain bike or hybrid with a sloping top tube is the better option for most women. See pages 12 and 13 for more information.

FAST ROAD BIKE

Fast road bikes have straight flat handlebars and short-reach stems, plus MTB-style handlebar gear changers and 27 speeds. But the frames are steeply-angled and lightweight, similar to the ones used on sports bikes. Most makers also fit light, 700C wheels with narrow tyres but others go for 550Cs with touring or slick MTB tyres. You can only position your hands on the handlebar grips, so you are forced into a fairly upright riding position. That is good for comfort over fairly short distances and gives you a good view of the surrounding traffic.

HYBRID BIKE

Hybrids frames are similar to MTB frames, usually with a sloping top tube for plenty of standover clearance. Hybrids tend to be slightly more expensive than basic MTBs, although you usually have to pay a little extra to get suspension forks and a sprung seat post. If you want mudguards, they are usually extra. When buying, look for brazed-on carrier fittings, a wide range of gears with convenient changers on the handlebars and light but robust wheels and tyres.

Men's bike set up

A good riding position is vital for comfortable and efficient cycling. Set the saddle height first and then adjust the position of the handlebars to get the angle of the back right.

Set your initial riding position following the advice on the opposite page. Then ride your bike for a few days while you get used to how it feels. If the riding position is roughly right, your weight should be shared fairly evenly between the saddle and the handlebars.

You must also find a comfortable position for the handlebars, allowing for a slight bend at the elbows to help absorb shocks.

On an MTB, set the handlebar height so that your back is roughly 45º to the ground. This position should feel very comfortable. But it may be difficult to achieve if your bike is fitted with an Aheadset-type stem, as they do not have a lot of adjustment for height. See pages 146 and 148 for advice.

On a sports bike, start with the top of the handlebar stem slightly below the top of the saddle. In that position, your back will be fairly flat when using the 'drops'. But there are alternative hand positions on the brake levers and the top part of the handlebars, which allow a more comfortable back angle of 30º to 40°. If need be, fit a stem with a longer or shorter extension or one that lifts the handlebars slightly.

You are most likely to feel uncomfortable where your bottom contacts the saddle. If so, check first that the saddle is horizontal. If it is, try moving it half an inch forward, then half an inch back – you have to find out what suits you. Some riders are more comfortable with the saddle nose pointed up or down just a fraction, but don't go any further than that. Try a different saddle if you can't get comfortable.

When buying a new bike or frame, go for the smallest one that fits you. As a guide, most of the seat post should be out of the frame when the saddle height is roughly correct. If you buy a frame that is too big, you will have to stretch too far to reach the handlebars.

UTILITY AND LEISURE BIKES
Frames on utility and leisure bikes are normally laid well back, so most of your weight inevitably falls on the saddle. There is no way of avoiding this completely but you could try lowering the handlebars or fitting straight ones if you are really uncomfortable. Toe clips are not usually fitted to utilities but you should still try to keep the ball of your foot over the pedal axle so that you can pedal fairly efficiently. As these bikes are mostly used for short journeys around town, the saddle can be set lower than normal. This allows the rider to plant one foot flat on the ground while sitting in the saddle, which is more comfortable when waiting at traffic lights and other hold ups.

Frame size

MOUNTAIN BIKES

MTBs are used for various purposes, so riders use many different riding positions. Set the basic saddle height in the same way as on a racer. But for cross-country riding, and even more for downhill, allow more bend at the knee so that you can easily put your foot down when it feels as if you are losing control. In addition, the back should be at roughly 45° to the ground. This allows you to see ahead without having to crank your head backwards. It also throws more weight onto the handlebars, holding the front wheel down and helping you to keep control over really rough ground or at high speed.

1 Frame size is usually measured from the centre of the bottom bracket axle to the centre of the top tube. But compact road frames are usually sold as small, medium or large. Take a test ride so you can check that a bike fits you properly, before buying.

2 Frames for racers, touring bikes and men's utility bikes are all roughly the same height from floor to top tube. You should aim for at least an inch and a half of clearance between the top tube and your crotch, when your feet are planted flat on the floor.

3 Mountain bike frames are built smaller and lower, so you should have at least three inches clearance over a horizontal top tube. But most MTBs have a sloping top tube, and with this shape of frame, top tube clearance should be at least 4in or 5in.

Initial riding position

1 To set saddle height, sit on the saddle wearing the shoes you will usually ride in. Move the seat post up or down until your leg is very slightly bent with the pedal at its lowest position. A few days later, try raising the saddle half an inch.

2 Then set the reach to the handlebars by hanging a weighted piece of string from the knee, with the cranks horizontal. Move the saddle backwards and forwards until the plumb line passes through the pedal axle.

BASIC SADDLE HEIGHT

Whatever type of bike you ride, set the saddle height so that when sitting on it with your leg stretched right out, you can comfortably place the ball of your foot on the ground. Your leg should then be bent a little when the pedal is at its lowest point. This is only the starting point, so try a few rides before deciding whether

moving the saddle up or down a little would suit you better. If you have not ridden much before, don't worry if it feels as if your leg muscles are being stretched. The stiffness should soon go away. But if you are still uncomfortable after a few days, see page 13 for tips on improving your riding position.

11

Women's bike set up

Women are a different shape from men. But only recently have bike and component manufacturers started taking this into account.

Women tend to be shorter and lighter than men, with proportionately shorter arms and smaller hands. On the other hand, women's legs are longer but the pelvis is a very different shape. Unless these physical differences are taken into account, cycling can feel like drudgery for females.

Your first step is to choose a bike with the smallest possible frame, taking your height into consideration. Women of average height will be fine with a 15in (38cm) MTB frame or a 19in (49cm) racing or touring frame, although taller women may have to go up to a 17in (43cm) MTB or a 21in (54cm) racer.

Traditional open frames that allow you to ride in a skirt are still around, both new and second-hand. But this type of frame is not stiff or strong enough for anything more than short city runs. Far better, even if you want the option of cycling in a skirt, is a hybrid or leisure bike with a steeply sloping top tube. Go for one with 26in wheels (same size as an MTB) if you are short or are not yet confident about dealing with the traffic. When bought new, these bikes are usually pretty comfortable, with suspension seat posts, comfy gel saddles, short-reach brake levers and an adjustable stem for the handlebars.

If you cycle for fun, not just to get around, go for a mountain bike designed specially to suit women. These tend to be more expensive than leisure bikes but short reach brake levers, special suspension to suit your lower body weight and short cranks should all be fitted as standard.

There are also road bikes built to a women specific design. If you go for one of these, shorter women should choose one with smaller 650C wheels. This type of bike is nearly always fitted with combined brake and gear levers. If you have to stretch your hand to reach the brakes, Shimano supply special plastic shims for their STi levers that bring the levers closer to the handlebars.

Whatever bike you are going to ride, set the initial riding position as for a man's bike on page 11 and then experiment with small alterations as time goes by. If a small frame does not allow you to raise the saddle enough, fit a longer seat post. Some women will also feel happier with short 165mm (6.5in) cranks, although these are expensive and you can often get away with standard 170mm items. If the handlebars are too much of a stretch, fit a stem that brings them closer and adjust the height of the handlebars so they are just a little below saddle height.

WOMAN-SPECIFIC MOUNTAIN BIKE
Compared to a man's bike, a woman-specific design has a frame with a shorter top tube and the bike is shorter overall. This gives less of a reach to the handlebars, and makes the bike lighter and more agile. The saddle is also shorter and wider; the handlebar grips are smaller in diameter; and the stem has a short extension, with enough lift to position the handlebars only slightly below the saddle height.

OPEN-FRAME WOMAN'S BIKE
Bikes with the skirt-friendly open-frame design are still available. The best ones are modernised, as here, using MTB-style components like a suspension seat post for comfort and a wide range of gears. The frames are usually made of steel, so they are heavy, and they inevitably flexes in the middle when cornering. This sort of bike should cost little more than a normal MTB.

Adjusting MTB brake levers

1 On an MTB, see if you can reach the brake levers, without changing your grip on the handlebars. Vee brakes only need a two finger pull for full power but the first joint should wrap comfortably round the lever.

2 If you cannot wrap your fingers round the lever easily, look for the reach adjuster screw in the angle between the brake lever and the handlebar. You will need a Phillips screwdriver or a hexagon key to adjust it.

3 Then wind the adjuster in clockwise until you can apply the brakes comfortably, just with two fingers. If there is no adjuster, or the adjuster does not have much effect, consider fitting a pair of short-reach brake levers.

Further modifications

1 To allow for proportionately longer legs, it is very simple to fit an extra long seat post to most frames. Seat post diameter does vary, so make sure you get the correct size. Narrower handlebars are also worth considering.

2 If your problem is discomfort over bumps, the answer is a suspension seat post. This fits in place of an ordinary seat post and absorbs the bumps with a strong internal spring. Fit a female-friendly saddle as well.

3 If you want to experiment with different riding positions, consider fitting an adjustable stem. Undoing the front bolt allows you to raise or lower the handlebars, which also alters the distance to the handlebars a little.

SITTING COMFORTABLY

Saddles for women are shorter and wider than standard, although wide saddles can lead to chaffing in some cases. They should also have plenty of gel padding, and maybe a cut-out. Be careful there are no sharp edges or ridges around the cut-out. However, some women find cut-outs increase the pressure on sensitive areas. Remember that most women prefer the saddle nose tilted down a little.

YOUR RIDING POSITION IS NOT RIGHT IF:

Your bottom is sore after a few miles.
Cure: check that the saddle is the correct height and not far from horizontal. Then try moving it forwards a bit. And fit a gel saddle.

You slip towards the nose of the saddle.
Cure: lift the nose of the saddle a little.

You feel stretched out over the frame.
Cure: raise the handlebars a bit and fit a shorter stem.

Your neck and shoulders get stiff or ache.
Cure: raise the handlebars so you can look forwards without kinking your neck.

Your wrists hurt.
Cure: raise the handlebars or lower the saddle.

Your knees hurt.
Cure: check saddle height is correct. Make sure the pedals turn freely and that your feet are not held too firmly in the toe clips.

Your feet hurt.
Cure: stiffer shoes, preferably proper cycling shoes. Do not overtighten your shoe laces or toe straps.

WOMEN'S BIKE SPECIALISTS

If you need advice on buying a bike, or want to buy special woman-sized components, accessories and clothing, there are now several shops specialising in serving female cyclists. Most bike co-ops also have women members who are keen to help female riders. If your budget is limited, they will advise you on how to adapt a man's bike. But if you cannot get comfortable, even on a bike specifically designed for women, there are specialist frame builders who build made-to-measure bikes for women. These usually have ultra small frames fitted with 26in wheels and shortened cranks.

Kids' bikes

When kids learn to ride a bike, they gain so many things: self-confidence, early mechanical skills, road sense, even adventure. Provided they get good training in road skills right from the start, it's a very positive experience.

Size counts a lot when it comes to children's bikes. You will be tempted to buy a bike that a child will grow into, but you should resist. They will find it much more difficult to gain confidence on a bike they can only just control.

Tiny, 14in-wheel and 16in-wheel bikes are usually fitted with a very crude chainset and steering bearings. Once you have reached the stage of looking at 20in wheel bikes, try to find one with adult-style steering bearings and chainset, especially if you are buying second-hand. You will find it much easier to get hold of replacement parts and easier to do routine maintenance as well. However, multi-speed gears are unnecessary and are likely to be a constant source of problems until the child can handle a 24in bike.

24in-WHEEL BIKES
From eleven onwards, a scaled-down adult bike is fine. If you go for one with a 14in or 15in (35cm or 38cm) frame and a sloping top tube, there will be plenty of step-over clearance and it will allow for several years of growth. Don't forget that you can fit a longer seat post in the years to come but toe clips should only be fitted from twelve onwards. If you plan to keep the bike for some time, it is worth going for a bike one or two steps up from budget level as the higher-quality components will need less maintenance and usually turn out to be much easier to work on.

20in-WHEEL BIKES

Suitable for girls and boys eight to eleven, this size of bike can either have a single gear, which means simplicity, crash resistance and low maintenance, or scaled-down adult equipment, including gearing. This is exciting but may not keep working for very long. The one shown has an immensely strong Y-frame, a design based on the latest adult MTBs.

PLAY BIKES WITH 14in WHEELS

Up to four years old. OK for giving the very youngest children a taste for cycling but do not leave the stabilisers on for too long as they can become a substitute for learning to ride properly.

16in-WHEEL BIKES

One stage up from play bikes, 16in wheel machines suit kids from $4^{1}/_{2}$ to $6^{1}/_{2}$. Mountain bike styling gives this bike a very robust character.

GIRL'S BIKE WITH 20in WHEELS

With a deep additional bracing tube across the frame, this type of girl's bike is very strong. Nevertheless, a boy's bike with a sloping top tube would do much the same job. Take a few minutes to explain how the gears work to the rider.

Kids' bike set up

Don't leave your child's riding position to chance or other kids. Set it up carefully for safety and easy control.

Until a child has achieved a high level of bike control and road awareness, insist on setting their riding position yourself and check it every few months as they grow. The main thing is to keep the saddle low enough to allow them to plant the balls of both feet firmly on the ground, while still sitting on the bike. When they get old enough to handle a 24in-wheel bike, set the saddle height as you would on an adult bike.

There should be at least 2in of standover clearance above the top tube on a conventional frame and 3in on a sloping-top tube frame. Less clearance than that means the frame is too large.

Don't forget to check the reach as well. If a child has to lean forward to reach the handlebars, maybe you should fit a stem with a shorter extension.

Whatever style of bike they ride, children should sit more upright than adults to encourage them to look ahead down the road.

Parents report that the easiest way to teach kids how to ride is to set the saddle height low enough to let them plant their feet on the ground with the bike upright and legs slightly bent, then remove the pedals as explained on page 86 and let the kid loose. They'll naturally start to scoot the bike along with their feet, learning how to steer and use the brakes as they go. Once they've gained some confidence, the saddle can be raised little by little until they're starting to lift both feet off the ground. At that point, introduce straight line and slalom exercises and once they can steer accurately, on with the pedals and away!

FEET FLAT ON THE GROUND

Until a child has pretty well perfect bike control, keep the saddle low so that they can slip off it and get their feet down quickly if necessary. This will help to prevent scraped knees and damage to the bike as well. This bike has 20in wheels with reflectors fitted between the spokes to draw the motorist's attention both day and night.

STAY IN YOUR PLACE

When you are out with the children, insist they ride in front of you so that you can see everything that's happening. Do not ride too close or you'll have to keep on braking and there is also the possibility of crashing into them, if somebody in front stops unexpectedly.

SLOPING TOP TUBE

The sloping-top tube design works well for younger children, giving plenty of standover height.

SPECIAL BITS

Most kids' bikes are small versions of an adult's bike. But some have special headsets and one-piece chainsets that are quite awkward to work on. The headsets are similar to the Aheadset featured on page 168, while the chainset and special bottom bracket is covered on page 101.

TINY BIKES FOR TINIES

An enclosed space or garden is best for very young riders, where they can pick up self confidence in complete safety. Lay on slalom tracks and figure-of-eight steering tests for fun and to develop and improve control skills.

BMX bikes

Riding a BMX develops fantastic bike control skills and opens up a world of excitement and friendly competition.

BMXs are designed for maximum bike control at fairly slow speeds. The frames are built for strength rather than speed and the basic design does not vary a lot, although there are various different styles of riding. The most popular ones are race, street and freestyle. Only one size of frame is normally available, though the saddle adjusts up and down to cater for riders of varying height.

There is only one gear on these bikes, which means you can only vary the gearing by fitting a larger or smaller chainring. However, basic BMXs use a one piece chainset, see page 101, so you cannot change the gearing on these anyway. Higher up the price range, the chainsets are similar to normal cotterless ones and it is possible to change the chainring, see page 92.

Maybe the hardest part of a BMX to understand is the braking system. Most BMXs are fitted with compact U brakes front and back. However, many tricks involve spinning the handlebars, impossible without a special device called a rotor head. This features a back brake cable that splits into two near the brake lever. The cable adjusters screw into a loose plate at the top of the headset with the nipples located in the middle plate. A second pair of cables connects to the middle and lower plates but join into one again before reaching the back brake. When you spin the handlebars, the stem and top plate revolve, but the bottom mounting plate stays still, so the cables do not get tangled up.

Some BMX riding styles place a very heavy load on the frame and mechanical parts, so bear in mind that the manufacturer's guarantee probably only covers normal riding.

SAFETY POINT

When a bike is being ridden on the road, including any BMX, the law says it must have two independent brakes, both of them in working order. Haynes strongly endorses this legal requirement.

However, riding BMXs without brakes is very popular on the streets. So we urge parents to check from time to time that the brakes have not been removed from any BMX bikes in their household, and to ground the rider until the brakes have been re-fitted.

Setting up a BMX bike

1 The front U brake is fitted with a cable pipe that fits into a socket on one of the brake arms. Check occasionally that the cable pipe still moves freely. When setting up the brakes, keep the straddle wire as short as possible, for maximum braking efficiency.

2 When front or rear pegs are fitted, you'll have to use a socket set with a 10in or 12in extension to tighten up or undo the wheel nuts. This is not the easiest task but if you get somebody else to steady the handlebars or the saddle, that will help a lot.

3 To check the chain tension, try lifting the chain at the mid-point of its bottom run. It is correct when you can lift it $\frac{1}{2}$in. To adjust, undo the wheel nuts, move the wheel to the new position, check it is central and finally, tighten the wheel nuts a little at a time.

4 To prevent distortion of the clamp when adjusting the handlebar angle, undo one nut half a turn, then the diagonally opposite one the same amount. Undo the other two in a similar way and continue half a turn at a time. Reverse the procedure when tightening.

Adjusting rotor rear brakes

1 Screw in the cable adjuster on the frame as far as possible. Then loosen off the straddle wire yoke and move it up the cable until it is about $\frac{1}{2}$in from the frame and retighten. This will help to reduce the amount of pull needed to apply the brakes.

2 Release one end of the straddle wire and run it round the yoke. Refit the straddle cable to the brake arm, tension the straddle wire with pliers and then tighten the clamp bolt. There should be a right angle between the brake arm and the straddle cable.

3 Now check the cable assembly just below the handlebars. Make sure that the middle plates are free to move, and lubricate lightly. Adjust the brake cables so that both moving plates are an equal distance apart at their ends and level with the ground.

4 Test the tension on the top section of the rear brake cables. If they are slack, increase the tension using the cable adjuster near the brake lever and the adjusters on the top plate. Then test the back brake, using the cable adjuster on the frame if necessary.

BMX PEDALS

If the frame or cage around the pedals gets bent or distorted, fit replacements immediately, or they can cause accident or injury.

As the pedals take a battering every time a BMX is dropped, and that can be quite often, fit good-quality replacements as they will take the punishment better.

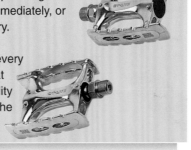

Personal safety

Helmet wearing is voluntary, not a legal requirement, but few bike riders are now bold enough to venture on to the roads without one.

Do not rush in and buy a helmet at the first shop you come to. Find one instead that has a good selection of helmets from a wide variety of different makers and employs experienced staff. Then ask them to advise you about the suitability of the different designs for your kind of cycling.

Try on plenty of types and makes of helmet and don't give up until you find one with a really good fit. One test is that if you are able to move the helmet backwards and forwards with your hands when the chin strap is properly adjusted and fastened, it is too big. Not only will it be uncomfortable, it will also give you much less protection and may even slip off if it is ever put to the test.

Look particularly for well-designed ways of adjusting the fit, such as interchangeable pads of varying thicknesses to fit in pockets around the edge of the helmet. The other feature to look for is a nape strap or retention bracket at the back of the neck.

Apart from the fit of the helmet, the other main factor governing rider comfort is ventilation. Make sure there are plenty of air channels running from front to back because although a helmet may not feel hot in the shop, it certainly will after ten miles of hard pedalling. However, too many full-length ventilation channels can weaken a helmet, so make sure there are plenty of strengthening elements running across the helmet as well.

The minimum legal requirement for any cycle helmet sold in the UK and the rest of Europe is that it must be CE certified and conform to the EN1078 European Standard. However, the Snell Foundation standard is generally regarded as even higher.

1 Make sure you buy a well-fitting helmet. If the fit is right, the helmet will sit quite low on your brow but high enough to allow unobstructed vision when you're looking upwards or sideways.

2 Inside the helmet, if a retention bracket is fitted, the touch-and-close fastening system enables you to position the bracket accurately, just below the bulge of the skull.

1 You will need a waterproof jacket sooner or later. It will only be used in bad weather, so a fluorescent yellow one with strips of reflective material is the best choice as it will help you to be seen.

2 Proper cyclists gloves are a good investment. Go for ones with gel-padded palms. The gel reduces vibration from the road while the glove protects your hands from abrasions in a crash.

3 Cycling gear for children is available in all sorts of designs. But the important thing is to buy a helmet that is endorsed by their particular hero, or their favourite story, so they wear it willingly.

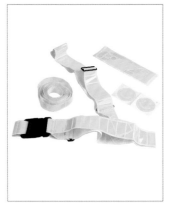

4 The best value in bike safety is a reflective belt and matching arm bands. They are effective night and day. But reflectors on the pedals are even more effective because they move all the time.

3 When properly adjusted, a retention bracket prevents the helmet tipping backwards. If this happens, it is irritating and reduces the effectiveness of the helmet in a crash.

4 The straps must fit naturally either side of the ears. If they don't, go for a different helmet. The adjusters should sit below the ear lobes and the buckle tucks under the chin.

5 Some helmets are fitted with an external adjuster to get the fit exactly right. But most manufacturers rely on interchangeable pads of varying thickness to do this.

CRASHED HAT

The foam shock absorbing material in a helmet compresses during a crash and doesn't regenerate. As a result, some manufacturers offer to inspect a helmet after a crash. The foam also becomes less effective over a period of time, so it is best to replace any helmet that has been in an accident, however slight. To encourage this, some makes offer free replacement after an accident. However, bear in mind that if you leave the cheapest helmets aside, paying a higher price does not necessarily get you a better product.

KIDS' HELMETS

To be fully effective, helmets for children have to be relatively larger than adult ones, so they sometimes look as if they are perched on top of the head. However, they must fit at least as well as any adult helmet and according to the same guidelines.

CHAPTER 2

TOOLS & TECHNIQUES

Before you rush out and buy a lot of new tools, take a look at the
ones around the house and in the garage already. You may have a
basic bike tool kit sitting there, just waiting to be used.

Basic tool kit

Most people spend more than half their bike maintenance time cleaning and oiling the chain and the gear mechanisms. If you spend less time than that, or no time at all, you are not doing it right.

Sooner or later you will need most of the tools shown on this page, although you are unlikely to need them all immediately. But you will certainly need a can of oil and some chain lubricant before you can do even the most basic maintenance. A general-purpose aerosol spray can be used for most other jobs but the specialised bike lubricants are more effective and last much longer, especially in the wet. The ones that leave a solid lubricant behind when they evaporate are probably best. For chains, however, many riders use a wax-based lubricant, perhaps backed up by an aerosol. So even if the top layer of lube gets washed off in a downpour, the waxy base layer will cling on longer and prevent excessive wear.

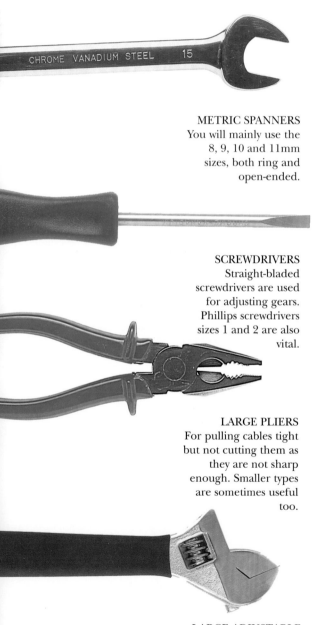

METRIC SPANNERS
You will mainly use the 8, 9, 10 and 11mm sizes, both ring and open-ended.

SCREWDRIVERS
Straight-bladed screwdrivers are used for adjusting gears. Phillips screwdrivers sizes 1 and 2 are also vital.

LARGE PLIERS
For pulling cables tight but not cutting them as they are not sharp enough. Smaller types are sometimes useful too.

LARGE ADJUSTABLE SPANNER
For use only on headsets and bottom brackets, although even for these jobs, a purpose-made spanner is better.

TEFLON-BASED AEROSOL LUBRICANT

CHAIN CLEANING MACHINE

SPECIALISED CHAIN LUBE

DRY LUBRICANT

CYCLE OIL

CLEANING BRUSH

SPROCKET BRUSH/RAKE

CHAIN MAINTENANCE

WAX-BASED CHAIN LUBRICANTS

OILS AND GREASES

HIGH QUALITY SPRAY LUBE

PTFE-BASED SPRAY LUBRICANT
Chases away water from chain and gears.

COPPER-BASED ANTI-SEIZE GREASE

GREASE INJECTOR PACK
For use on bearings and brake pivots

WATERPROOF GREASE
For packing bearings

TOOTHBRUSH
You will sometimes find it easier and quicker to degrease components with a toothbrush than anything else.

UTILITY KNIFE
For cutting handlebar tape, electrical insulation and cable tidies.

HEXAGON KEYS
The long ball-ended type is shown here. Use the ball-end for working in awkward corners and the plain end when you have to undo something really tight.

ENGINEER'S HAMMER
A 16oz or 20oz hammer is excellent for sharp, accurate blows. This type of hammer is much less likely to slip than others.

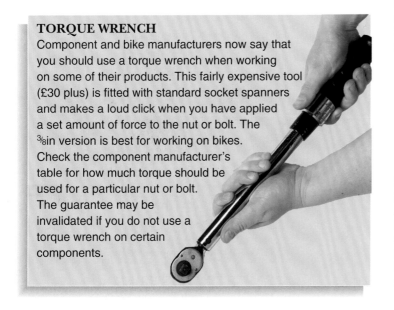

TORQUE WRENCH
Component and bike manufacturers now say that you should use a torque wrench when working on some of their products. This fairly expensive tool (£30 plus) is fitted with standard socket spanners and makes a loud click when you have applied a set amount of force to the nut or bolt. The ³⁄₈in version is best for working on bikes. Check the component manufacturer's table for how much torque should be used for a particular nut or bolt. The guarantee may be invalidated if you do not use a torque wrench on certain components.

Working techniques

Once you have got your tools together, you have to learn how to use them without damaging the components you are working on.

Nuts and bolts have a six-sided shape, usually spoken of as a hexagon. If you damage the hexagon with a badly fitting spanner, it will be a nuisance until the day you replace it. To avoid this, use a tightly fitting ring spanner whenever you can. If you have to use an open-ended spanner and it feels loose on the hexagon, find one with a better fit. If you cannot, try wedging a small coin or a washer in the jaws of the spanner to make it tighter.

The length of each spanner is related to the amount of force needed to tighten each size of nut, so there is no need to use a lot of muscle. You should be able to tighten up anything sufficiently using the pull of three fingers. If the amount of effort required to tighten a nut or bolt suddenly increases, stop tightening immediately as the bolt is probably about to break or you are damaging the thread.

You can apply a bit of extra force when tightening a nut or bolt that keeps on coming loose. But here it is better to fit a self-locking nut or use Loctite thread-locking compound.

Socket head bolts (also known as Allen bolts) look great because they are so neat. But, unlike nuts or bolts, which you can always remove one way or another, damaged socket head fixings are very difficult to remove. So check that the socket is clean to ensure that the hexagon key goes to the bottom of the socket and make sure also that the hexagon key is an exact fit. Do not use cheap, silver-painted hexagon keys as they are too soft. If you have a handful of various hexagon keys and not a proper set, only use the ones with a metric size engraved on the side. That should ensure they are strong enough.

Phillips screwdrivers are quite likely to damage the screw heads unless you use one with a hardened tip. And push hard on the end of the handle to prevent it slipping.

1 Whenever possible, use a ring spanner or socket in preference to any other type. They grip a nut or bolt on all six corners, so if you are careful, there is little chance of the spanner slipping and damaging the hexagon.

2 Compared to a ring spanner, an open-ended one is more likely to slip because they only grip on two corners. When you have to use an open-ended, try to prevent it slipping by steadying your hand against another component nearby.

5 Socket head fixings tend to fill with mud. So clean them out and check that the hexagon key goes all the way to the base of the socket, before using any force. Otherwise the hexagon key may slip round in the socket and damage it.

6 When a socket head fixing is buried deep in a component, you will only be able to reach it with the long leg of a hexagon key. Slip a close-fitting length of tubing over the shorter end, so you have enough leverage.

GOOD SPANNER WORK

Always try to pull a spanner towards you as that reduces the chances of injury if the spanner slips. When you push a spanner away from you and it slips, your hand can end up anywhere, gouging a lump out of your knuckle on the way.

3 A set of open-ended spanners comes in very useful when you need to hold a bolt still while you undo the nut. You have to do this when a bolt turns before the nut comes undone, and when working on some cable clamps.

7 Phillips screws often crop up on gear mechs and pedals. Check the screwdriver isn't worn and position it in a straight line with the screw before you apply pressure, or it might slip and make it difficult to remove the fixing at all.

4 Socket sets are not usually regarded as bike tools but they are ideal for jobs where the nut is buried. On some pedals, for example, you can only reach the cone lock nut with a socket and extension. They are also good on crank bolts.

8 When steel gets distorted, it is often possible to bend it back again, gripping it in a vice or using a couple of adjustable spanners. But this rearranges all the molecules in the metal and tends to harden it. This work-hardening process takes effect right away, so it is always best to put the damage right in one go. Try to avoid using a series of separate small adjustments.

Working on cables

If the brakes and gears do not operate smoothly, your bike will never feel right. But if you use the right cables and fit them carefully, you can bring back that feeling of precise control.

When new brake or gear cables are required, take a look at the outer casing as well as the inner wire. You can usually get away with replacing just the inner. But if the outer casing is kinked or damaged in any way, or the plastic covering is peeling off, that should be replaced as well.

Only buy stainless steel inner cables because they are naturally slippery. As a result, they will only need a light coat of bike oil when you assemble them and a few more drops of oil if they ever become stiff or sticky. They are also stretch resistant, which makes the brakes less spongy. It also improves the operation of the indexing on the gears.

If you have to fit a new outer casing as well, remember that the diameter of the outer brake cables is noticeably bigger than the one for the gears. You can buy the inner and outer as a package or separately. Either way, go for high quality outer cable because it is less squashy than the cheaper types. That will again reduce sponginess in the operation of the brakes and improve the way the gears work. And fit metal ferrules around the ends of the outer cables as that prevents them unravelling. It also improves the operation of the gears.

You can also buy top quality cables as complete sets. In these, the outer cable is usually lined with a low friction material, or there is a separate low friction liner made of something like Teflon. This means they do not need lubrication of any sort, although the exposed part of the gear cables should be wiped clean with an oily rag to prevent grit finding its way along the cable. Some sets even have rubber seals around the ends of the outers to keep water out. These high-quality cables are worth paying a little extra for, especially if you ride a lot off road or through the winter.

The short cable running from the frame to the rear gear mechanism is more likely to get contaminated with dirt and water than any other. So when replacing the rear gear cable, always fit one of the specially made-up replacements to ensure that the rear gear operates smoothly.

There are two types of brake cable, one has a pear-shaped nipple and the other a drum-shaped one. They are sometimes supplied fitted to the opposite end of a cable, allowing you to just cut off the one that is not needed. If the nipple is a very tight fit in the brake lever, smooth off the edges lightly with a file.

Inspecting cables

1 The most likely place for a brake cable to fray is below the cable clamp. This does not immediately affect the strength of the cable, but you could have problems tightening up the cable by pulling more through the clamp bolt. Fit a new cable as soon as convenient because the fraying will eventually weaken it.

2 When just a single wire has unwound from a brake cable, you can often get away with cutting off the loose wire with a sharp pair of cable cutters. But eventually the cut end inside the outer cable will lift and stop the cable moving smoothly. Fit a new inner cable immediately, if you suspect this has happened.

3 Gear cables are thinner than the ones for brakes, so they should be replaced when they come untwisted. To prevent this happening, fit a cable cap on the end of the cable. And keep the exposed parts of the gear cables clean, not forgetting the cable guides under the bottom bracket.

Cutting standard outer cables

Most recent bikes have slotted cable stops so you can pull out the outer cables without undoing the inners. This makes it easier to squirt lubricant down the outer cable.

1 To cut standard outer cable, squeeze the cutter lightly so the jaws slide between the coils of wire first. Then squeeze harder to cut the metal part.

2 If the wire cutter leaves a jagged end (bottom cable), clean it up with the cutters or a grinder so it is smooth like the top one.

3 When replacing outer cable, use the old one as a pattern so you get the length right. Or cut slightly too long and measure against the bike.

4 Outer cables should be fitted with a metal ferrule at each end. They prevent any fraying and ensure that the outer cable is seated correctly and firmly in the cable stops.

5 Do not try to fit a new inner cable into a damaged outer as it will soon start to fray. If this happens, pull the inner cable back and cut off the damaged end of the outer.

TOOLS FOR WORKING ON CABLES

SIDE CUTTERS
◆ You need a good pair of side cutters before you start replacing cables. Ordinary pliers often include wire cutters but they tend to squash the cable, not cut it.

SPECIAL CABLE TOOL
◆ Purpose-made cable cutters, as supplied by Shimano, Park and Cyclo amongst others, work better than side cutters. They work neatly and cleanly on both inner and outer cables.

CABLE PULLER
◆ Better than a third-hand tool as they work on gears as well as brakes.

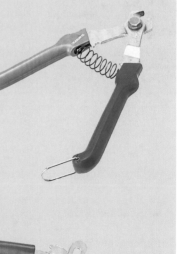

Finishing touches

1 Once you have fitted a new cable and checked that the gears or the brakes are working properly, use heavy pliers to squeeze a metal cable cap onto the end of the cable.

2 Leave about 2in of spare but bend it slightly to make sure it cannot get caught up in the mechanism. If you do this, a gear or brake cable should last for years of normal use.

Problem solving

Maybe you ride an old bike that somebody else has butchered. Maybe you cut loose with a hammer yourself. Luckily, most bike problems can be fixed.

Stick to the instructions and advice in this book and, theoretically, you should not have any problems. But sooner or later you will have a crash or forget your bike for a few months and then you may find yourself in trouble.

To get home after a crash, bent stems can usually be straightened out if you hold the front wheel between your legs and twist the handlebars. If one side of the handlebars is bent, lay the bike on the ground, place one foot on the other side and pull hard. As always when straightening metal, it is best to exert a slowly increasing amount of force and not make a sudden wrench. If that does not work, try levering the handlebars straight with a length of wood or a fallen branch. Once the metal starts to move, keep the pressure on until it is straight. Fit new parts before you ride the bike again.

In a frontal crash, the top and down tubes often get bent, usually only slightly. It is usually the forks that take the brunt of the impact, sometimes bending right back to touch the down tube. This certainly puts your bike out of action. To get yourself home, try straightening the forks using a piece of tubing slipped over the end of the forks. Or use a large pair of Stillson's and lots of muscle.

Nevertheless, there are various problems best left to professionals. A good bike shop can remove cranks that have seized onto the bottom bracket axle, straighten bent cranks and extract a corroded seat post without damaging the frame.

They should also be able to check and correct frame alignment after a crash, organise a respray for a frame looking past its best and clean up any damaged threads. When fitting a cartridge bottom bracket, you should get the bottom bracket threads recut as a matter of routine.

On the other hand, an engineering or engine reconditioning shop would probably be better at dealing with any nuts and bolts that you just cannot move. But check the likely cost as it will often be cheaper to replace a component than to salvage it.

Dealing with stuck parts

1 Alloy seat posts often corrode and jam in the seat tube. To get one out, remove the seat bolt or seat clamp and apply penetrating oil around the bottom of the seat post every few hours for a couple of days. Then try again.

2 If that fails, try to get the seat post moving by turning it from side to side using grips. Then apply more penetrating oil and pull it out. Or fit an old saddle and thump the side with a mallet to break the seal.

5 You always need a long spanner to shift the pedals but if you cannot move them, extend the spanner with a tube. However, one of the reasons why people have trouble is that they forget the left-hand pedal has a left-hand thread.

3 When a crank or something similar gets stuck, cushion it with cloth or a piece of wood and strike it several times with a hammer. If that does not shock it free, try riding a couple of miles with the crank bolt missing.

4 If somebody has tried undoing the wheel nuts with an adjustable spanner or used the wrong size spanner, the best way to undo the damaged nut or bolt is to use a surface drive socket. These grip the sides of the hexagon, not the vulnerable corners.

6 Do not use too much leverage as you could rip the thread out of the crank. Instead, try soaking the end of the crank with spray lube. Do not forget to spray the end of the axle where it shows on the inside face of the crank.

7 Sometimes the spanner flats on the pedal axle get damaged. In that case, strip the pedal and clamp the axle in a vice. Then pull on the chainring to unscrew the pedal axle but check you are turning in the right direction.

SAW POINT

If you are desperate, you can sometimes shift obstinate components using a hacksaw. In most cases the junior size will be fine but a full-size one is better for really heavy jobs. Fit a new blade and oil it lightly before you start as that will make the whole job much easier.

Where something is held in place with a nut and bolt, slip the saw blade in behind the nut and cut through the bolt. If you are very tight for space, you may find yourself cutting through the back of the nut as well, but that does not matter. If you are dealing with something like a cable clamp with a damaged socket head fixing, cut a deep slot across the socket head and then try undoing it with a screwdriver. If you have good access to a nut, make two diagonal cuts across opposite flats. Then open up the cuts with a cold chisel and hammer – the nut will usually fall apart. If all else fails, see if the local engine reconditioner can help.

CHAPTER 3

INSTANT
BIKE CARE

**If you take a few minutes to clean and oil your
bike, you can forget about breakdowns.**

Quick lube routine

There are many points that need lubricating on a bike but most of them need only occasional attention.

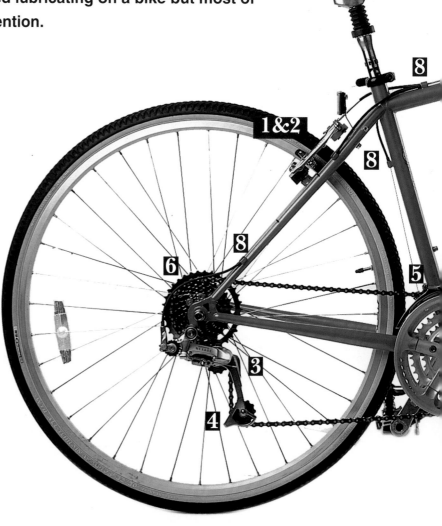

As they whiz round, chains tend to throw off any oil you put on them. They also get covered with dust and any oil that manages to cling on will get washed off by the rain eventually.

If a chain is then allowed to run dry, the chain, chainring and sprockets will all wear out much faster than if they were lubricated. It will also become harder and harder to change the gears. You can prevent this by lubing (lubricating) the chain frequently and by cleaning it thoroughly, as soon as you can see dirt and dust starting to build up on the links. If you spot a similar build-up on the jockey wheels of the rear gear mechanism, you have left it too long. Full instructions on cleaning chains appear on page 76.

For regular commuters, frequently means once a week in winter, maybe once a fortnight in summer. Back this up by drying and spraying the chain with water dispersing lubricant when you have been riding in the rain. Leisure riders should lube their bikes after any cross-country trip and soon after any ride over 40 miles on the road.

That leaves the question of when to lube the rest of your bike. If you use this schedule and go through the whole lube routine every time your chain needs cleaning, your bike certainly will not be under-lubricated. But wipe off any surplus on the surface.

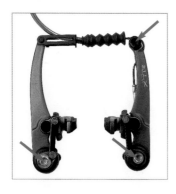

1 Vee brake pivots should be assembled with a spot of grease but need a shot of spray lube to keep water and rust at bay. Give the cable attachments a very occasional shot as well.

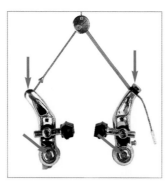

2 Standard cantilevers also need a shot of lube to protect the pivots and just a trace to ensure that the straddle cable does not seize or fray where it joins the brake arms.

3 Rear gear mechanisms need a shot of lube on each of the main pivots, the top pivot and the chain cage pivot. In other words – if it moves, spray it, but only lightly.

4 Jockey wheels do not pick up much oil from the chain. So they need a squirt to shift any dirt, a wipe and a second shot on the bearings to keep them turning smoothly.

7

8

1&2

BRUSH OFF
When using your bike in dry weather, dust collects in all the nooks and crannies. If you do not have time to wash the bike before starting the lube routine, remove all the dust with a dry, one-inch paint brush, but be careful to cover the chain while you do so. This prevents any abrasive dust being carried into the chain bushes and inner links when you lube the chain.

WHICH LUBRICANT?
There is a never-ending procession of new and ever more expensive bike lubricants trying to find room in bike shops. The problem is that nobody can tell straightaway if the new ones are any better than the old, let alone whether it is worth shelling out for the really expensive ones. Unless you enjoy trying new things and do not mind a bike shed full of half-empty tins, it is probably best to stick to products that have been around at least a couple of years. At least that proves somebody else thinks they are worth the money.

5 The front mech needs a squirt on all the pivots, then a quick wipe round the chain cage. Lube the gear shifters and also wipe any bare inner cable with an oily rag.

6 Lubricating the chain and sprockets is number one priority. And scrape any dirt off the sprockets and chainring with a small screwdriver, wipe with a cloth and then lube.

7 The brake levers need a shot on the pivots, on the inner cable with the lever pulled back for access and on the cable adjusters. Also check the brake pads for wear.

8 Give all inner cables a squirt where they exit from the outers, especially the rear mech cable. Where necessary, free the outer cables from the stops and fire lube down them.

Big clean-up

Mountain bikes need a good scrub down after a muddy ride but any bike looks better after a wash and polish.

The most convenient product to wash your bike with is washing-up liquid. It will work fine if the bike is really oily because the strong detergent will strip off most of the oil as well as the dirt. The trouble is that it will also remove any wax or polish on the frame, leaving it looking horribly streaky because of the phosphates left behind. You will have to shine it up with bike or car polish if you want to put the gleam back.

Washing-up liquid will not work on really oily areas like the gear mechanisms and the chainwheel. Here you will have to apply a water-soluble degreaser, work it around with a washing-up brush and then wash again.

If your bike is just normally dirty, car shampoo will work better than washing-up liquid. It is less likely to cause streaks and leaves a light coat of wax on the paintwork.

Do not wash your bike in the sun as the water will dry off too quickly, leaving you with very dull paint and a lot of streaks.

Never use a pressure washer. Bike bearings are just not designed to keep out water under pressure. For the same reason, keep the pressure down if you use a hose, just letting the water cascade over the bike. Do not squirt it directly at the hubs, bottom bracket, gears or headset.

And keep the bike upright, whether it is standing on its own wheels or in a bike stand.

Cleaning kit

WATER DISPERSING LUBE

SPRAY DEGREASER

BRUSH-ON DEGREASER

WASHING-UP LIQUID

1 Squirt plenty of washing-up liquid or a sachet of car shampoo into half a bucket of hot water. Apply a first coat to the whole bike using an old sponge or washing-up brush, but give it time to work.

2 Wash the whole bike again. This second wash will shift most of the dirt, but there may be areas where the dirt is more stubborn. Use a bottle brush, a tooth brush or a paint brush for the nooks and crannies.

WHEN YOU NEED TO DO THIS JOB:
◆ After a muddy cross country-ride.
◆ Every two or three months in dry weather

TIME:
◆ One hour to do the job properly including cleaning and lubricating the chain. Ten minutes if you're in a real hurry.

DIFFICULTY:
◆ Dead easy. There is no excuse for not keeping your bike gleaming.

SPECIAL TOOLS:
◆ Bottle brush, washing-up brush, toothbrush, close-textured sponge, old sponge for the chain, chamois leather.

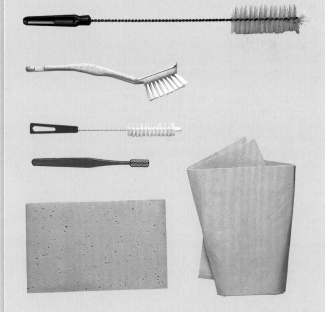

3 Wherever the foam seems to form droplets and roll off, use a degreaser to break down the film of oil. Do the same to the chain. Work it with a brush to ensure the dirt and oil mixes with the degreaser.

4 If you have time, get a bucket of clean warm water and rinse the foam away. Use a sponge to cascade water over the frame, the mudguards and the chain. And run the chain through a wet sponge.

5 Dry the frame, mudguards, saddle and handlebars with a clean rag or a chamois. Then squirt spray lube over the chain, gears, hubs and headset to drive out any water that has got in. Then lube the chain.

WASH, LUBE AND GO
When you have finished washing your bike, even if you have sprayed it with aerosol lubricant, there is still a chance that water has got into the bearings. On the other hand, if you oil your bike without washing it, there is a chance that dirt will get into the bearings. So treat washing and lubing as two parts of the same job and allow about an hour for the combined effort.

10-minute bike check

Go through this routine occasionally to check your bike is safe and likely or not to let you down any time in the near future.

1 If the brakes are adjusted properly, you will only have to pull the lever half-way for them to be fully on. Although the 'sponge' in the system will probably allow you to pull it closer, using more force.

The first four steps in this test routine cover the brakes, including disc brakes. If you find any defects here, do not use your bike until you have put things right. Otherwise you will be a danger to yourself and other road users.

Next comes some checks on the structure of the bike, particularly the stem and handlebars, plus the suspension forks if fitted. If you spot any cracks, pinholes or other serious defects, it would be foolhardy to ride your bike until they are dealt with. You are most likely to spot a crack in the handlebars close to the clamp, while pinholes are most likely to occur in the welds.

As for the steering, it will be obvious if the stem and handlebar are out of line with the front wheel, but not so easy to tell if the headset is loose or worn. And you must take care to tell the difference between wear in the suspension forks and a loose headset.

However, if you hear or feel a jolt when you lunge the bike forward and then apply the front brake, the headset almost certainly needs adjusting. But if there is only a little slack, you might find it easier to detect if you wedge your finger between the frame and the fork. Adjust or replace as soon as possible because a loose headset wears out fast.

The chainset comes next. If you can detect movement on just one crank, do not ride the bike until you have tightened it up. If you do use it, you can easily wreck the loose crank. But it is OK to ride short distances when the cranks feel tight or gritty when you turn them, or with a loose bottom bracket, a bent chainring or bent cranks, but these problems will certainly slow you down.

Gear cables tend to fray in similar places to brake cables, but they also fray under the bottom bracket on road bikes. However, badly adjusted rear gear mechanisms are the main cause of unreliability on nearly all bikes. So check that there is a quick reliable change between all gears. If the chain jumps off at any point, you will have to adjust the rear mech from scratch. Check the indexing as well – changes should be crisp and instantaneous.

Finally, check that the bolts on the saddle clip, the seat post clamp and the handlebar stem are all tight. Avoid overtightening because it is only too easy to damage alloy components.

Ideally, do your 10-minute check before the Quick lube routine but after the Big clean-up on earlier pages. That way you will be working on a clean but not oily bike. However, leave time to lube the bike thoroughly when you have finished the checks.

5 Where suspension forks are fitted, check for cracks in the brake arch. Wipe the chrome upper fork tubes and spray with the specified aerosol lube. Then apply the front brake and see if there is any slack in the forks. If so, fit new bushes.

6 Inspect the handlebars and stem for cracks. If you can feel any movement between the forks and the frame, adjust the headset soon. Then go round checking that the bolts on the stem, handlebars and handlebar brace are all tight.

10 On rear mechs, inspect the cable for fraying and turn the jockey wheels to check they are not seizing up or worn. Shift from top gear to bottom and back a few times to check the gear change is swift, accurate and quiet.

2 Look at the brake pads next. There should be plenty of rubber left and at least 1mm between the pad and the top edge of the rim. Curved pads should follow the curve of the rim.

3 Check the brake cables for fraying near the cable adjusters and where they exit from the outer cable. If it takes a lot of pressure to apply the brakes, fit new inner cables and possibly new outers.

4 If mechanical disc brakes are fitted, check the cable as in Step 3. On hydraulic discs, look for leaks and check the fluid level on open systems. On both types, check the calipers are still firmly bolted to the frame or fork.

7 Hold one of the cranks still and try to move the other one. Then swap round. If you feel any movement on one of them, the crank bolts need tightening. If the cranks move equally both sides, your sealed bottom bracket needs replacing.

8 Lift the chain off so you can turn the cranks easily. If necessary, take out the back wheel to give you enough slack. Then spin the cranks to check that the bottom bracket turns smoothly and with very little friction or noise.

9 While you turn the cranks, look down from above to see if the chainrings and cranks are both straight. Then check that all the chainring bolts are tight. Finally, make sure the pedals revolve freely, without any cracking noises.

11 Inspect the front mech cable for fraying and make sure the chain cage is parallel to the chain. Then check that there is no more than a 1 to 3mm gap between chain cage and large chainring. The change should be quick and reliable.

12 Check that the riding position is comfortable and that your leg is almost fully extended when pedalling. Then check the seat clip bolt or bolts but take care not to over tighten them because the alloy threads are easily damaged.

13 Try to twist the saddle from side to side. If it moves, tighten the seat post clamp bolt. Then check that the handlebar stem is in line with the front wheel. If need be, tighten the stem clamp bolts so it does not move again.

Wheel and tyre servicing

Follow up the 10-minute check on the previous page by spending another five minutes on the tyres and wheels.

When you spin the front wheel, it should keep on turning for quite a while and there should not be any kind of grinding or cracking noise. If it seems to slow quite quickly or you can hear odd noises, the hub probably needs stripping down and regreasing. If you can feel any side-to-side movement at the rim, the hub bearings need adjusting – see page 138-139.

As the wheel turns, use the brake pads or use your thumb to check if the wheel rim moves from side to side or up and down. If you can see that the rim is buckled, see page 140. In addition, all the spokes in a wheel should be at roughly the same tension. If there is a buckle, some of the spokes will probably be loose, but if they all seem to be slack, the wheel needs completely re-tensioning or even re-building by a professional bike mechanic.

No tyre runs absolutely true but if the tread wanders from side to side a lot or the tyre bulges, try taking it off and refitting it more carefully. If that does not improve things, the tread of the tyre may have been put on crooked during manufacture or it may have been damaged. Whatever the explanation, the only solution is a new tyre.

When you are checking the tyre tread for flints, look also for sponginess, deep cuts and an excessive number of cuts. If there are more than a dozen or so cuts, or you can see the individual threads in the sidewall, the tyre is coming to the end of its days. At that stage, punctures are much more likely.

Five-minute tyre and wheel check

1 Lift the front wheel off the ground and give it a spin to check the hub bearings. Then use the brake pads as a fixed point so you can gauge if the rim or tyre is not running straight. If disc brakes are fitted, carefully position your thumb close to the rim and use that as the fixed point.

Inflating tyres

1 To pump up a Presta valve tube, undo the knurled nut all the way and push in the stalk a fraction until you hear a hiss of escaping air. This ensures that the valve is not stuck. Try wiggling the stalk if it is hard to pump up the tyre.

PRESTA VALVE

SCHRAEDER
VALVE

BUBBLE TROUBLE
If a tyre keeps going down but you cannot find the puncture, the valve may be slowly leaking air. This will show up if you remove the tube and dunk it in water, but there is a way of checking without going that far. Just fill an egg cup or yoghurt pot with water and dip the valve in. If there is a stream of bubbles, you will have to fit a new tube if it is a Presta valve, or screw in a new insert if it is a Schrader.

2 If the tyre isn't running straight, take it off and re-fit it, fitting the beads right into the well of the rim. Then, whether it is buckled or not, stretch each pair of spokes with your finger and thumb to see if they are evenly tensioned.

3 Go round the tyre with a small screwdriver next, prising out any flints stuck in the tread. Look out for deep cuts, whether or not there is a flint embedded in them. It is best to fit a new tyre if there is any serious damage.

4 The tyre wall should be evenly coloured, with an unbroken coat of rubber all the way from the rim to the tread. If the fabric is showing or there are any cuts or splits, let the tyre down so you can see how bad the damage is.

5 Try turning the axle with your fingers. If it feels gritty or tight, strip and regrease. If it feels like the bearings are dragging but are running smoothly, run two drops of oil into the bearing or, better still, strip and regrease.

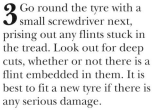

2 Utility and mountain bikes often use a Schrader valve, which is much fatter than a Presta. Some pumps fit both types but you may need an adaptor, so check. Do not use garage air lines on Schrader valves – it is dangerous.

3 Most pumps just push onto the valve but the air will escape if you push the adaptor on too far. If you are having trouble, check that the adaptor is square onto the valve and steady your hand with a finger round the valve or a spoke.

4 When you have fully inflated a tyre with a Presta valve, check that the valve is at right angles to the rim and do up the valve nut finger tight. Do not tighten it more than that as it might cause the valve to leak. Then fit the dust cap.

5 Pump up MTB tyres until they are firm, not hard. Set them to 30 to 40 psi with a tyre pressure gauge. Hybrid tyres should be fairly hard (50 to 70 psi) but sports bike tyres should hardly dent with thumb pressure (90 to 120 psi).

10 hard-to-spot faults

The 10-minute bike check should reveal most common problems. This spread is to help you pick out the more unusual faults.

The 10-minute bike check will tell you if your bike is safe and whether it is likely to breakdown in the near future But it will not help you trace the minor but niggling problems that can make the difference between a bike that is just OK and one that is a pleasure to ride.

First of all, do not neglect your riding position. Most people just get the saddle height roughly right and leave it at that. They forget about adjusting the saddle fore-and-aft, and the possible need to fit a different saddle. Do not forget about the distance you have to stretch to reach the handlebars. And the need to match the width of the handlebars to your own body. Look back to Chapter 1 for guidance on these points.

The biggest source of problems is the gears. If they are not working properly and minor adjustments do not help, go back and rework the adjustment from scratch - pages 48-53. If that does not work, you will have to fit a new chain and sprockets and possibly new chainrings and a new mech.

You may also have to splash out on some new tyres. Just because there is a millimetre of tread left, it does not mean that the tyres are in roadworthy condition. High-quality tyres are the easiest and best upgrade for any bike. You will go even faster and suffer fewer punctures if you keep them pumped up properly.

The better the bike, the more likely it is that you will come across various creaking noises, because they are caused by different metals rubbing together. Do not try to eliminate them by overtightening bolts because there is a chance you will rip the thread out. Undo them, clean the surfaces where they touch and coat everything lightly with copper anti-seize grease.

Brakes next. Again, just because there is a millimetre of rubber left on the pad, it does not mean that the pad is gripping the rim properly. Adjust them so that they toe-in slightly at the front – see page 122, although the new pads may well have instructions covering this point. Do not expect the new pads to generate full power immediately – the pads usually have to lay a coating of the new material on the rims and wear into the shape of the braking surface before they reach full power.

Finally, there are the forgotten bearings like the bottom bracket and hubs. If a bike is getting on a bit, close inspection may reveal that these components are just worn out.

1 Too much effort needed, aches and pains or a feeling of poor control over the bike can all be caused by a bad riding position. Go back to the basic set up in Chapter 1 and then experiment for yourself.

2 The chain is worn if you can almost lift it off the chainring. This will not cause clear-cut problems but the chainrings and sprockets will wear fast and the gear change will be sloppy and inaccurate.

5 Tyres may look good from a distance, but it takes a close examination to get at the truth. If a tyre wall looks past it, try letting the tyre down so you can squeeze it flat and check for splits and cuts.

6 Bikes should be silent. If yours creaks, the noise probably comes from steel bolts in alloy threads or vice versa. Apply anti-seize to the stem, chainring and saddle clamp bolts to silence them.

3 If there is a regular noise that stops when you stop pedalling, the indexing on the rear mech is probably not quite right. Try turning the cable adjuster on the rear gear one half turn anti-clockwise.

4 You can prevent the chain jumping off the sprockets by readjusting the rear mech from scratch. If that does not fix things, check the chain is not too long. When the chain is on the smallest sprocket and the biggest chainring, the chain cage should be at an angle of roughly 90° to the floor.

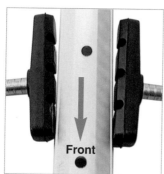

Front

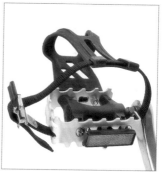

7 Poor braking may be due to contaminated brake pads. Try fitting new ones. The braking surface may be dirty as well. If so, scrub them using a green nylon abrasive pad and some degreaser, then rinse.

8 Snatchy and noisy braking can be caused by badly fitted brake pads, especially if each pad is aligned differently. Try fitting them so that the front edge is 1mm closer to the rim than the back edge.

9 To check the headset for freeplay, wrap your fingers around the top steering bearing, put the front brake on and rock backwards and forwards. Any movement means the headset must be checked.

10 Pedals with grinding bearings or bent axles make it impossible to pedal correctly. Check the axle is straight by eye, then spin the pedal so that you can check that it turns freely.

CHAPTER 4

GEAR SYSTEMS

Every day and every road is different. But thanks to
modern gear systems, most bikes have enough gears
to strike a balance between speed and effort,
whatever the conditions.

Types of gears

Nearly all bikes are fitted with either derailleur or hub gears. Derailleur systems have a front mech to shift the chain between two or three chainrings and a rear mech with up to ten sprockets. Hub gears have fewer speeds and need occasional workshop maintenance.

NINE SPEED MOUNTAIN BIKE REAR MECH
These mechs have a long chain cage to allow for a very wide range of gears, and are controlled by a handlebar mounted gear shifter. They can also be used on hybrid and touring bikes, which need very low gears for hill climbing and load carrying.

REAR MECH

NINE SPEED RACING BIKE REAR MECH
Sports and racing rear mechs for use with double chainsets (see left) have a short chain cage for low weight and a better gear change. Rear mechs for use with triple chainsets (see above) have a medium length chain cage to allow for a wider range of gears. Both types are controlled by combined brake and gear levers, or by shifters on the down tube of the frame.

ECONOMY REAR MECH
These are made of steel, not alloy, usually with a bolt-on hanger for use on budget frames not fitted with a gear hanger. Short cage models are also available.

HUB GEARS

With optional built-in coaster brake. Designed as easy-to-use gears for city and leisure bikes, they are controlled by a click shifter on the handlebars. Hub gears need little day-to-day maintenance and up to fourteen speeds are available.

HUB GEAR

THREE-SPEED HUB GEAR

Mainly for utility bikes. These hub gears need occasional adjustment to the cable tension, but the latest versions do not even need oiling. Controlled by a click shifter, usually on the handlebars, they can be combined with a derailleur to give a wide range of gears on leisure and utility bikes.

FRONT MECH

MOUNTAIN BIKE AND HYBRID FRONT MECH

MTB front mechs have a deep, heavy duty chain cage so they can cope with triple chainrings and big differences in chainring size. This particular type has a very rigid chain cage mounted at the top of the mech for a lighter, better change. Separate top pull, bottom pull and combined models are all available.

RACING BIKE FRONT MECH

Racing front mechs are fitted with a light chain cage, with separate models for double and triple chainrings. Most types bolt on to the down tube with a clamp but high-grade road frames have a special brazed-on fitting for bolting the front mech to.

Rear mech: care and inspection

To make the most of your bike, you need a 100% reliable gear change.

All rear derailleur mechanisms (rear mechs) need frequent lubrication and occasional servicing to keep them working sweetly. So give the rear mech a few shots of aerosol lube every time you lube the chain. Also spend a few minutes cleaning it when dirt starts to build up, or if the gears stop working properly.

You will need to know if the rear mech is indexed or has friction changers. Some older bikes have friction gears but these are now rare. With these, you have to judge how far to move the gear lever each time you want to change gear. Once you have got the hang of them, each change should be crisp and reliable, and makes just one slight clonk.

But most bikes now have indexed gears, with between seven and ten speeds. If you can feel and hear a slight click when you move the gear changer, and a tiny answering clonk as the chain jumps onto the chosen sprocket, you have index gears.

Indexed rear mechs are usually fitted with a top jockey wheel that moves from side to side a little. This allows the chain cage to run slightly out of line with the sprockets, so the indexing will work even if the adjustment is not quite dead-on.

If your rear mech throws the chain off the sprockets, it needs cleaning and adjusting, as explained on this page. But with indexed gears, you may hear a continuous metallic rattling sound in most of the gears. Maybe you will not be able to get bottom gear, or maybe there is a noise in top gear. All of that means the indexing needs attention - in which case, see page 50.

If you just cannot get the gears to work right, bear in mind that Campagnolo and Shimano sprockets are spaced differently, it is possible that someone has fitted a Campag rear mech and a Shimano cassette or the other way round.

HOW TO USE YOUR GEARS

REMEMBER: bottom and the rest of the low gears are for climbing hills. Top and the other high gears are for descents.
AT THE BACK WHEEL: the small sprocket is top gear, the large sprocket is bottom.
BUT AT THE CHAINWHEEL: the small ring is low gear, the big ring is high gear.

1 If you have to clean the chain due to a build up of dirt, the rear mech will need cleaning as well. Give it a squirt of aerosol lube or grease solvent and wipe it thoroughly with a cloth. Then lube the main pivots and top pivot bolt.

2 Pay particular attention to the jockey wheels because they pick up hard-packed dirt from the chain. Soften the dirt with solvent and scrape off with a small screwdriver. Wipe, and then lightly spray lube into the centre of both jockey wheels.

4 The jockey wheels wear out more quickly than any other part. So pull the chain cage forward to free the bottom jockey from the chain, then test for movement by trying to wiggle it. Check also that the jockey wheel turns freely. If it does not, strip and grease.

5 Pull the chain away from the upper jockey wheel next and do the same check. On most indexed mechs, the top jockey wheel moves sideways a bit, so look for the wobble that indicates wear. If the jockey wheel just moves sideways, that is OK.

WHEN YOU NEED TO DO THIS JOB:
◆ Steps 1, 2 and 3 – every time you clean the chain.
◆ Steps 4, 5 and 6 – every time you give the chain a thorough clean. It is also worth going through 4, 5 and 6 when checking over a second-hand bike.

TIME:
◆ 1 minute to lube the rear mech when you do the chain. 5 minutes to check wear and crash damage.

DIFFICULTY: 🔧🔧
◆ Quite easy, but you are liable to get your hands pretty dirty. Consider wearing latex gloves.

3 The cable should instantly transmit each movement of the gear lever. To make sure it does work like this, lubricate the inner cable, then operate the gear lever a few times so that the lube works its way right down the outer cable.

6 Hanging down beside the back wheel, rear mechs are often get damaged when a bike falls over or is in a crash. To check for damage, clamp the bike in a workstand or get somebody to hold it upright. Then position yourself behind the back wheel, your eye level with the hub. You should be able to see if the gear looks out of line with the frame. If you suspect it is, check the gear hanger for cracks or chips in the paint – a sure indication that it is bent. It is also worth checking that the chain cage looks straight. If it is, the top and bottom jockey wheels will line up exactly with the sprockets. If the chain cage is out of line, the rear mech may be damaged or just worn out.

GEAR HANGER

MOUNTING BOLT

CABLE ADJUSTER

LOW GEAR LIMIT SCREW - L

HIGH GEAR LIMIT SCREW - H

CABLE CLAMP

TOP JOCKEY WHEEL

CHAIN CAGE

BOTTOM JOCKEY WHEEL

EXTRA LOW GEARING
Shimano Megarange and some other wide-range rear mechs can cope with any size bottom sprocket right up to 34 teeth. They can do this because the rear mech is mounted slightly further back than usual and has a bottom jockey wheel with 13 or more teeth. This extra large jockey wheel has to be used to cope with the extra long chain. Some Megarange gears use the Rapid Rise design. If so, go to page 52 for special instructions on adjustment.

Rear mech adjustment

Most rear mechs are indexed, so gear changes should be fast and reliable. If you are having problems, a few easy adjustments or a new cable should put things right.

The first step when you are adjusting any rear mech is to make sure that the inner cable is free of friction as it moves in the outer cable. This applies when fitting a new cable, or a new rear mech or re-using the existing bits. The most likely cause of any friction is the short length of outer cable that connects to the rear mech. So to avoid problems, some experts fit a new one every time they fit a new inner cable.

You then adjust the upper and lower limit screws, which control the movement of the chain cage from side to side. If you ever find that the chain has jumped off the sprockets and got jammed in the spokes, the limit screws probably need adjusting. The same applies if the chain jams between the top sprocket and the frame.

On mountain bikes and hybrids, you select the gears with either a rotary changer built into the handlebar grip, or a trigger-type changer. But nearly all modern sports bikes and racers have combined brake and gear levers (pages 62-63). Older road bikes have indexed levers on the down tube, in the same place as friction gear changers.

For an indexed rear mech to work, the gear changer has to move the cable exactly the same amount for each gear change. But this set amount can only be transmitted accurately to the rear mech if the cable is under a lot of tension. If the cable stretches or the outer cable compresses, reducing the tension, the indexing stops working sweetly.

You will probably notice the noise of the chain running slightly out of line when this happens. To increase the cable tension again, give the cable adjuster one half-turn anti-clockwise. If that does not work, go through Step 5 on this page to re-adjust the indexing. But if you still cannot get the gears to change smoothly and precisely, fit a new inner and outer gear cable (pages 61-65), then go back to Step 5.

Adjusting the indexing

5 To see how the indexing is working, give the bike a road test. First check that the chain runs silently in top gear on the biggest chainring. If it makes a rattling noise, turn the cable adjuster (large arrow) – not the H and L limit screws – half a turn anti-clockwise if the chain is trying to jump off the top sprocket. But if it is trying to climb onto the second sprocket, give the cable adjuster half a turn clockwise. Keep on road testing, changing up and down through the gears and adjusting the cable tension, until the bike runs silently in top.

Next, change down to second gear with the gear lever and turn the cable adjuster one quarter-turn anti-clockwise at a time, until you hear a metallic clattering sound as the chain tries to climb onto the third sprocket. Then turn the adjuster clockwise until the clattering noise stops, but absolutely no further than that. Road test again to make sure that the gear changes are quick and accurate. But when you are checking out the gear change up onto the biggest sprockets, change down to a smaller chainring.

Be very careful when changing down into bottom gear the first few times as you might 'overshift' the chain off the biggest sprocket and into the spokes. If you cannot get the gears to shift properly, lubricate the outer cable again. Better still, fit a complete new inner and outer cable. Also check the adjustment of the B screw, see page 57.

REMEMBER, AT THE BACK WHEEL:
The smaller the sprocket, the higher the gear. So adjust the screw marked H for High.
The larger the sprocket, the lower the gear. So adjust the screw marked L for Low.

BUT AT THE CHAINWHEEL:
The larger the chainring, the higher the gear. So adjust the screw marked H for High.
The smaller the chainring, the lower the gear. So adjust the screw marked L for Low.

Indexed gears: adjustment

WHEN YOU NEED TO DO THIS JOB:
◆ Rear mech is noisy.
◆ Gears will not change smoothly and accurately.
◆ Chain jumps off into spokes or jams between sprocket and frame.

TIME:
◆ 30 minutes from fitting new mech to completing adjustment of indexed rear mech.
◆ 5 minutes to fine-tune the indexing, including test ride.

DIFFICULTY:
◆ Basic adjustment is quite straightforward, but getting the indexing working perfectly can take a bit of patience.

1 Check that the inner cable is not weakened or frayed anywhere. And make sure that the outer cable is not kinked or damaged, especially the short cable down near the rear mech. Then spray some aerosol lube down each section of outer cable. Do not forget to check the cable guide under the bottom bracket. Now lift the back wheel and select top gear, turning the pedals slowly so that the chain jumps down on to the smallest sprocket

2 Undo the cable clamp to free the gear cable, if necessary. Then pull the rear mech backwards to make it easier for you to see the position of the jockey wheels. On index gears, a vertical line through the middle of both jockey wheels should line up with the outside edge of the smallest sprocket. To move the jockey wheels to the right, turn the H for High limit screw anti-clockwise. To move the jockey wheels to the left, turn it clockwise, the opposite way.

3 Make sure that the gear lever is still in top gear position. Then screw the cable adjuster in most of the way and fit the gear cable, pulling it as tight as possible with pliers before you tighten the cable clamp. Using the gear lever, change down slowly until the rear mech is in bottom gear. The jockey wheels should line up with the MIDDLE of the bottom sprocket. If they are to the right of that point, or the rear mech will not change down to bottom, turn the L for Low limit screw anti-clockwise. Turn the limit screw clockwise if the chain cage is to the left of the largest sprocket

4 If you have trouble finding the H (top) and L (bottom) limit screws, they are usually on the top or back of the rear mech. But on budget Shimano and most Campag gears, they are on the side, near the cable clamp. If the limit screws are not labelled H and L, you will have to use trial and error to sort out which one is which.

NON-INDEXED GEARS WITH FRICTION LEVERS

Friction gears are controlled by levers on the down tube. When setting them up, check first that the right hand lever moves smoothly. If not, loosen the centre screw slightly. But if the lever action feels loose, tighten the centre screw very slightly.

Set the limit screws next. Use the same method as outlined in Steps 2 and 3 above, EXCEPT that the H limit screw must be adjusted so that the chain cage is directly below the centre line of the top sprocket.

Fit the cable and then road test the bike. When changing gear, move the lever a little until you feel and hear the chain jump to the next sprocket. Adjust the position of the lever slightly if the gear makes any noise as you pedal.

In top gear, the chain should run almost silently. If there is a slight but regular metallic clacking or coughing noise, try adjusting the H limit screw one eighth-turn anti-clockwise. If that makes the noise worse, turn the H limit screw clockwise a little until the noise goes away.

Now change down carefully, one gear at a time, until you get to bottom gear. Turn the L limit screw clockwise if there is a clacking or coughing noise. If that makes the noise worse or the chain jumps down onto the next sprocket, adjust the L limit screw anti-clockwide one quarter-turn at a time until the chain runs silently on bottom gear.

If in doubt about any of this, check the chain cage from behind to see if it has moved too far to the left, or too far to the right, and then adjust the limit screws as required.

If the gears run quietly at first but get noisier, or they keep jumping to a higher gear, tighten the centre screw of the lever very slightly. But if the top jockey wheel seems to get tangled up with the bottom sprocket, adjust the B screw as explained on page 57.

Rear mech adjustment: SRAM & Shimano Rapid Rise

There are important differences between the way you adjust these two types of rear mech and the mainstream types. Nevertheless, it is worth reading the previous spread before starting this one to get an understanding of the basics of rear mech adjustment.

Shimano Rapid Rise rear gear mechanisms work the other way round from all other types. That means the rear mech automatically moves into bottom gear when the tension on the cable is released and not into top gear as on all other rear mechs. This is claimed to be an advantage because it is always harder to get the chain to climb up onto a larger sprocket than to drop down onto a smaller one. With Rapid Rise, the more difficult change down onto the bigger sprockets is assisted by the pull of the spring.

SRAM ESP-type gears also work on a very different principle from others. With this design, if you pull the cable 1mm, the rear mech moves 1mm. SRAM call this the 1:1 actuation ratio. On all other designs, moving the cable 1mm moves the rear mech 2mm, which means that the cable must be adjusted very accurately. The 1:1 ratio also does away with the need for the top jockey wheel to move from side to side. It is claimed that the practical effect of all this is that SRAM gears do not need such frequent maintenance as other types and that the indexing works more reliably.

SRAM gear

1 Provided the chain is the correct length – see pages 80-81 for details – adjust the H limit screw so that a line between the centres of the jockey wheels lines up with the outer edge of the smallest sprocket. Then move the chain onto the smallest chainring.

Rapid Rise adjustment

1 When the cable tension is off, a Rapid Rise rear mech moves to the left. So first, select bottom gear, and turn the pedals until the chain climbs onto the bottom sprocket. Adjust the L limit screw so that the chain runs silently, with the top jockey wheels in line with the centre line of the bottom sprocket.

2 Next, change slowly up to top gear and adjust the H limit screw until the jockey pulleys are in line with the centre of the smallest sprocket. Fit the cable, then road test to check that the change from top to second is fast and reliable. If necessary, increase the cable tension by turning the cable adjuster anti-clockwise.

RAPID RISE
The Shimano Rapid Rise concept first came onto the market at the top of the MTB range. The early version had a complex pulley mechanism on the cable but this has now been eliminated. The budget Nexave groupset for leisure bikes features the only other Rapid Rise rear mech on the market at the moment.

adjustment

2 Turn the pedals with one hand while you push the rear mech towards the bottom sprocket with the other. Once the chain has jumped up onto the biggest sprocket, hold the mech in that position and adjust the L screw so that the jockey wheels line up precisely with the centre line of the biggest sprocket.

3 Holding the the gear in the same position, measure the distance between the point where the chain leaves the biggest sprocket and where it contacts the top jockey wheel. That distance should be 6mm on the latest SRAMs and three chain rivets on earlier ones. Adjust the 'B' screw with a 2.5mm or 3mm hexagon key until you get the distance right. This adjustment is not so important on other makes but it is vital on SRAM. Fit the cable and then check and adjust the indexing as you would on any other type of rear mech.

4 To change the cable, flip off the cover beside the cable adjuster. Then cut the old cable and push it out through the cable entry. Insert the new cable and feed it through the cable entry, the adjuster and along the outer cable. When it emerges, pull the rest through, make sure it lies in the cable track and snap the cover back on. For top-of-the-range models, push back the escape hatch near the adjuster, undo the 2.5mm socket-headed cable retainer inside and push the old cable out. Feed the new cable in, pull it tight and refit the cable retainer.

5 Fit the new cable to the rear mech in the normal way. But if a Nightcrawler cable seal is fitted, feed the new cable through the pointed end of the long rubber bellows first, next the rubber seal, then the small nozzle of the plastic rigger. Continue feeding the inner cable through the second rubber seal and into the normal outer cable. Snap the rigger onto the cable stop and push all the parts together to form a continuous waterproof seal. Again, fit the new cable to the rear mech in the usual way.

SRAM REAR MECH

SRAM rear mechs are for MTBs, hybrids and touring bikes with a very wide range of gears. The main body of the gear is arranged so that the jockey wheels and chain cage stay as close as possible to the sprockets as you changes up and down the gears. This is why the B screw adjustment is so vital. In addition, the top pivot of the gear is not sprung as on other designs.

The cable is wrapped round the semi-circular cable guide at the top and pulls directly on the inner link for a snappier change.

The latest X.0 rear mechs have new alloy main links and large diameter, stainless-steel ball bearings for the jockey wheels. They are also fitted with rubber seals for a long life.

SRAM/GRIPSHIFT GEAR CHANGERS

Gripshift rotational shifters are made by SRAM. Their ESP shifters only work with SRAM gears also made to the ESP design. Non-ESP Gripshift designs work well with other rear mechs including Shimano. The latest 'half pipe' shifters have a bigger grip for easier gear changing, plus a better internal mechanism.

Normally, Gripshift shifters need no maintenance. If one becomes stiff to operate, fit a new inner and outer cable. Then check that the plastic washer between the handlebar grip and shifter moves freely. If neither of those things reduces the amount of effort needed to shift the gears, flip off the cable cover or open the escape hatch and spread a match head size bead of Jonnisnot lubricant around the cable track and another round the ratchet. Do not use any other lubricants or degreasers because they might swell the plastic.

Rear mech: overhaul

If you have checked the adjustment but the gears still do not work nicely, the rear mech needs a strip-down.

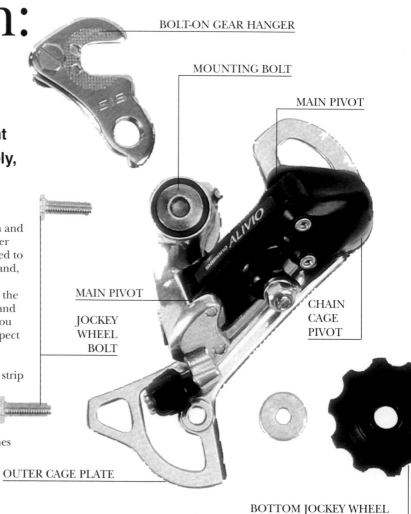

BOLT-ON GEAR HANGER

MOUNTING BOLT

MAIN PIVOT

MAIN PIVOT

JOCKEY WHEEL BOLT

CHAIN CAGE PIVOT

OUTER CAGE PLATE

BOTTOM JOCKEY WHEEL

There is no set period of time, or number of kilometres, after which you should strip down and clean a rear mech. The kind of mountain biker who cannot keep away from muddy tracks might need to do it once a month, or even sooner. On the other hand, many riders leave the gears untouched for years.

That is leaving it too long. Over that sort of time, the jockey wheels will probably have started to seize up and the gear change will have deteriorated, all without you noticing. To prevent this happening, you should inspect the rear mech occasionally, maybe when you are cleaning the chain. If it looks as if the teeth on the jockey wheels are starting to wear down, it is time to strip and clean the rear mech.

Most gears can be broken down into more parts than shown in the diagram. But you do not need to go any further than separating the chain cage plates and the jockey wheels. Jockey wheels sometimes have deeper washers on one side than the other, so make a note of which side they fit. Any remaining parts like the springs and H and L limit screws can usually be cleaned with solvent, while they are still in place.

That leaves the question of how badly worn the rear mech is. To check while the mech is still on the bike, hold the bottom of the chain cage with two fingers and see how far you can move it without forcing it. If it moves more than 10mm, investigate further.

This is done by stripping the mech and gripping it above and below the two main pivots. Then see if you can feel any movement or play between the top part of the gear and the bottom part. The movement you are trying to detect from front to back. Do not confuse this with the normal sideways movement. If you can feel more than the slightest amount of play, fit a new mech as shown on pages 56-57.

The easiest way of removing the rear mech from the frame is to undo the jockey wheel bolts, which frees the mech from the chain. Then just undo the top mounting bolt. Use this method whenever possible because it saves having to break the chain. Nevertheless, if you cannot undo the jockey wheel bolts, and they are sometimes almost impossible to budge, you will have to split the chain, shown on page 78.

Clean and dry all the parts thoroughly before re-assembly. And remember that the top jockey wheel is usually designed to move from side to side a little. So if the pulley is marked 'Centron' or has a metal bush moulded into it, it is the top jockey roller. Half fill the centre of both jockey wheels with waterproof grease, before putting the washers in place. And use anti-seize grease on the jockey wheel bolts to make sure it is easy to undo them in the future.

Rear mech details

Campagnolo

Shimano

Campag only make gears for road bikes, mainly with Ergopower combined brake and gear levers. They can only be used with Campag cassettes because of the spacing of the sprockets. Campag also make gears for Miche.

Shimano make gears for MTBs, racers and utilities. But most Shimano rear mechs can be used with most other Shimano components. They can also be used with most SUNTOUR bits and non-ESP Gripshift changers.

TOP JOCKEY WHEEL

JOCKEY WHEEL BUSH

CHAIN CAGE PIVOT

SHAPED WASHER

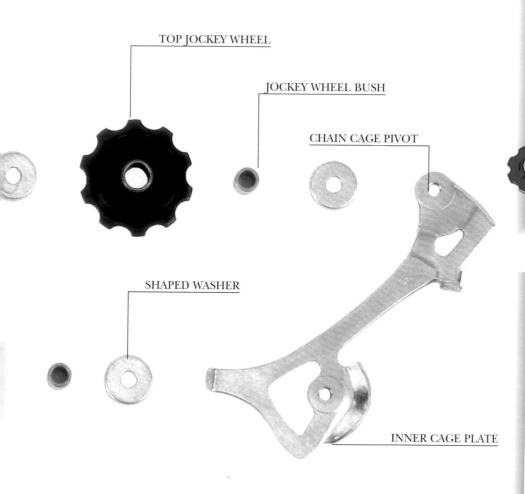

INNER CAGE PLATE

WHEN YOU NEED TO DO THIS JOB:
◆ Poor gear changing indicates rear mech needs cleaning.
◆ Inspection reveals jockey wheels are worn.

TIME:
◆ About 1 hour to remove, thoroughly clean and refit a rear mech.

DIFFICULTY:
◆ It is sometimes hard to reassemble the jockey wheels correctly. Try making a drawing as you take the chain cage apart so you do not mix up the various washers and bushes.

SPECIAL TOOLS:
◆ It is very important to have a well-fitting spanner or hexagon key to undo the jockey wheel bolts.

SRAM

SRAM rear mechs are now made of metal but earlier designs were mostly plastic. They are very different from any other design, so should only be used with other SRAM parts. ESP rear mechs can only be used with ESP changers.

Sun Race

Sun Race is a budget alternative to Shimano. They are adjusted in the same way and you can use Sun Race with any Shimano-compatible components. So far, all Sun Race rear mechs are steel but alloy ones are on the way.

SUNTOUR

SUNTOUR is back in the market with new Swing Arm designs that can only be used with their own changers. But older SUNTOUR rear mechs are adjusted as Shimano and can be used with Shimano cassettes and changers.

Rear mech: removal and refitting

You will have to remove and refit an old rear mech to do an overhaul. Or fit a new one from scratch when the old one is worn out.

There are three different ways in which the rear mech is fitted to a frame. On good-quality bikes, the mounting bolt is screwed straight into a threaded hanger that hangs down from the rear drop-out.

Be careful to keep the bolt straight as you screw it in. If it goes in at an angle and you force it, that could strip the thread in the hanger. If you do this on a steel frame, you will have to get it tapped out by a professional bike mechanic. It is also worth getting the threads tapped out after a respray, in case the threads are choked with paint. On the other hand, if it is an alloy frame, you just fit a new gear hanger - see the Blue Box opposite.

A similar method is shown on page 49 and usually found on leisure and hybrid bikes. Here a small extension plate is bolted onto the gear hanger and the mech itself is fitted to the rear end of the extension. This places the rear mech further back than usual, which allows much larger sprockets to be fitted. To remove the rear mech, undo the socket-headed bolt as if it was the mounting bolt.

The final way of fixing the rear mech to the frame is shown on page 46. This method is used on budget bikes, which do not have a built-in gear hanger. Instead, a separate steel gear hanger is bolted to the rear end, with an oval nut on the inside, shaped so that it fits into the drop-out. On budget hybrids, the bolt-on bracket is extended like the extension plate described above.

To remove a rear mech fitted using a bolt-on bracket, first remove the back wheel. Then remove the bottom jockey wheel or break the chain. Finally, you loosen the fixing bolt at the rear of the bracket and pull the mech forward, away from the frame. When re-fitting, make sure the oval nut fits into the slot for the wheel in the drop-out. As you tighten the bolt, stop the oval nut turning by holding it with a spanner on the flats. There is no need to overtighten because the bracket is held in place by the wheel nuts as well as the fixing bolt.

Whatever the method of fixing, lightly coat the thread of the mounting bolt with anti-seize grease. And if you are fitting a new rear mech, bear in mind it is always best to fit a new chain as well. Set the correct chain length as explained on page 81.

Finally, set the B screw adjustment as explained in the Blue Box on page 57. This ensures that the jockey wheels and sprockets do not touch when you go down into bottom gear.

1 This shows the way to remove a rear mech by breaking the chain. Hold the mech with one hand while you undo the pivot bolt with a long hexagon key as it may be tight.

2 If you intend to re-fit the mech, take the opportunity to do a quick strip down and clean – see page 54 Always clean the jockey wheels, then lube with waterproof grease.

5 Fit the gear cable now, tensioning the inner before you do up the cable clamp. Snip any spare inner cable off close to the clamp and fit a cable cap to stop it fraying.

6 Turn the pedals slowly and change gears one by one down to bottom gear. Adjust the L limit screw if the chain does not jump onto the largest sprocket or run there silently.

Fine-tuning index gears

1 If the indexing is having an off-day, increase or decrease the cable tension by turning the cable adjuster a quarter-turn. Experiment to find out which way is best.

2 Racing bikes with STI and Ergopower combined gear changers usually have a thumb adjuster on the down tube so you can alter cable tension when riding along.

3 When fitting a rear mech to the frame, it is easier to screw the top pivot bolt into the gear hanger if you steady it by tucking your forefinger behind the gear hanger.

4 Now fit the chain - see page 80. Then adjust the throw by turning the H limit screw until the jockey wheels align with the outer edge of the top sprocket.

DAMAGED GEAR HANGERS

Hanging off the side of the frame, the rear mech and gear hanger often get damaged when a bike falls over. To prevent this happening, you can replace the standard top pivot bolt with a breakaway bolt. This provides a weak link that snaps off to stop the mech getting damaged. For an easy way to straighten the hanger on a steel frame, see page 27. Other materials are less forgiving and so frames are often fitted with a replaceable gear hanger, retained by a short socket head bolt. However, each frame needs a different hanger, so ask for a spare when you buy a new bike.

7 Check that the outer cable is arranged in smooth, large radius curves. Then go through the final indexing adjustment on page 50 and give the bike a road test.

WHEN YOU NEED TO DO THIS JOB:
◆ The old rear mech is worn out.
◆ A rear mech has been stripped down completely.

TIME:
◆ 30 minutes to fit a new rear mech, plus another 30 minutes to adjust and test gear change

DIFFICULTY:
◆ Care is needed when screwing the pivot bolt into the gear hanger. Otherwise it is easier than overhauling a rear mech.

SPECIAL TOOLS:
◆ None.

THE B SCREW ADJUSTER

As well as the two limit screws, nearly all rear mechs have a third adjuster, usually known as the B screw, also referred to as the chain adjuster. You do not normally need to touch it.

But if you fit a large bottom sprocket, 28 teeth or more, the top jockey wheel sometimes touches the sprocket and interferes with the gear change. If this happens, select the smallest chainwheel and sprocket, then adjust the B screw to give the smallest possible gap between the jockey wheel and sprocket. Increase the gap slightly if bottom gear does not run smoothly.

For SRAM gears, see page 52. On SUNTOUR MTB mechs, you set the gap at 6-8mm but on their road mechs, you adjust the B screw so that the main plates are parallel with the chainstay.

Front mech care and adjustment

Front mechs are not temperamental like rear mechs can be – they often go for ages before needing attention

Front mechs all work on the same principle but there are many small variations. Most MTBs have a front mech indexed like a rear mech, with a 1-2-3 indicator on the shifter. But a few old MTBs and road bikes have a front mech that works with a friction gear changer.

Many MTBs use a front mech cable that pulls from the top and is routed along the top tube. This protects the cable from damage and the filth and mud thrown up from the road. But plenty of MTBs have bottom-pull front mechs, as do nearly all road bikes, and they tend to give a slightly better change. You can even get front mechs that adapt to either top or bottom pull.

MTBs usually have a big jump between the smallest and largest chainring. To make sure they can cope with this, the front mechs have a deep, heavily stepped chain cage.

On the other hand, double chainrings on road bikes usually have a smaller jump between them. So lighter and narrower chain cages are always used. Even narrower chain cages are now fitted to front mechs designed to work with the super-narrow chains required for 9 and 10 speed cassettes.

But now that triple chainsets for the road are becoming popular, there is a new breed of front mechs to suit, with light but wider and deeper chain cages. Do not try to make an MTB front mech work on a road bike, or the other way round.

1 When fitting a new front mech or tuning up an old one, position the outer plate of the chain cage between 1mm and 3mm above the teeth of the outer chainring. The red tab on a new mech is to help you get this right.

2 Arrange the outer plate of the chain cage exactly in line with the chainrings, then tighten the clamp round the seat tube. The chain should be fitted at this point but has been left out here to make it easier to see what is going on.

3 Fit the chain onto the inner chainring and adjust the L limit screw of the front mech so that the inner plate of the chain cage is about 0.5mm clear of the chain. Spin the cranks to check that the chain does not touch the chain cage.

4 Next, lift the chain up onto the big chainring and operate the front changer with your fingers. Then adjust the H limit screw of the front mech so that the outer plate of the chain cage is also 0.5mm clear of the outer edge of the chain.

5 Fit the cable at this point, checking that the inner cable moves freely and that the outer is not kinked. Make sure also that it is seated correctly in the cable stops. Lube the inner cable and the mech.

6 Feed the inner cable between the chain stays and tension it with one hand and tighten the cable clamp with the other. Now check that the front mech changes from ring to ring without delay.

7 On an indexed front mech, road test the bike to check if the indexing is working well. The big test is the jump from the middle to the biggest chainring, with the chain on the second biggest sprocket. If that change does not go through quickly and accurately, increase the cable tension by turning the cable adjuster half a turn at a time until you get an instant change with one click of the shifter. If you find the chain rubs on the chain cage in some of the gears, try making small adjustments to the H and L limit screws. But when you use the biggest chainring with one of the biggest sprockets, or the other way round, the chain nearly always rubs lightly on the chain cage. To stop the noise, 'trim' the chain cage left or right a fraction using the gear changer as you ride.

WHEN YOU NEED TO DO THIS JOB:
◆ If the chain jumps off when you are changing from one chainring to another.

TIME:
◆ 10 minutes to adjust or remove the front mech.
◆ Another 10 minutes to check adjustment with a test ride.

DIFFICULTY:
Much easier than dealing with the rear mech.

FRONT MECH ADJUSTER SCREWS
Sometimes the limit screws on front mechs are marked H = High = the biggest chainring, and L = Low = the smallest chainring.

This is similar to a rear mech, but the letters are often so small or so hidden that it is very hard to read them. To identify which screw is which, just give the outer one an experimental half-turn and make a note of which direction the chain cage moves.

Front mechs: continued

A front mech with a clamp that fits round the frame is known as a band-on front mech. When buying one, you will need to know the exact diameter of the seat tube or take the bike with you to the shop. However, there are so many variations that shims are often used to adjust for varying diameter seat tubes.

Frames with oversize seat tubes, especially good-quality road frames, often have a brazed-on fitting to carry the front mech. This overcomes the problem of finding one with the correct size clamp but you have to fit a specially-designed braze-on front mech.

If you are out on your bike and find the chain rubs lightly on the chain cage when you select particular gears, adjust the position of the chain cage slightly using the gear changer. This is known as 'trimming' the front mech. On many front mech shifters, there is a special halfway position so you can trim the front mech.

Fitting a front mech

1 To remove a front mech without breaking the chain, loosen the cable clamp and pull the inner and outer cable away. Undo the clamp bolt to release the clip round the frame and then move the front mech back along the chain to improve the access.

2 Turn the front mech upside down so you can get at the back of the chain cage. Remove the nut and bolt holding the chain cage together and pull the plates apart. Slip the front mech off the chain. Reverse this process to fit a new front mech.

On most road bikes and some MTB's, the front mech cable runs under the bottom bracket. But these cables can get damaged easily, so check in case of problems with the front mech. If the cable has a sleeve to reduce friction, make sure you transfer it when fitting a new cable.

BOTTOM BRACKET FRONT MECH

To save assembly time, some bike manufacturers fit the front mech on a bracket that is held in place by the sealed bottom bracket cartridge. This is not a problem, apart from the fact that you cannot adjust the position of the front mech at all. If you ever want to fit a larger or smaller chainring, consider replacing this type with a conventional band-on front mech.

Braze-on front mech

1 To fit a braze-on front mech without breaking the chain, remove the nut and bolt from the chain cage, as shown left. Pull the cage plates apart and fit the front mech over the chain. Replace the nut and bolt. Then slide the front mech up or down the bracket until there is no more than a 1mm to 3 mm gap between cage and chainring. Tighten the bolt.

2 Unlike a band-on front mech, you do not have to align the chain cage with the chainring, unless something is bent. So with the chain on the smallest chainring, set the L limit screw. Then fit the cable and lift the chain onto the outer ring. Adjust the H limit screw and road test. Adjust the limit screws to minimise the amount of trimming needed.

Gear shifters

Friction gear levers are easy to strip down. But index shifters have so many tiny parts that you should never try to open them up.

Nearly all mountain bikes are fitted with index gears controlled by shifters mounted on the handlebars. Index shifters work with either a ratchet, or on the stroke principle. You can tell if it is a ratchet lever because there is a sharp click that you can feel and hear when you move the gear lever. Do not take ratchet changers apart because it is very difficult to re-assemble them, and you could lose half the parts doing so.

Stroke shifters are more complicated than ratchet ones. But you can sometimes undo the central screw, remove the cover and then clean and lubricate with light grease. You should never attempt to go any further. Where gear indicators are fitted, you usually have to remove two small screws to take off the indicator unit, then undo the central socket head screw. You can then separate the shifter from the brake lever.

Nearly all road bikes more than about four years old have gear levers mounted on the down tube. Most of them are friction changers, with a central screw that applies pressure to the lever. This holds the gear lever in position until the rider moves it to change up or down a gear. The centre screw has to be adjusted carefully because if it is too tight, it will be impossible to change gear. On the other hand, if the centre screw is too loose, the rear mech will become noisy or jump out of gear

Friction levers can be stripped down without difficulty but they seldom give problems. It is usually only necessary if they have been given too much lube, or if a bike has not been used for a while and the gear levers have seized up.

There are also a few road bikes with down tube levers that are indexed. They must not be stripped down - it only takes an occasional shot of lube to keep them working sweetly.

A few road bikes have down tube levers that allow you to choose between index and friction. Turning the centre screw enables you to select between them. Again, the only maintenance required is a quick shot of aerosol lube on the outside.

1 On simple trigger shifters, maintenance consists of an occasional spray with aerosol lube, then a wipe over. Try to direct the spray at the cable nipple, then operate the gear lever a few times to spread the lube around.

2 Rapidfire Plus levers have a separate lever for up and down shifts. Do not strip them down because they are spring loaded. To lube, remove the rubber cap over the nipple, if fitted, and squirt aerosol lube into the nipple recess.

3 If you find it awkward to use a gear shifter combined with the brake lever, try altering the angle at which the whole assembly is bolted to the handlebar. Loosen off the clamp bolt and move it to a more comfortable position, then retighten firmly.

4 On sports bikes with indexed down tube levers, aim one shot of aerosol lube at the outside edge of the central housing. When you apply the lube there, it more likely to find its way into the ratchet mechanism, where it is needed. Wipe off any surplus.

FRICTION SHIFTER

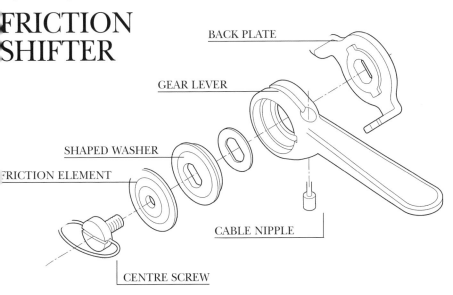

BACK PLATE

GEAR LEVER

SHAPED WASHER

FRICTION ELEMENT

CABLE NIPPLE

CENTRE SCREW

5 Most down tube shifters screw into bosses fixed to the frame, though a few have a band-on fixing. To remove, undo the central screw and pull off. To refit, make sure you locate the square cut-out on the back plate correctly.

STi and Ergopower levers

Combined gear and brake levers are much easier to use than down tube levers. But the internal components are tiny, so you must not strip them down unless you are an experienced bike mechanic.

Shimano make STi combined or integrated gear and brake levers for road bikes with drop handlebars. Campagnolo make Ergopower. But although they do exactly the same job, bits from one system must not be mixed with components from the other because they just will not work together.

When fitting STi levers to the handlebars, look for the groove on the outer edge of the brake hood. Feed a hexagon key down this groove to loosen and tighten the installation screw as necessary.

Adjusting any Shimano rear mech with STi levers is entirely normal, except that you must operate the smaller or B gear change lever behind the main lever at least eight times before fitting the gear cable, to ensure that you have selected top gear. You will not be able to see the cable hook or nipple housing in any other gear.

As for fitting brake cables to STi levers, it is much easier to thread the cable into the nipple housing if you pull the main or A lever to one side. Then feed the rest of the cable into the nipple housing and out through the back of the hood. Make sure the nipple is nicely seated in the housing.

With Ergopower levers, you also adjust the rear mech in the normal way. But access to the socket head installation screw is by pulling the brake lever. It is in the same position as on a normal hooded lever, and the brake cables are fitted in more-or-less the normal way - see the diagram on the opposite page.

When fitting the gear cable, you first press the smaller gear change lever or button down to its lowest notch, changing up to top gear and ensuring the lever is in top gear position. Then lift the edge of the hood rubber and feed the inner cable through the cable port. Provided you keep pushing it along gently, the cable should automatically find its way into the outer cable.

When fitting and servicing both of these systems, bear in mind that the performance of the cable is the main factor governing the quality and reliability of the gear change. So use only top-quality inner and outer cables, either the maker's own or a branded alternative. Keep them clean and free of grit during installation and lube them with a wax chain lube or similar if they are dry. If any of the nipples do not seat properly in the nipple housing, or are very tight, smooth off any rough edges with a knife or some abrasive paper.

WHEN YOU NEED TO DO THIS JOB:
◆ When fitting a new combined brake and gear levers
◆ If the gear changing or braking has got worse and will not respond to tweaking, indicating new cables are required.

TIME:
◆ Allow a couple of hours in case you have to sort out problems with the outer cable as well as the inners.

DIFFICULTY: ✄✄✄✄
It is not difficult just to fit the inner cable. But if the outers also need work, it starts to get a bit ticklish.

STi combined levers

1 When fitting the lever to the handlebar, loosen the clamp with a 5mm hexagon key if necessary. Find a comfortable position for the levers, with the tops of the hoods roughly horizontal.

2 Check you feel comfortable riding with your hands on the hoods, then finally tighten the installation screw. Bear in mind that you change up with the smaller or B lever and down with the main or A lever.

3 When fitting the inner cable, operate the B lever at least eight times to make sure that the internal gear-change mechanism is in top gear position. Then pull the main lever towards the handlebars.

4 You should now be able to see the nipple housing or cable hook (arrow) clearly through the cable tunnel. If you cannot, operate the B lever again until you can see where the inner cable fits.

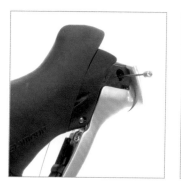 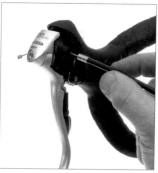

Ergopower combined levers

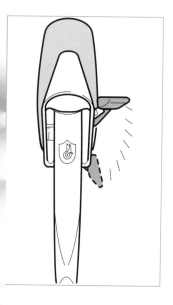 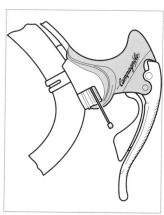

5 Thread the end of the inner cable through the nipple housing. Then pull the main part of the cable through from the other side. Do not seat the nipple in the housing at this stage.

6 Slide the outer cable over the inner and bring the end up close to the lever. Now pull the last section of inner through and check the nipple is seated evenly. Do not pull the cable tight until it is.

Release the inner cable from the rear mech and then lift the outer edge of the rubber lever hood so that you can push the old nipple out. Feed the new cable in through the cable port, taking it slowly at first so that the end of the cable enters the outer cable without any problem. Seat the lever hood back down carefully.

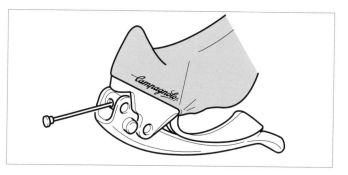

To fit a new brake cable, first press in the quick release button on the brake lever itself, then pull the lever right back. You will then be able to see the nipple housing and thread the brake cable through into the outer cable that should be taped to the handlebars.

Turn the pedals and change up to top gear - the smallest sprocket - using the lever or button on the inside edge of the lever.

Fitting new gear cables

When they become frayed or sticky with congealed oil, gear cables must be changed. Unfortunately, there is a vast variety of different gear shifters, so read the pages covering gear shifters first, then go through Steps 1 to 5 until you find the design nearest to yours.

All inner cables look very similar but that can be misleading. So when buying, specify whether you have indexed gears or not. The high quality cables for indexed gears are stiffer than normal ones and both inners and outers are often specially treated to reduce friction. That means it is OK to use indexed cables on ordinary gears, but not the other way round. If you use non-indexed cables on indexed gears, it will affect the gear change and you will have to adjust them more often.

The next problem is that Shimano use one type of nipple while Campag and SUNTOUR use a slightly different one. So you also have to specify the make of gear but even then, you sometimes have to file the nipple a little until it fits snugly into the shifter.

When fitting new inner cables, check the outers for kinks and breaks as well. On indexed gears, it is best to use ready-made outers with metal ferrules rather than making complete cables up yourself. Anyway, special outer cable is made for indexed gears. This has separate wires running the length of the cable, held together by a plastic cover. This kind of outer cable does not compress when the inner is fully tensioned, so it does not affect the way the indexing works.

Many cable clamps are designed so that the inner cable wraps around the clamp bolt slightly. There is usually a shallow groove to fit the cable into, but you should make a mental note of the old cable path before removing the old inner cable, just in case. If the gears do not work well after fitting a new cable, you may have fitted it on the wrong side of the cable clamp.

Lubricate inner and outer cables with silicon, mineral oil and synthetic lubricants only, not grease.

CABLE SEALS

The length of outer cable between the frame and the rear mech can get filled with dirt and water and this has a major effect on the performance of the rear mech. Fit a new outer cable every time you fit a new inner and fit a cable seal as well to prevent the gear change deteriorating again.

MTB and hybrid

1 Some handlebar shifters have a partly hidden cable recess. Look for it by moving the lever forward, then tracing the path of the cable round the lever. If you screw the cable adjuster right in, the nipple may pop out of the recess.

2 On underbar set-ups, the best way to get at the inner cable is to take the bottom cover off. In most cases, it is held in place by two or three tiny Phillips screws.

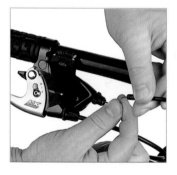

7 When the end of the cable emerges from the cable adjuster, feed the end into the outer cable and keep pushing it through until it pops out the other end. Then pull it tight, carefully seating the end of the outer in the cable adjuster.

Run the outer cable from the frame to the rear mech in a smooth curve. Carefully feed the inner through the cable adjuster and clamp, then seat the outer in the cable adjuster.

3 With the cover out of the way, check that the inside is not choked with old grease. If so, wipe it all away. Then give the inside a short spray of aerosol lube. Do not overdo it.

4 You also have to remove the cover to change the inner cable. Then pull the outer cable out of the adjuster and push the inner cable towards the shifter, freeing the nipple.

5 On some other designs, including rotary shifters, access to the inner cable is by a screw-in plug. Unscrew the plug and spray lube in there, or pull out the old cable .

6 When fitting a new inner cable, you may find it easier to work from underneath, as here. Hold the cable between finger and thumb and gradually feed it into the changer.

Sports bike gear cables

1 Move the lever to top gear position and separate the old inner cable from the rear mech. Then pull it out of the outer cable and the cable guides, if fitted. Push the nipple up and out of the recess, using pliers if necessary.

2 With down tube shifters, check that the guides under the bottom bracket are not damaged or blocked. Carefully uncoil the new cable to prevent any kinks and, if you are reusing the old outer cable, make sure it is OK.

3 Check that the gear lever is in top and that the chain is on the top sprocket. Feed the new inner cable through the nipple recess in the lever, slot it into the cable guides and thread it through the cable stop down by the rear mech.

4 Feed the inner cable into the outer and take it in a smooth curve down to the cable adjuster on the rear mech. Check which side of the cable clamp the cable should run, pull it tight with pliers and tighten up the clamp bolt. .

WHEN YOU NEED TO DO THIS JOB:
◆ If the cables are frayed or sticky, leading to a heavy gear change.
◆ When there is a mystery fault with the indexing and lube does not help.

TIME:
◆ 30 minutes to fit a rear mech cable, less to fit a front mech cable.

DIFFICULTY: ///
◆ Easy to fit new cables on a racing bike with down tube shifters, but handlebar and twist grip shifters are very fiddly.

TOOLS:
◆ A cable cutter is desirable.

READY-MADE CABLES
Once the cable from the frame to the rear mech has started to deteriorate, there is no point trying to clean it out again with thin wire or aerosol lube. Replace with a short length of outer cable made for this job and sold individually. No need to buy a complete cable set.

Sturmey Archer and Torpedo hub gears

Too many utility bike riders struggle along because their hub gears do not work. Yet they are the easiest gears of all to adjust and work really well in city traffic.

Inside all hub gears are a lot of carefully machined parts that have more in common with the automatic gearbox on a car than with anything else on a bike. Fortunately these internal parts seldom go wrong and on the rare occasions when there is a fault, it is probably due to wear and a complete new unit is usually the answer. You should never try to strip down a hub gear by yourself, as it is unlikely that you will ever get it back together again correctly without special tools and know-how.

The commonest problem on a Sturmey is finding that you can only pedal in one gear – somehow you are in neutral when the gear lever is in other positions. The other big fault is slipping in the gears – there is a coughing noise, the pedals jerk round suddenly and then go back to normal. This happens more often going uphill. These and most other faults are more often caused by incorrect adjustment of the cable, a broken cable or a broken control chain than anything else.

Follow the basic process given in Steps 1 to 3 to fit new cables or control chains and to keep the gears in adjustment. New cables come complete with inner and outer and on older bikes, the outer is positioned with an adjustable heavy-duty frame clamp. If you ever find that you cannot adjust the cable correctly, adjust the position of the frame clamp. If the cable runs over a pulley, check that it turns freely.

The latest Sturmey Archers are sealed and do not need oiling. But if there is a black plastic oil port on the hub body, feed a few drops of light oil into the hub every couple of weeks.

Wheel bearings are cup and cone type, adjusted in the usual way, but you will probably need a special spanner. Adjust on the opposite side from the drive chain.

Remove back wheel

1 On hub gear bikes, the gear cable connects with the back axle, so the first step is to separate them. Undo the knurled wheel on the gear cable one quarter-turn, then undo the adjuster about twelve turns to release the cable.

2 Slacken both wheel nuts with a spanner, then undo them the rest of the way with your fingers. To prevent the axle turning, special washers fit around the axle and into the frame. Place the wheel nuts and washers to one side.

New cable and adjustment

1 Check first that the control chain moves freely and is screwed right into the axle. Undo it one half-turn at the most to align it with the control cable. If the chain is stiff or broken, simply unscrew the old one and screw in a new one.

2 Put the gear lever into low and prise out the nipple of the old inner cable, then unscrew the outer from the back of the lever. Fit the new cable, clamp the cable at the correct length and tighten the adjuster up to the knurled nut.

3 Select N or 2 on the gear lever and look through the inspection hole in the axle nut. Clean out if necessary. Screw the adjuster up or down until the shoulder is exactly in line with the end of the axle – see the diagram opposite.

WHEN YOU NEED TO DO THIS JOB:
- ◆ Cable is broken.
- ◆ Control chain is stiff or broken.
- ◆ Gears will not engage. Or they slip (step 3 only).

TIME:
- ◆15 minutes to fit new cable.
- ◆ 2 minutes for step 3.

DIFFICULTY:
- ◆ It is easy to fit a new cable but adjusting the gears can be awkward.

TOOLS:
Special cone spanner.

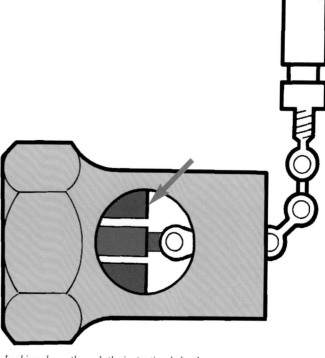

Looking down through the inspection hole, the arrow indicates where the shoulder of the control rod should be aligned with the end of the axle.

3 Push the axle forward with your thumbs, but try to hold the wheel as it drops away to stop it bouncing around. Now support the frame with one hand while you lift the chain off the sprocket and put the wheel to one side.

4 When refitting, replace the shaped axle washers. Then do up the wheel nuts lightly, pulling the wheel back so that it is centralised, with about 12mm of play in the chain. Tighten the wheel nuts, giving each side a turn at a time.

Torpedo hub gears

1 Check that the control chain flexes easily and that it is screwed fully home into the axle. Also make sure that the cable is undamaged and is not frayed where it goes over the pulley. Select H or 3 position on the gear lever.

2 The Torpedo cable comes in one piece, with a plastic ratchet that clicks on to the control chain. The length of the inner cable is adjusted with a hexagon key via the cable clamp, so that the ratchet just reaches the control chain.

3 Bring the end of the control chain and the ratchet together, then push the ratchet onto the control chain as far as you can using minimum force. Check that the cable feels fairly taut but not under high tension.

Nexus and Sachs hub gears

Torpedo hub gears are similar to Sturmey Archer but the new generation of multi-speed hubs opens up a new era for city bikes.

Torpedo hub gears – see previous page – are very straightforward three-speed units. Unlike a Sturmey Archer, they will always give you drive – you may not get the gear you want but at least you can always get one. The main thing that can go wrong is the cable. It will either need tightening up or you will have to fit a new one. Use Steps 1 to 3 to help you with both these jobs. If you need to remove the back wheel, disconnect the gear cable as in Step 4, then use the same procedure as when removing a Sturmey wheel.

Shimano Nexus gears have either four or seven speeds. The seven-speed version has a very wide range of gears, right down to a crawler gear for steep hills.

The main problem with Nexus is the cable going out of adjustment, which is indicated by unusual noises or inability to select a gear. If a hub brake is fitted and there is an unusual noise when using the brakes or the brakes are very sharp, there is not enough grease in the brake.

Either get it topped up by your local bike shop or fill the brake body with brake grease through the topping-up hole on the outside of the brake unit. You have to get the gear refilled with grease and serviced every six months anyway.

When removing a wheel with a Nexus hub, select first gear. Then disconnect the cable and the brake arm, if fitted.

Most of these hub gears are sealed and do not need lubricating, but check with the supplying dealer if you are not sure.

Fitting a new cable and

1 When fitting a new cable or adjusting the gears, select fourth gear on the gear shifter using the rotary hand grip before doing anything else. The figure '4' must appear in the round indicator window.

2 To remove the old gear cable, undo the three tiny Phillips screws holding the cover onto the gear shifter. The screw heads fit from underneath, so be careful not to let them drop on the floor.

5 Thread the new inner cable round the three rollers in the gear shifter and feed the end through the cable adjuster and the outer cable. Push the slack through and seat the nipple carefully.

6 Push the inner cable down through the outer and the cassette. When it emerges inside the rear drop out, lead the cable round the pulley and through the cable clamp. Pull the inner cable tight.

7 Tighten the cable clamp grub screw to keep the cable under tension. Then screw the cable adjusting bolt at the end of the outer cable in or out until the two red lines line up. Road test the bike to check that the gear changes go through easily and that the gear is silent, apart from when changing gear or a second or so afterwards.

Adjusting Nexus gears

3 Working from the top, lift off the silver cover. This allows you to prise the cable nipple out with a screwdriver. Cut the inner cable at a convenient point and pull it all out of the outer cable.

4 That leaves the rest of the cable clamped to the hub. Undo the socket head grub screw and pull out the remaining part of the old inner cable. To fit the new cable, start at the shifter end.

WHEN YOU NEED TO DO THIS JOB:
◆ Control chain has broken or gone stiff.
◆ Cable has frayed or broken.
◆ You cannot find all the gears.

TIME:
◆ 10 minutes to fit new cable on either Torpedo or Sachs 7-speed.
◆ 5 minutes to adjust Torpedo cable.
◆ 2 minutes to check click box location.

DIFFICULTY:
◆ Very easy – much easier than adjusting Sturmey Archer.

Sachs 7-speed hub gears

Hub gear combined with rear brake, showing the brake reaction arm that bolts onto the frame on the right.

1 If you suspect that the cable or lever on a seven-speed Sachs hub gear has been damaged, it can only be replaced as a complete unit. So undo the lever clamp, pull it off the handlebars and undo all the cable fastenings.

2 There is no need to adjust the cable as it is sealed into the click box. This in turn fits onto the end of the axle. Check by loosening the mounting screw occasionally and pushing the click box onto the axle, retightening the screw by hand.

3 Sitting on the end of the axle, a click box is quite vulnerable to damage when a bike falls over. Park your bike carefully to prevent this happening and always fit the guard when you refit the back wheel, just in case.

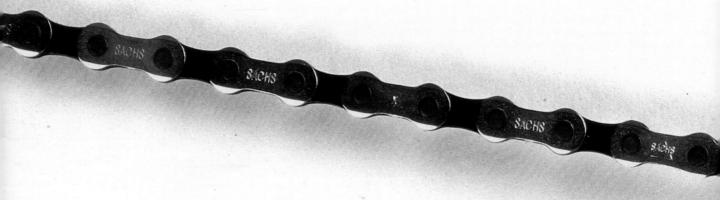

CHAPTER 5

CHAIN, PEDALS & CRANKS

The secret of cycling is the conversion of muscle power into mechanical power, as efficiently as possible. It is the chain and cranks that make this possible.

Drive systems: components

Try to identify the type of chainset and bottom bracket you are dealing with, before you start work. More and more types are coming onto the market. If you do not have the correct tools to deal with them, you are wasting your time.

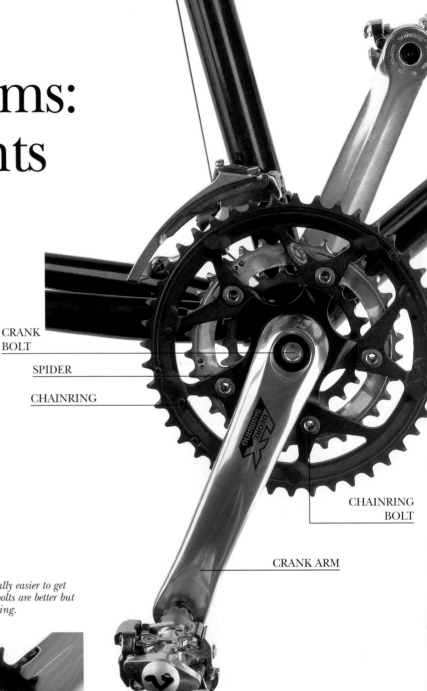

CRANK BOLT

SPIDER

CHAINRING

CHAINRING BOLT

CRANK ARM

Four-bolt chainsets are very popular, although it is usually easier to get hold of five-bolt replacement chainrings. In theory five bolts are better but the real difference between them is just a question of styling.

This five-bolt LX chainset is cotterless and is removed by undoing the crank bolts anti-clockwise with a long hexagon key and using a crank extractor tool. Various sizes of chainring can be bolted on, depending on the gearing you want. They can also be replaced reasonably cheaply if they become worn.

1 This chainset is a modern cotterless design, identified by the socket-headed crank bolt. Older types of cotterless have standard hexagon crank bolts, which are often fitted with a slotted dust cap as well.

2 Standard bottom brackets have an axle supported by ball bearings that run in one bearing cup each side. Frequent stripping and greasing is desirable. Usually fitted with a toothed lockring.

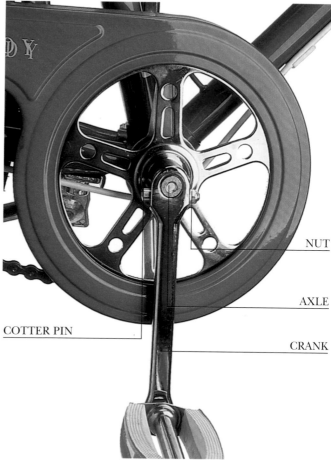

NUT

AXLE

CRANK

COTTER PIN

3 Some standard bottom brackets have a six-sided lockring and adjustable bearing cup requiring a large spanner. Others have two neat pairs of holes in the adjustable cup, so they can be adjusted using a pin spanner.

4 You can identify a cottered chainset by the cotters that are pressed into holes in the cranks, locking them to the axle. This type of chainset is found on elderly and budget bikes only and they are nearly always made of chromed steel. Cottered chainsets are fitted to a standard adjustable bottom bracket.

5 Wear trainers or some other type of lightweight shoe with standard pedals and toe clips. On budget bikes and kids' bikes, the pedals are often made of plastic and cannot be stripped down or adjusted. You have to fit new ones if the old pedals start to grind. If you upgrade to metal pedals with proper bearings, they will last longer and work more efficiently.

6 There are many designs of clipless pedals around. They all allow you to pedal much more efficiently and in greater comfort. But you can only use them with special shoes, which can be a problem if you have to walk in them.

7 When buying, get advice from a reliable bike shop or an expert rider. Take care that the shoes are a good fit and are feel right. BMX and some MTB clipless pedals (above) are double-sided for easy use in the heat of the moment.

DOUBLE-SIDED PEDALS

A popular type of MTB pedal has a clipless mechanism on one side and a toothed platform on the other. Good in town or cross country when you are on and off the bike.

Drive system: care and inspection

As the miles go by, wear gradually builds up in the drive system. To maintain maximum efficiency, check it over every few months.

It is the build-up of gritty, oily dirt on the chain, sprockets and chainring that causes most wear in the drive system. Keep the chain clean and well lubricated and it will slow down wear enormously. But if you allow the dirt to sit there undisturbed, the gritty deposit acts as an abrasive paste.

As a result, every time the chain rubs against the teeth of the chainring or sprockets, a tiny fragment of metal will be worn off it. Multiply that by the number of times the chain slips on and off the teeth of the chainring in 100 miles and you can see that the amount of wear will soon become significant.

Chainrings are usually made of an aluminium alloy. The cheaper types are quite soft but luckily they pick up a hard layer on the surface as they are used and this slows down the wear. The more expensive chainrings are made of harder alloys or are anodised to combat wear. Either way, the chain and sprockets usually wear faster than the chainring.

Once a new drive system has done a thousand miles or so, the chain will be starting to wear. If you fit a new one at that point, it will prevent the more expensive sprockets and chainrings starting to wear as well.

You may get away for a while without ever changing these components. But eventually you get to the point where there is a regular cough or jerk as you turn the cranks, particularly when putting on the pressure. You then have to replace the complete transmission which means the chain, chainring and sprockets.

1 Chain rings are usually fixed to the spider of the chainset with four or five bolts. So the first part of the inspection is to check they are tight. The sleeve nut at the back of the chainring may turn as you do so – stop it turning with a screwdriver.

2 If the cranks are loose on the axle, they sometimes creak as you ride along. But it is better to test for movement by holding one crank while you wiggle the other. If you feel either one moving, tighten the crank bolts immediately.

3 The next check is for wear in the bottom bracket bearing. This is easier if you slip the chain off the chainrings. Hold each crank near the pedal and try to move them diagonally. If both cranks move the same amount, the bottom bracket needs changing or adjusting.

4 Check also that the cranks turn smoothly and quietly. Strip and investigate if not. Then, using the chainstay of the frame as a fixed point, turn the crank so you can see if the gap between the chainring and the frame varies. If it does, remove the chainring so you can see if the spider is bent.

LOOSE CRANKS

If the left-hand crank is worn and you cannot tighten it enough to stop it moving, try filing or grinding some metal off the reverse side of the square hole, where it fits on the axle. Assemble with Loctite and tighten as hard as you can.

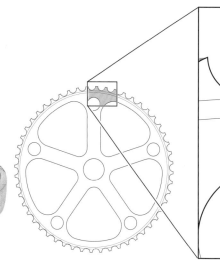

5 Look closely at the chainring for wear. If the outline of the teeth is blunted, now is a good time to fit new chainrings. By the time the teeth have become even slightly hooked, as shown above, the chainring is very badly worn. The chain, sprockets and all the chainrings must be replaced.

CHAINLINE AND GEAR SELECTION

You get minimum wear when the chain runs in a straight line. But derailleur gears work by making the chain run out of line, so the best thing is to set up a bike so that a line through the middle of the chainrings hits the middle of the sprocket cluster. Check the chainline by eye and if it seems to be out, ask a professional mechanic to check whether the wrong length of bottom bracket axle, the rear hub or mis-alignment of the frame is putting things out.

Smallest sprocket

Smallest chainring

Biggest sprocket

Biggest chainring

Avoid selecting gears where the chain has to bend in a noticeable curve as the chain will wear very fast, as shown on the left. You will also waste a lot of energy because of the extra friction created in the chain. If you use these extreme gears by mistake, change gear again as soon as you can.

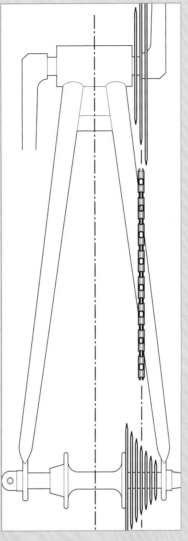

Perfect chainline on a bike with 21 speeds – seven sprockets and three chainrings.

WHEN YOU NEED TO DO THIS JOB:
◆ Every few months on a bike in regular use.
◆ When you are overhauling a neglected bike to bring it back into regular use.
◆ To assess how much you will have to do to bring a second-hand bike up to scratch.

TIME:
◆ 15 minutes for a complete inspection, to include checking chain wear and chainline.

DIFFICULTY:
◆ The hardest part is working out exactly which one of the various possible problems with the cranks is causing a problem.
◆ It is also quite hard to check the chainline absolutely accurately, although it is certainly worth doing on bikes with 14 gears or more.

TOOLS:
◆ Clearly marked steel ruler.
◆ A one-metre steel ruler makes it much easier to check the chainline.

Chain: clean and lube

A clean new bike chain transmits 98 per cent of the power you produce to the back wheel. So keep it that way.

Nearly all modern bikes have a $^3/_{32}$ in chain. Although if derailleur gears are fitted, you can be certain it is a $^3/_{32}$ chain. The only exceptions you are likely to come across are kids' bikes, hub gear bikes and track bikes. All these types usually have $^1/_8$ in chains, which are slightly wider. The width of the teeth on the chainring and sprockets matches the width of the chain, so you have to stick to either $^1/_8$ or $^3/_{32}$ components.

If you are buying parts for a bike that could have an $^1/_8$ chain, look for the spring link – see page 79 – or compare it with the chain on a bike with gears. If you reckon a bike has a $^1/_8$ chain, tell the retailer so he knows what sort of components you need.

Most new chains are fitted with Power Links or similar devices, which are special, hand-operated joining links – see the Blue Box on page 80. But the only way to shorten a chain when fitting a new one is to use a proper chain tool. You will also need a chain tool if you want to remove an old chain.

Basic $^3/_{32}$ chains are suitable for use with old six sprocket gear systems. The more expensive $^3/_{32}$ chains are narrower and more flexible, so they work fine with seven speed and eight speeds. Bikes with nine speeds need highly flexible, very narrow chains able to run a long way out of line. Eight-speed systems also tend to work better when fitted with a nine-speed chain. Do not try using a standard chain with an eight or nine speed system. The gears will not work well and the chain will wear out fast.

The latest ten-speed cassettes require a still narrower chain, plus their own special chain tool. But Wippermann make a suitable chain that can be joined with a special Connex link.

There is no need to use Campag chains with a Campag sprocket cassette or Shimano chains with a Shimano cassette. Makers like SRAM and Wippermann produce high-quality chains that will do the job at least as well and much cheaper.

Automatic chain cleaner

If you have to service your bike in the house or somewhere else where it is vital to keep the floor clean, a chain cleaning machine is very useful. First, you take the top off and position the machine on the bottom run of chain, near the rech mech. Then you hook the arm behind the bottom jockey wheel and re-fit the top. The machine must now be filled with solvent. To help this process, there is an automatic measuring system.

Finally, you just turn the pedals backwards and as the chain runs through the machine, it is scrubbed clean by several sets of revolving brushes. Dispose of the used solvent responsibly.

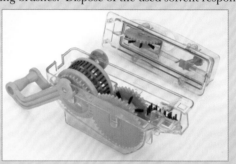

What chain?

If you do not know which type of chain is fitted, clean the side plates and check the brand name. Sedis, SRAM, Sachs and Taya are the most common brands of standard chain. The rivets can easily be pushed out to shorten the chain using almost any chain tool.

Shimano chains are marked UG, HG or IG. Unlike other chains, the rivet heads are slightly larger than the hole in the side plate. So when a rivet is pushed out, the rivet hole becomes enlarged. That means special black joining rivets must be used to join the chain up again.

SPECIAL CLEANING FLUIDS
Chain cleaning machines are often sold with a bottle of cleaning fluid as a special offer. But once that bottle is finished, any standard degreaser, normally used with a brush, should work fine in the machine and probably cost a lot less. However, you must dispose of these solvents in the dustbin, preferably pouring them onto a wad of newspaper so that they are absorbed. Do not ever pour them down a sink or road drain where they may leak into the ground water and contaminate the environment. You could use a more environmentally-friendly citrus alternative but the residue still has to be disposed of carefully as it will be contaminated with the hydrocarbons used in chain lubricants.

Easy chain cleaning

1 If your chain is caked in mud, hose it clean first. But if it is just covered in oily dirt, remove the worst of the clag with a cloth. Take care to clean the back of the chain as well.

2 Use the edge of a cloth and a screwdriver or a special C-shaped brush to scrape out the muck between the sprockets. Also wipe the teeth of the chainrings with the cloth.

3 The cloth will not reach between the chain rollers, so spray with solvent and scrub with an old toothbrush next. Then flush away with an old sponge and plenty of water.

4 When the chain is clean, dry with a rag. Then spray with aerosol lube to drive out the water. Next day, complete job with chain lube, preferably either wax- or teflon-based.

Checking chain wear

1 As chains wear, they also stretch. So as a basic check, try lifting one rivet only at the front of the chainring. If that opens up a visible gap between the chain and the chainring, the chain is badly worn.

2 Measuring the length of a known number of chain links is a more reliable method of gauging wear. Use a steel ruler as they are easy to read, then position the zero of the ruler on the centre of a rivet.

3 Count out twelve links of chain. Twelve links of new will measure 12in to the centre of the rivet. A badly worn chain, one that is ready for the dustbin right away, will have stretched out to $12^1/_8$ in.

4 The easiest and most straightforward way to assess the condition of a chain is to use a Wipperman gauge. Just fit the hooks at each end in the space between the links, 20 links apart. If the chain is in good shape, the tool will form a triangle, with a gap between tool and chain. If it is worn out, the tool will lie flat along the top of the chain.

WHEN YOU NEED TO DO THIS JOB:
◆ Every month when the bike is in daily use.
◆ When the chain is visibly dirty.
◆ After a ride through mud or heavy rain.

TIME:
◆ 15 minutes to clean a dirty chain; another 15 minutes to clean your hands. Consider using disposable latex gloves, obtainable from motor spares suppliers.

DIFFICULTY:
◆ No special problems.

TOOLS:
◆ Chain cleaner machine, old toothbrush, lots of cloths, newspaper or old carpet to absorb any drips.

Chain: remove and replace

Sometimes you have no choice about splitting the chain. But try to avoid doing so because it always introduces a weak link.

SHIMANO CHAIN TOOL

REPLACEMENT RIVET

When you are faced with a really dirty or rusty chain, it is usually best to fit a new one. But if you want to bring an old chain back into use, try soaking it in paraffin or diesel oil, until it is as clean and flexible again. Either way, you have to take the chain off the bike, so first identify which type of chain you are dealing with – see page 76.

Once you know that, you can pick the correct method of removal and refitting. If you are dealing with a Shimano chain, you will need a replacement rivet or pin to rejoin the chain. You cannot use the old one. There might be a spare one concealed in the chain tool but if not, you will have to get a new pin from a bike shop before you can do this job. These replacement rivets are black and have a long stalk that has to be broken off with pliers to complete the job. Unfortunately there are several different types, so take your bike to the shop with you so that they can identify the one you need.

When you are choosing which rivet to push out, take care you do not pick one of these black rivets. If you do so, it will weaken the side plates and the chain will probably break at some time in the future. Look for a silver-headed rivet and push that out instead. If you are dealing with a super narrow nine or ten speed chain, you may find that it takes a lot of force to push the rivets out, so only use a top quality chain tool.

Standard chai[n]

1 Wind the punch out and position the chain on the guides furthest from the punch. Shimano chain tools work fine on standard chains – you just have to adjust the support screw so that it presses on the back of the chain.

WHEN YOU NEED TO DO THIS JOB:
◆ The chain is badly worn.
◆ The chain is rusty.
◆ You cannot undo the jockey wheel bolts.

TIME:
◆ Allow 20 minutes the first time you split the chain as you will need to take your time and check each stage carefully.

DIFFICULTY: ✓✓✓✓
◆ You will have to use quite a lot of force to push out the rivet, which makes this job a bit nerve wracking until you're used to it. Also, when working on a Shimano chain, you must be very careful to press out a normal silver-headed rivet, and never a black-headed joining rivet.

TOOLS:
◆ Standard or Shimano chain tool.
◆ Hefty pliers and small file.

Shimano HG and IG chain

1 Select a silver rivet – never a black-headed one – to push out. Fit the chain onto the guides furthest from the punch and adjust the support screw so that it firmly supports the back of the chain plate.

2 Check the punch is centred and then start pushing the rivet out. You will probably be surprised at how much force is needed. Drive the rivet right out, undo the chain tool and separate the two halves.

STANDARD CHAIN TOOL

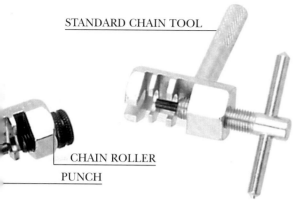

CHAIN ROLLER

PUNCH

Prising open master link on ⅛in chain

1 Utility bikes fitted with ⅛in chains often have a chainguard to protect the chain from dirt. It is nearly always easier to take the chain off if you remove the chainguard first.

2 Turn the cranks until you spot the master link. Lift the tail of the spring clip off the head of the rivet with a screwdriver. Take care or it will fly across the garage as you do so.

3 With the spring clip out of the way, dislodge the loose side plate by flexing the chain. Then pull out the rivet part of the spring or master link as well.

4 Re-join the chain by reversing the process for taking it off. The closed end of the spring clip must point in the direction in which the chain moves.

2 Make sure the chain is seated securely on the guides. Next, wind the punch in until the pointed end hits the dimple in the centre of the rivet. Check the punch is exactly centred, then screw it in just under six full turns. It will be stiff at first but become easier after the first half turn.

3 That forces the rivet out but not all the way. Then flex the chain to separate it. If it is still tight, push the rivet out a bit further but not right out. Leave a short length of rivet inside the chain plate so you can snap the chain back together. Then carefully push the rivet back into place.

3 To rejoin the chain, push the new rivet into both holes in the side plate so that the tip is just visible. Slot the chain into the chain tool, then screw in the punch until it hits the centre of the new rivet.

4 Wind the new rivet in until the groove in the replacement rivet emerges the other side of the chain. Snap off the bit that sticks out. If it does not break off cleanly, smooth the end with a file.

STIFF LITTLE LINKS
If you hear a regular cough or feel a regular jump through the pedals, one of the chain links is probably stiff. You can sometimes loosen up a stiff link by flexing the chain backwards and forwards with your thumbs, either side of the rivet. But if the rivet sticks out farther on one side than the other, fit the chain tool with the punch touching the rivet that sticks out. Then push the rivet in a tiny fraction by turning the handle about sixty degrees.

Fitting a new chain

Fitting a new chain is a bit more complicated than refitting an old one because you usually have to shorten it.

With a new chain, you get around 114 links. All 114 might be needed if your bike has a very large chainring or sprocket. But normally, you have to shorten a new chain and that means you have to gauge the correct length.

This is important because the chain tensioning mechanism on a rear mech can only cope with a certain amount of slack. It normally has to deal with the difference between the chain running on the big chainring and big sprocket, and the small chainring and the small sprocket. But additional links of chain can be too much for it, causing the chain to jump off the chainring occasionally and slowing down the gear change.

The easiest way to decide chain length is to run the new chain round the big chainring and the biggest sprocket, then add two more links. Or, select the biggest chainring and the smallest sprocket. Then set the chain length so that the chain cage points roughly 90º to the ground.

But if the bike has a bottom sprocket with 26 teeth or more, it is probably best to fit the chain on the biggest chainring and sprocket, then shorten the chain so that the chain cage points at 40º or 45º to the ground.

On bikes with rear suspension, you have to find the point in the suspension travel where the chain is tightest. This is best done by using your weight to compress the suspension and watching the rear mech swing forwards. Note where it swings furthest forward and set the length of the new chain so that the chain cage is 45º to the ground at that point.

If you have a bike where the chain jumps off a lot or the chain cage on the rear mech swings right back in bottom gear, you can try removing two links to see if that improves things.

Most Shimano transmissions are designed to be used with HyperGlide (HG) chains. But they also make super narrow 9-speed HG and InterGlide (IG) chains. However, SRAM, Wipperman and other makers now produce chains that work perfectly well with eight and nine-speed HG components as well as any type of Campagnolo, SUNTOUR and SRAM derailleur system.

POWER CHAIN AND SIMILAR JOINING LINKS

Breaking a chain with a chain tool, so you can remove it, is a nuisance and creates a weak link. To get round this problem, most new chains can be joined up and broken apart without a chain tool. Although you still need a chain tool if the chain has to be shortened.

To join a Power Chain, bring the ends together and thread both pins of the connecting link through the holes in the inner links. The ends of the pins should stick out slightly from the side plates. Then pull hard in opposite directions. The groove in each rivet will click into the narrow section of the opposite side plate. To separate the chain, clean it first. Then press the side plates together and force the inner links towards each other.

The KMG MissingLink II is similar to a Power Chain. But once you have assembled it, you pedal forwards and listen for the audible click as it comes together.

Wipperman chains with Connex joining links are very similar but have slightly curved slots in the sideplates. It is best to position the Connex link at right angles to the rest of the chain when joining and breaking it.

There is also the KMC Snap-On joining link which you flex with your thumbs to break apart. To rejoin, you fit the sideplate with two fixed rivets, add the loose sideplate and flex again.

Connex link

Power Chain

Setting correct chain length

1 To fit a new chain, select bottom gear on the rear mech and the big chainring on the front mech. Thread the new chain through the chain cage, then round the biggest sprocket and chainring.

2 Bring the two ends of the chain together - it is usually easiest on the bottom run. Then count the number of links to see how far they overlap with the rear mech chain cage at roughly 45º to the ground.

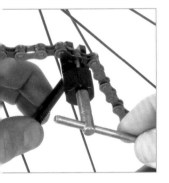

3 Shorten the chain by the number of overlapping links that you counted. Do not push the rivet right out - leave enough so that you can snap the other end into place.

4 Lift the chain onto the biggest chainring and biggest sprocket. If all seems to be well, push the chain rivet in the rest of the way. Check that the link is not tight, then road test.

5 An alternative way of gauging chain length is to fit the chain to the largest chain wheel but the smallest sprocket. Bring the ends together and overlap until the chain cage points at a right angle to the floor. Count the number of overlapping rivets as before, shorten the chain and then rejoin it. Check and road test.

BIKES WITH ONLY ONE SPROCKET

This category includes bikes with hub gears, single freewheels and fixed wheels. You can only adjust the chain tension on these by moving the back wheel. So when fitting a new chain, position the wheel in the middle of the slot in the rear drop out. Then remove the spring link – see page 79 – and wrap the chain round the chainwheel and sprocket. Pull the chain tight and grip the link where the ends overlap with two fingers. Remove the surplus chain with a chain tool and join the ends with the spring link. Finally, move the back wheel backwards or forwards until there is about 1/2in of slack in the middle of the bottom run when you lift it with your finger.

FIXED WHEEL

When riding a fixed wheel, you have to pedal all the time. This is an interesting change from being able to freewheel. But you can only ride a fixed wheel bike safely by fitting wheels with special track hubs. The fixed sprocket screws onto the larger thread on the hub. The lock ring has a left-hand thread and screws onto the smaller one. Alternatively, some riders use an adaptor that fits onto the hub. The sprockets are splined onto the adaptor, which makes it a little easier to swap them around.

Multiple Freewheels

You can still buy screw-on freewheels and hubs. But for eight, nine and ten-speed transmissions, the cassette or freehub design is better.

Sprockets are the toothed discs fitted to the back wheel that the chain runs on. Although non-cyclists usually call them cogs. When combined together into a multiple freewheel, they are sometimes called a 'cluster' for short.

If you find yourself struggling to get along or pedalling too slowly, particularly up hill, the gear ratios fitted to your bike may not suit you. Luckily it is easy enough to fit different size sprockets – or a complete new multiple freewheel and chain. But take expert advice before deciding which ratios to go for.

With screw-on freewheel or 'blocks' each separate sprocket screws onto the freewheel body. The body then screws onto the hub, so the whole thing is fairly heavy. You change the sprockets by holding the freewheel stationary with one chain whip and unscrewing the sprockets with a second chain whip.

In a modern cassette, the freewheel mechanism is inside the cassette body, which is fixed to the hub. The sprockets fit onto grooves machined in the outer surface of the cassette body, which are held in place with a lockring.

Screw-on multiple freewheel

There is a series of ridges around the centre of the freewheel body. The serrated part of the remover fits into them, so you can unscrew it using a spanner. Each sprocket tooth is shaped to speed up gear changes, working with the ramps on the side.

WHEN YOU NEED TO DO THIS JOB:
◆ Sprocket teeth are worn.
◆ Freewheel is noisy and feels gritty.

TIME:
◆ Allow 10 minutes to remove a screw-on freewheel as it is best to take your time.

DIFFICULTY: ⚒⚒⚒⚒
◆ Take care – it is easy to damage the cut outs.

SPECIAL TOOLS:
◆ Only attempt this job if you have the correct freewheel remover for the type of block and it is completely undamaged.

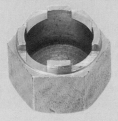

Cassette freewheel

Cassettes are better sealed and so have a longer working life than a screw-on freewheel. They carry eight, nine or ten sprockets, all with carefully-shaped sprocket teeth and large chain ramps to speed up the gear change and minimise the shock as the chain jumps from sprocket to sprocket.

REMOVING SINGLE FREEWHEELS

To remove a single freewheel, position a blunt cold chisel in the recess in the centre and hit it with a fairly heavy hammer. The freewheel unscrews in the normal, anti-clockwise direction. Take care not to cut into the centre of the freewheel with the cold chisel. On fixed wheel bikes, undo the lock ring in a clockwise direction, then unscrew the sprocket anti-clockwise using a chain whip – see page 84.

Removing a screw-on freewheel

1 Undo the hub nut or the friction nut on the quick release. Then fit the remover into the cut outs in the block centre. Carefully check that it fits perfectly. If it does not, you could wreck both the block remover and the cut outs.

2 Once you are satisfied that everything is OK, refit the hub nut or friction nut. Do it up finger tight so that it holds the freewheel remover in place. If you have a firmly mounted workshop vice, clamp the remover tightly in the jaws.

3 With the wheel in the vice, turn the rim an inch or so anti-clockwise. Alternatively, use an adjustable spanner to turn the remover about an inch anti-clockwise. Slacken the hub nut a little, then unscrew the cluster a bit more.

4 Keep loosening the hub nut and the cluster bit by bit until it will unscrew by hand. When re-fitting, spread anti-seize grease on the threads and be careful – the thread is very fine and it is only too easy to cross-thread it.

Freehubs and sprockets

The only way to find enough space for eight, nine and ten sprockets on the back wheel is by reducing the width of the rear hub. Then the only way to stop the axle breaking is to fit a bearing inside the freehub body.

Hubs with screw-on freewheels have been replaced by freehubs because of the number of sprockets that are now being squeezed into the narrow distance between the chainstays. That is 130mm on road frames and 135mm on MTB and hybrid frames. This can only be done by making the rear hubs narrower and narrower. But on hubs with screw-on freewheels, this means placing the axle bearings closer together as well, leaving the end of the axle unsupported. As a result, the axle can break and maybe cause an accident.

The freehub design overcomes this weakness. Instead of being screwed on as a separate component, the freewheel forms part of the hub. The axle bearing can then be fitted inside the extension of the hub that carries the freewheel body, with an extra one in the centre of the axle in some designs. Axle breakage is therefore almost unknown now that freehubs are standard.

On some early Campag and SUNTOUR freehubs, the sprockets are held in place by a threaded top sprocket. In this case, the top sprocket is unscrewed using two chain whips, or chain whip and removing tool. But both of these makers now use a serrated lockring design, as used by Shimano.

When they first came onto the market, only the big manufacturers like Campag and Shimano made freehubs and suitable sprocket cassettes. Now other makers have climbed onto the band wagon, supplying sprocket cassettes and even adaptors which allow Shimano sprockets on Campag hubs.

To save weight, the largest sprockets have an open spider design and are bolted or riveted together. Sometimes you can open up the cassettes to change individual sprockets but this is really a job for experts as there are many minor variations.

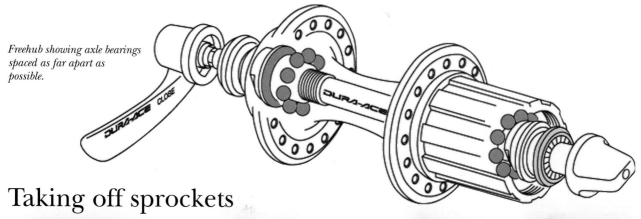

Freehub showing axle bearings spaced as far apart as possible.

Taking off sprockets

1 Check that you have the correct, undamaged removing tool. Fit the tool into the lockring and hold it there by screwing the friction nut back onto the quick release skewer.

2 Position the chain whip on the bottom of the middle sprocket and wrap the long chain around the rest of the teeth, allowing you to exert force in a clockwise direction.

3 Rest the wheel on the floor and hold the sprocket still with the chain whip while you undo the serrated lockring in an anti-clockwise direction using a large spanner.

4 It takes a lot of force to shift the lockring. But once it has moved, slacken the friction nut and the lockring bit by bit, until you can undo the lockring with your fingers.

Freehub body

1 Once you have removed the sprockets, take off the lock nut and cone on the plain side of the wheel and pull the axle out through the hub. Take the ball bearings out of the hub, and wipe off any surplus grease in the working area.

2 You should now be able to see the six-sided socket in the head of the bolt that holds the freehub body to the hub itself. Check that the socket is clear and undo the bolt. You will then be able to lift the freehub body away from the hub.

3 While the freehub body is off, clean the interior surfaces of the hub and freehub body with solvent. Then apply anti-seize grease to the retaining bolt to make it easy to remove next time. Reassemble by reversing the procedure.

4 While the freehub is off the wheel, take the opportunity to clean the cassette thoroughly and flush the body through with solvent. Then oil with heavy mineral oil through the gap between the inner and outer bodies at the back.

Campag freehub body

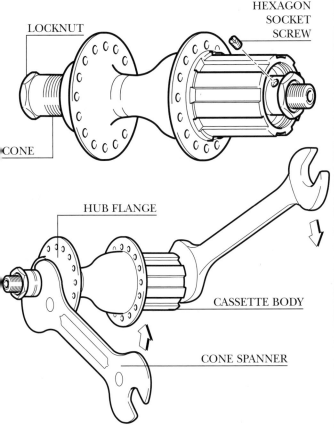

You can remove a Campagnolo freewheel body by first undoing the hexagon screw that acts as a safety device. Then undo the large locknut on the axle, holding the axle still using a cone spanner on the other end.

WHEN YOU NEED TO DO THIS JOB:
◆ New sprockets may well be needed if you have not fitted a new chain for thousands of miles.
◆ Different size sprockets may be needed if you go climbing mountains.
◆ The freehub body may need cleaning with solvent or replacing if it will not freewheel smoothly.

TIME:
◆ 15 minutes to remove sprockets.
◆ 10 minutes to strip out hub axle, if necessary.
◆ 5 minutes to remove freehub body.
◆ 1 hour to put everything back together again.

DIFFICULTY: 🔧🔧🔧🔧🔧
◆ One of the most difficult jobs you are likely to encounter on a bike. Removing the lockring is hardest, so your tools must be in good condition. The hub must be reassembled with great care.

TOOLS:
◆ Correct lockring tool, in undamaged condition.
◆ Chain whip.
◆ Large adjustable spanner.
◆ 10mm Allen key, preferably a long one.

LOCKRING TOOL

Pedals: removal and refitting

If the pedals creak and grind as you ride, you will never develop a smooth, efficient pedalling style. And if you are unlucky, they can even cause knee trouble.

When they are doing the budget for a bike, makers often leave the choice of pedals to last, when all the money has been spent. As a result, lots of bikes leave the factory fitted with the cheapest possible pedals. They are often made of cheap plastic, without proper bearings.

This is not good because you will never be able to pedal efficiently with pedals that do not rotate freely or are broken. And if the bearings suddenly seize or the cage suddenly falls apart completely, you can easily be pitched off into the road. To prevent problems, replace the pedals right away if you suspect they are unsafe.

Even when decent bearings are fitted, they are often given only a quick dab of grease at the factory and this soon gets washed away. This makes it worth stripping and greasing the pedals as a precaution, even if your bike is new or only a few months old.

Clipless pedals are removed and refitted the same way as ordinary pedals. But the bearings are usually sealed and special tools are required to remove and replace them. Leave it to the professionals, although luckily the bearings have a long life. Just concentrate on keeping them clean.

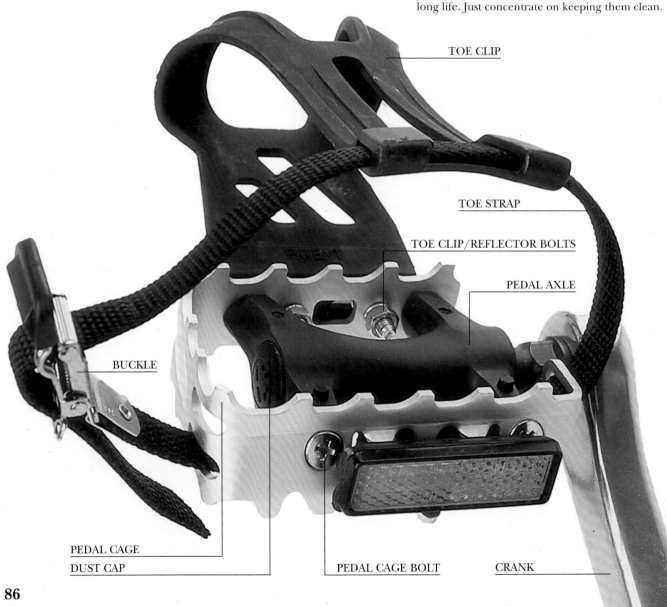

TOE CLIP

TOE STRAP

TOE CLIP/REFLECTOR BOLTS

PEDAL AXLE

BUCKLE

PEDAL CAGE

DUST CAP

PEDAL CAGE BOLT

CRANK

1 To remove the pedal on the chain side, fit a narrow 15mm or 17mm spanner onto the flats on the pedal axle. A proper pedal spanner as in the picture is the best tool for the job. Undo in the normal, anti-clockwise direction.

2 You may find it difficult to shift the pedal. Try spraying the axle end with aerosol lube from both sides. Leave for a while and try again. If that does not work, turn the crank until the spanner is roughly parallel with the floor.

3 Hold the saddle and handlebars and put your foot onto the end of the spanner – be careful, as it will probably move suddenly. If that does not work, use a length of tube to extend the spanner, and try once more.

GETTING STARTED WITH PEDALS

The weight of the pedal often makes it awkward when you are trying to get the pedal thread to start screwing into the thread in the end of the crank. So use both hands, taking the weight of the pedal with one hand while you turn the axle to screw it in with the other. Vary the angle of the pedal axle to the crank a bit at a time until the pedal thread engages the thread in the crank.

4 Now for the left-hand pedal: this is very unusual because it has a left-hand thread, designed to stop it unscrewing as you ride along. You therefore undo a left-hand pedal by turning it clockwise – the opposite way from normal.

5 To make it easier to remove the pedals next time, coat the thread on the axle with anti-seize grease. If you do not have any anti-seize grease, use some ordinary heavy oil. This is particularly important if the cranks are made of alloy.

LOOK FOR THE HEXAGON SOCKET

Nearly all pedals have flats for a spanner on the axle. But some pedals also have a hexagon socket formed in the end of the axle – easily spotted if you look at the back of the cranks. If you are working on pedals with a hexagon socket, it is usually easier to undo the pedals with a long workshop hexagon key than with a spanner.

LEFT AND RIGHT HAND PEDALS

Pedals are nearly always marked L for Left and R for Right, on the spanner flats by the crank end of the axle. There is a faint chance of you coming across ones marked G for gauche meaning Left and D for droite meaning Right.
NOTE:
Left-hand pedal: unscrew clockwise.
Right-hand pedal: unscrew anti-clockwise.
Reverse direction when refitting.

WHEN YOU NEED TO DO THIS JOB:
◆ If you are fitting new pedals.
◆ When stripping and greasing pedals.

TIME:
◆ 5 minutes.

DIFFICULTY:
◆ The most testing part is remembering about the left-hand thread on the left-hand pedal.

TOOLS:
◆ Long narrow spanner or purpose-made pedal spanner, or long Allen key.

Pedals: strip, grease and reassemble

Though similar to most other bearings, pedal bearings are small and can be awkward to work on.

On a wet day, pedals get showered with water. Most manufacturers try to stop this water getting into the pedal bearings by fitting a rubber seal between the bearing and the end of the axle. This usually works quite well but it is seldom completely effective.

Nevertheless, when stripping down a pedal, take care to avoid damaging any rubber parts and to put them back, without twisting, in the groove or wherever else that they came from. When the seal fits into the pedal cage around the inner bearing, it is sometimes best to stick it in place with ordinary clear glue. This makes assembly easier and prevents the seal falling out in the future.

The other way to combat water is to coat the bearings with plenty of water-resistant grease. Once you have assembled and greased the pedal bearings properly, they should not need attention again for many miles. Do not worry if you find the axle or cones are slightly pitted. They will still run smoothly despite a certain amount of damage.

It is sometimes difficult to refit the dust cap as they usually have a very fine thread. But if it is missing, the pedal bearings will fill with water. See if the dust cap from an old pedal will fit as they sometimes do. If not, try covering the open end of the pedal with adhesive tape.

When re-assembling, adjust the bearings so that the pedals turn smoothly - see pages 138-139 for how it is done with hubs. But take extra care with the lock nut. If it is not tight enough, the bearings could fall apart, the pedal will then disintegrate and maybe leave you sprawling in the road.

You will also find that smooth-turning pedals help you develop a good pedalling technique. There is no one pedalling style but as a guide, your foot should be positioned roughly horizontal at the top of the pedal stroke. You then apply as much power as you comfortably can on the down stroke, which is when you put most of the power in. Some people keep the heel slightly below the horizontal, others keep it slightly above. But these variations can be sorted out by experiment.

On the upstroke, most riders find it best to lift the heel slightly, to offer minimum resistance to the other foot that is making the power stroke.

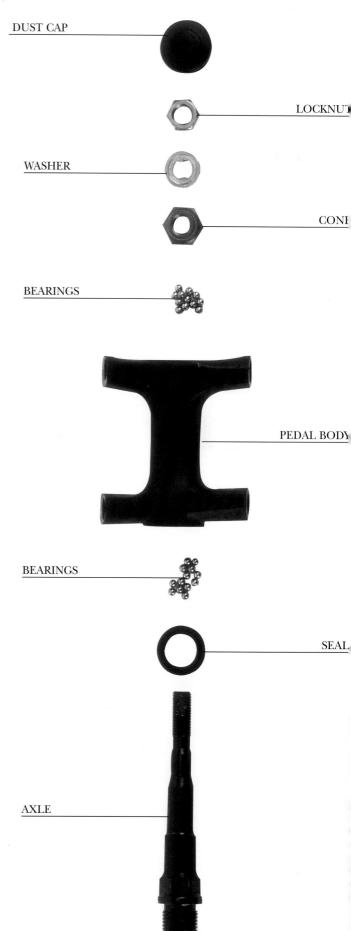

DUST CAP

LOCKNUT

WASHER

CONE

BEARINGS

PEDAL BODY

BEARINGS

SEAL

AXLE

1 Some pedals have a cage that can be separated from the pedal body. The cage certainly makes it awkward to work on pedals, so strip it off whenever possible. It may be easier if you use a vice.

2 The cage is usually fixed with Phillips or socket-head screws with countersunk heads. Loosen all four fixings a little before you remove the screws. Be careful not to distort the cage as you take it off.

3 Dust caps with domed centres are easy to prise out. But sometimes they fit flush and you have to use a tiny screwdriver. Unscrew metal dust caps with pliers or grips with wide-opening jaws.

4 Where there is a separate pedal cage, use either a socket spanner or a ring spanner to undo the locknut. On many types, only a socket will reach far enough into the pedal to slacken it off.

5 Once you have loosened the locknut, you can usually undo it the rest of the way with your fingertips. If it will not come off easily, spray the axle with aerosol lube to clean the threads.

6 Take out the lock washer next. Sometimes this is quite difficult if there is a tag that fits into a groove on the axle. Tip the pedal down to shake it off the axle.

7 The cone is now ready to be unscrewed. If there is a slot across the face of the cone, use a screwdriver. Or slide a small screwdriver between the cone and the pedal body and force it round.

8 While unscrewing the cone, hold the axle in the pedal body with your index finger, or you will get showered with greasy ball bearings. Or hold the axle in a vice by the spanner flats.

9 Catch all the loose bearings in a tin or on a piece of newspaper. Some will not drop out, so scrape them out with a pen top or similar. Clean and inspect all the minor parts but do not worry about minor pits in the bearing surfaces.

10 To re-assemble, stick the ball bearings into the inner bearing with grease, then lower the axle in. Holding the axle, turn the pedal up the other way, stick the outer bearings in, and re-fit cone, washer and locknut.

WHEN YOU NEED TO DO THIS JOB:
◆ With new pedals, in case they are not properly greased.
◆ If the pedal bearings feel rough and gritty.
◆ When the pedal bearings are loose.

TIME:
◆ 20 minutes per pedal, if you have a vice.
◆ 30 minutes per pedal if not.

DIFFICULTY: 🔧🔧🔧
◆ There can be problems getting to the outer bearing if you cannot remove the cage from the body. Otherwise stripping the pedal bearings is very good practice for greasing and adjusting other bearings. Do not overfill with grease.

TOOLS:
◆ Vice, wide-opening pliers or slip-jointed gland pliers.

1 There are nearly always circular holes in the pedal cage for the toe clip bolts. If not, toe clips are usually supplied with a backing plate to overcome this problem. But when buying, remember that pedals with built-in toe clip fixings look much neater.

Toe clips, straps and clipless pedals

Riding a bike without toe clips is a bit like riding a horse without a saddle – it can be done, but you are more likely to fall off.

Riders are sometimes put off using toe clips because they look unsafe. But experience shows that although it takes a little while getting used to them, clips and straps are a safety feature. On a bike with toe clips, your foot cannot slip off the pedal and cause a sudden swerve or loss of control. But that is exactly what can happen without toe clips. And if you fall off with your feet in toe clips, you seem to instinctively pull your foot out before you hit the ground.

The other advantage of toe clips is that they help you position the ball of your foot over the axle of the pedal. This makes it easier to flex your ankle at the top of the stroke, and directs all the power of your legs into the pedal.

Seldom do you need to tighten the toe straps. Most of the time, they just steady the toe clip – you only pull them tight when a major effort is needed, such as going up a steep hill. You can even buy short toe clips without straps, if you feel a 'halfway house' would help you get used to using them.

When buying toe clips, check that you get the right size for your foot and pedal combination. As for the pedals, go for ones with proper toe clip mounting holes and, preferably, a tag at the back of the cage to help you pick up the toe clip more easily when you are starting off from rest.

If you are looking at clipless pedals and the shoes that go with them, they come in a huge variety of designs. You will need advice from an expert on the combination of shoes and pedals that will suit you. You also have to consider the amount of 'float', which allows your foot to move a little and so takes the pressure off your knees.

Clipless pedals

1 The first clipless pedals were like the bindings used on skis. A cleat on the bottom of the shoe clicks into the pedal giving a firm connection. When it is time to get off your bike, you just twist your foot a little and it is free.

2 SPD-style clipless pedals are more compact than other types. Their best feature is the cleat 'buried' in the sole of the shoe, making it quieter and easier to walk in them. The spring clamping the shoe to the pedal can be adjusted.

2 Some road bikes are fitted with lightweight platform pedals. These are sometimes made of resin, sometimes alloy. Fit the special toe clips using the countersunk screws that come with the pedal. No nuts are needed, the holes are threaded.

3 To fit nylon or leather toe straps, feed the strap through the slots cut out of the sides of the pedal cage. If tight, pull through with pliers. On quality pedals, there is a tag on the pedal cage to stop the strap rubbing against the crank.

4 Pull the toe strap tight and position the buckle just outside the pedal cage. Leave enough slack between the buckle and the cage to slow down the pedal cutting into the strap – this is where they tend to break eventually.

5 The buckles are not intended to hold the toe strap firmly. Just pass the end under the knurled roller, then through the cut-out in the sprung part. Tighten the toe strap, when necessary, by giving the free end a jerk.

6 Fitting reflectors to the back of the pedals is particularly effective. They are almost unmissable to motorists and other road users because the twinkling light from the reflectors is constantly on the move. Most reflectors have a simple two-bolt fixing, similar to toe clips.

3 Mud and grit tends to clog all designs of clipless pedal, and it always takes a second or so to click the shoe into place. So to make it easier to use clipless pedals, there are several new designs with an extra large platform.

4 You can only use clipless pedals with shoes that have screw fixings for the cleats built into the sole. Some SPD shoes are fine for use on ordinary pedals but cleats can be fitted by simply cutting out an area of the rubber sole.

WHEN YOU NEED TO DO THIS JOB:
◆ When equipping a new bike.
◆ Getting the bike ready for winter.

TIME:
◆ 15 minutes to fit toe clips and straps.
◆ 5 minutes to fit reflectors.

DIFFICULTY: 🔧🔧
◆ No real problems, but you will sometimes find that the toe straps are very tight in the slots.

Chainrings and cranks

If you are not sure which type of chainset and bottom bracket you are dealing with, refer back to the beginning of this chapter.

A lloy cotterless chainsets are fitted to nearly all modern bikes. In most cases, they have replaceable chainrings. That works out very much cheaper when the teeth have worn down badly and need replacing or if you want to change the gearing. However, it is not always easy to get replacement rings from the chainset manufacturers.

Instead, you may have to ask your dealer to get hold of new rings from a specialist supplier. The French firm TA is the best known and can supply chainrings to fit almost any crank. But not only do the number of fixing bolts vary between different designs, so does the pitch circle diameter (PCD). The PCD is the diameter of a circle joining all the fixing bolts - see page 99.

The PCD on Shimano MTB cranks is usually 104mm. But on their road cranks it is 130mm, while Campag use 135mm. The smallest possible chainring on these has 38 or 39 teeth unless you fit a triple or Stronglight road cranks, with a 110mm PCD.

Older chainrings can be bolted to the crank spider in any position. But the oval type that was popular a few years ago must be fitted in a set position in relation to the crank. Look for the fitting marks on the back of the chainring and crank spider.

Many chainrings are fitted with pick-up pins to speed up gear changes. They also have a much larger pin to prevent the chain dropping into the gap between the chainring and the crank. The teeth often have varying profiles, to help the chain climb on and off when changing gear. So before unbolting the chainrings, make a note of exactly how they fit and check the fitting marks. The large pin on the outer face of the large chainring must be always be positioned beside the crank arm.

Some cotterless cranks are fixed to the bottom bracket axle with a fairly ordinary-looking hexagon-headed bolt. The cranks are fitted to the axle and removed with a special extractor tool. Later types have socket-head crank bolts that are self-extracting. You must tighten them hard with a long hexagon key. To remove them, you undo the socket bolts anti-clockwise. Better still, use a torque wrench to ensure they are correctly tightened. This point will come up very quickly if you ever try to claim warranty.

Socket-head bolts are also used on Shimano Octalink cranks. But the end of the axle is a complicated shape with eight splines, very different from the standard tapered axle. Octalink is claimed to give a more rigid, more secure fixing. Similar claims are made for the latest design of crank fixing known as ISIS (International Spline Interface Standard). This was devised in the United States but is intended to become the industry standard.

Cottered chainsets used to be found on most budget utility bikes – but even these are now fitted with steel cotterless chainsets. Nevertheless, you can still buy new cotter pins if the old ones get damaged. But remember, there are several types and size of cotter pin, so take the old one along as a pattern.

Finally, some BMX, kids' and utility bikes are fitted with a one-piece chainset. That is both cranks and the axle, all in one piece. This is not a good design but see page 101 for servicing.

Removing chainrings

1 Nearly all chainrings are bolted to the crank spider with chrome or alloy socket head bolts. Undo the first bolt half-a-turn, then the next one half-a-turn, continuing until all of the fixing bolts are loose enough to undo by hand.

2 The socket-head bolt shown fits into a sleeve nut that extends through all three chainrings plus the crank spider. Pull off the outer ring by pulling gently on opposite sides – it is a tight fit to prevent unwanted movement.

Removing one-key-release

1 Wind the crank fixing bolt in an anti-clockwise direction with a long, 6mm or 8mm hexagon key. Stop the cranks moving with your other hand. You will need to use quite a lot of force to do this.

2 Pull the crank a little to finally detach it from the axle. In this case, an Octalink bottom bracket axle is fitted but you are more likely to find a bottom bracket with a square taper axle for the cranks.

WHEN YOU NEED TO DO THIS JOB:
◆ Chainrings are worn or bent
◆ Bottom bracket bearing needs checking

TIME:
◆ 20 minutes for chainrings.
◆ 10 minutes to remove socket bolt cranks.

DIFFICULTY: 〃〃〃〃
◆ Changing a chainring requires care to prevent bending or distortion. Removing socket bolt cranks is easier than other cotterless types requiring an extractor.

SPECIAL TOOLS:
◆ Extractor tool not required to remove socket bolt cranks.

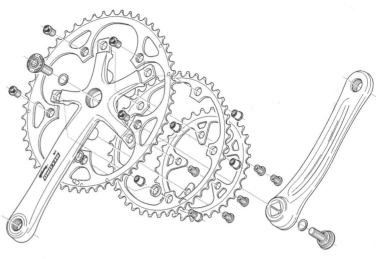

3 Check for spacers or washers between the chainrings, then lift the outer ring away for cleaning or straightening. The other rings usually remain in place until you draw the sleeve nuts out of the holes in the cranks.

4 In some cases, the small inner ring is bolted in place with a separate ring of bolts. Undo them all and the inner ring will come off. You may find that the smallest ring is made of steel so that it does not wear too quickly.

Many chainsets have only four spider arms, the fifth bolt screwing into a threaded boss on the crank. To keep the bottom bracket axle short, the cranks are low profile (S-shaped). And on triples, the smallest chainring is bolted into place with a second ring of bolts.

cranks

3 Collect the protective outer cap, crank fixing bolt and narrow washer together so that you do not lose them. The washer sits in the recess in the crank, so you may have to pick it out with your fingernail.

4 Check the bottom bracket is running silently and smoothly, then carefully clean all the old grease off the minor parts. Re-grease the fixing bolt and washer with good quality grease

5 Locate the crank on the end of the bottom bracket axle, slip the washer in the crank recess and fit the crank fixing bolt. Tighten the crank bolt with a torque wrench to the maker's specified figure.

6 Check the outer cap ring is tight using a pin spanner. Take great care to fit the cranks exactly 180° opposite each other on Octalink chainsets as it is only too easy to get it wrong.

TORQUE WRENCH
Bike and component makers now say that you should always use a torque wrench when fitting a nut or bolt. Torque wrenches measure the amount of force being applied to a nut or bolt via a standard socket spanner. The sockets fit on the torque wrench in the usual way but the ³⁄₈in size is best for bikes. A certain amount of force is set down for each individual nut and bolt on a list in the maker's handbook. When tightened to the force specified, nuts and bolts should never break or come loose. The attraction for manufacturers is that if they are faced with a warranty claim, they can reject it unless the claimant can show that a torque wrench was used when working on the item.

Crank removal

Taking off cotterless cranks can be nerve-wracking, but once you have done it a couple of times without problems, you are on your way to becoming a good mechanic.

The bottom bracket axle for most cotterless cranks has square taper ends. The axle, as well as the tapered hole in the crank that fits onto it, has to be made very accurately. But thankfully, the square taper shape is standard across pretty well all makes of crank and bottom bracket.

When refitting, reverse the process for removal, assembling the crank and axle with the lightest possible film of grease on the surfaces where they touch. This prevents corrosion between the steel axle and the alloy crank, making it easier to get the cranks off later. Some people claim you should assemble the cranks dry but majority opinion seems to agree that a film of grease is best. Tap the cranks home lightly with a soft mallet, or a hammer with a piece of wood as a cushion.

Once fitted, tighten the crank bolts up as hard as you can. The extractor tool usually has a socket spanner for this part of the job but you can get more leverage if you use a socket and ratchet handle from a normal automotive $^3/_8$in socket set.

Tighten up the crank bolts every hundred miles or so for the first few hundred miles after fitting, in case they loosen under pressure.

Do not ride a bike with loose cranks as the hard steel axle easily damages the soft alloy. Once the square taper in the crank has been damaged, it may not be possible to tighten it properly again. If your cranks just will not stay tight, try using Loctite stud adhesive on the spline. If that does not work, you can at least buy spare left-hand cranks.

CRANK LENGTHS FOR NORMAL CYCLING	
Under 5 foot 10 inches	170mm
5 foot 10 inches to 6 foot	172.5mm
Over 6 foot	175mm
Go for slightly shorter cranks if you have creaky knees. Bear in mind also that most riders find 170mm cranks work fine.	

Removing square taper cran

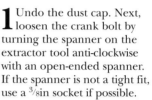

1 Undo the dust cap. Next, loosen the crank bolt by turning the spanner on the extractor tool anti-clockwise with an open-ended spanner. If the spanner is not a tight fit, use a $^3/_8$in socket if possible.

2 Undo the crank bolt the rest of the way with your fingers, then pull it out. Check that you do not leave the large washer behind or it could prevent you screwing in the extractor tool far enough.

COTTERED CHAINSET WITH BOTTOM BRACKET

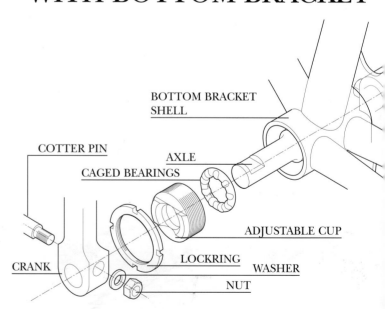

BOTTOM BRACKET SHELL

COTTER PIN

AXLE

CAGED BEARINGS

ADJUSTABLE CUP

CRANK

LOCKRING

WASHER

NUT

3 Get ready to remove the crank by checking that the thread on the extractor tool and the internal thread round the crank bolt recess are clean and undamaged. Slowly screw the extractor into the thread.

4 Check that the extractor is going in straight. If it seems to tighten up after the first couple of turns, the extractor is probably going in at an angle. Take it out, oil the thread lightly and try again.

5 When you are sure the extractor is installed OK, tighten the extractor bolt. You will find it takes quite a lot of force to push the chainset off the axle at first. Hold one crank stationary as you work.

WHEN YOU NEED TO DO THIS JOB:
◆ For access to the bottom bracket.
◆ When the bike needs a thorough overhaul.

TIME:
◆ Allow 30 minutes the first time, so that you can check carefully as you go.
◆ 10 minutes once you are used to the job.

DIFFICULTY: ⚒⚒⚒⚒
◆ You need a delicate touch when screwing the extractor into the crank, and quite a lot of force when actually pushing the crank off the axle.

TOOLS:
◆ Correct crank extractor with undamaged threads. A socket set may also be useful.

ISIS cranks

1 ISIS cranks fit onto an axle with 10 tapered splines.

2 Special tools are needed to service ISIS components.

3 ISIS design is expected to reach budget bikes soon.

Cottered chainset

1 Remove the nut and washer on the cotter pin, then give it one sharp blow with a mechanic's hammer. If that does not fire the cotter pin right out, find a 1in diameter metal bar, place on the pin and hammer on that instead.

2 You can re-use the old cotter pin if it is not damaged. If you have to fit a new cotter, take the old one to the bike shop as a pattern. When you are ready to refit the chainset, test-fit the new cotter pin and see how well it fits.

3 Slip the washer on the threaded end of the new cotter pin and tighten the nut as far as it will go by hand. If there isn't enough thread to reach the end of the nut, file some metal off the flat part. Repeat if necessary.

4 Fit the cotter pin so the nut is under the crank when the crank points backwards. Bash it right home with a medium hammer, then fit the washer. Tighten the nut hard with a spanner. Fit the other cotter the opposite way.

Cartridge bottom brackets

The most heavily-loaded component on any bike is the bottom bracket axle. Fit a new one as soon as you can detect any wear.

Most bikes are fitted with a cartridge or sealed bottom bracket at the factory to speed up assembly. This is also good for bike owners, because they have rubber seals around the axle that keep out water better than a standard bottom bracket with loose bearings and separate cups.

But not surprisingly, cartridge bottom brackets cannot be opened up for maintenance purposes. So once they start to wear, that is it. They cannot be greased or adjusted – you just have to fit a replacement, preferably a better quality one.

Replacement cartridge bottom brackets are supplied by chainset manufacturers and by many independent makers. Some independents only produce extremely light but expensive units made out of titanium and other fancy materials. Others produce original equipment quality ones, often more cheaply than the big makers. You tend to get what you pay for but the life of a cartridge bottom bracket is hard to predict.

Budget bottom brackets can wear out in a couple of thousand kilometres or less, while the most expensive units like the Royce more-or-less last for ever. But mountain bikers riding cross-country in all weathers should expect to wear out bottom brackets much faster than normal.

The main variable when buying spares is the length of the axle. This depends on the number of chainrings, plus the design of the cranks and the frame. To avoid problems, always take the old unit to your bike shop as a pattern.

If you find that the threads in the frame are too tight for easy fitting, clean them up with aerosol lube and by screwing an old bottom bracket cup in and out a few times. Cut a vertical hacksaw slot in the bearing cup to help get rid of any dirt in the threads.

Sealed brackets can be fitted to almost any bike as an upgrade. No modifications to the bottom bracket shell are required, although slots to let water drain away are sometimes provided.

ASSEMBLY VARIATIONS
The sealed unit shown on page 97 is a budget version from Shimano, with the collar fitted from the chain side. Many other types, including later Shimano, are assembled the opposite way, with the collar screwed in from the non-chain side. If you have trouble fitting a sealed unit, check the instructions in case you should be fitting it from the other side. Check also if the part that will not screw in has a left-hand or a right-hand thread.

Octalink bottom brackets

1 Clean inside the bottom bracket with aerosol lube, then lightly coat the threads on the main body sleeve with grease. Fit the special tool in the recess around the axle and screw the unit in anti-clockwise from the chain side.

2 Switching to the non-chain side of the bike, screw the collar or adaptor into the bottom bracket shell in a clockwise direction with your fingers. Work it backwards and forwards if it is tight and check it is going in absolutely straight.

3 Tighten the main body using the special tool and spanner as hard as you can. It is fully home when the edge of the threaded portion is flush with the edge of the bottom bracket shell. The main body screws in anti-clockwise.

4 Finally, from the non-chain side, tighten the adaptor clockwise until it meets the end of the main body, locking it into place. When fully tight, the adaptor will be almost invisible, fitting neatly into the bracket shell.

SEALED BOTTOM BRACKET
Budget cartridge bottom brackets are usually threaded at the chain side of the main body sleeve so it can be screwed straight into the bottom bracket shell. The other end is located with a threaded adaptor but this is a fairly heavy arrangement. More expensive types have two separate adaptors, which is much lighter. The special fitting tool engages with the internal grooves of the adaptor.

Square taper bottom brackets

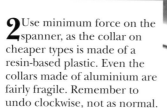

1 With the bottom bracket tool slotted into the adaptor, fit a big adjustable spanner onto the hexagon and turn clockwise. This should undo the collar that locks the sealed unit into the bottom bracket shell.

2 Use minimum force on the spanner, as the collar on cheaper types is made of a resin-based plastic. Even the collars made of aluminium are fairly fragile. Remember to undo clockwise, not as normal.

3 Now move to the opposite side of the bike, and again fit the special tool. In this case, unscrew the cartridge in the normal, anti-clockwise direction. This is not as tricky as removing the collar.

4 The unit can now be pulled out of the bottom bracket shell. Check that the rubber axle seals, where visible, are in good condition, and that the axle revolves smoothly and easily. Clean the threads.

5 Clean up the inside of the bracket also, using a squirt of aerosol lube. Screw the collar in anti-clockwise with your fingers, from the chainside, to check the threads are clean. Remove, then screw the cartridge back into the bracket shell and lock it in place with the collar. Coat all the threads with anti-seize grease as you go.

FAG SEALED UNITS

Giant bearing manufacturer FAG produces one of the cheapest sealed units. The axle and bearings are made of steel but the collars are made of resin. FAG units are often badged as their own by other makers including Campag. You can fit and remove a FAG bracket with a large pair of grips but the special tool makes the job very much easier.

WHEN YOU NEED TO DO THIS JOB:
◆ Upgrading from a standard bottom bracket.
◆ Fitting a new chainset.

TIME:
◆ 40 minutes – mainly because you have to clean up the threads.

DIFFICULTY: ✓✓✓✓
◆ Calls for the same combination of delicacy and force as when removing cotterless cranks.

TOOLS:
◆ Bracket tool, long spanner, old bottom bracket cups.

Cup and axle bottom bracket: 1

One standard bottom bracket can look very different from another, but they all strip down in the same way.

Standard bottom brackets need fairly frequent maintenance. Once-a-year is the minimum for a road bike used frequently. But unlike most bike components, it is only too easy to ignore the bottom bracket until it has almost seized up.

The main problem with cup and axle bottom brackets is water penetration. When that happens, the movement of the bearings churns the grease, oil and water into a sticky non-lubricating mess.

If you are lucky, the bottom bracket will then develop an annoying squeak, telling you that something is wrong. By that time, however, the bearing tracks in the cups will probably be pitted and some of the hardening will have worn off the axle. This will show up as an area of small pits, where the underlying metal is a different colour.

If you find any of these problems, fit new parts. Luckily you can fit a new axle with old cups. Or new cups with an old axle. Or even mix different makes of axle and cups. The only point to watch out for is that Italian frames often have a different thread in the bottom bracket shell.

Final adjustment is easier if you fit the chainwheel and crank first, and then screw the adjustable cup in or out until you can feel only a slight movement at the end of the crank. If you tighten the lockring at this point, it will pull the adjustable cup out slightly. This is often enough to make up for the way the adjustable cup usually turns slightly when you finally tighten the lockring.

When you strip a bracket, you may find eleven separate bearings, or the bearings may be held in a cage. Both arrangements work OK but separate ball bearings are probably better because the load is shared between a larger number of bearings.

Pack the bearings cups with plenty of grease. But do not use automotive grease as it tends to thicken up and is not waterproof. The best kind to use is a waterproof teflon-based grease or something similar.

Strip and overhaul

1 After removing the cranks, start work on the non-chain side. If the lockring has a series of square cut-outs, find a suitable drift or cold chisel that roughly fits them. Then, with an engineer's hammer, tap the lockring anti-clockwise.

2 As you tap the lockring, it may drag the adjustable cup round with it. After a turn or two, you should be able to unscrew the bearing cup with your fingers. Catch any loose ball bearings as you remove the cup, followed by the axle.

5 When you re-fit the bearing cups, only the grease stops the ball bearings falling out. Once all eleven are in place, cover them with more grease, but scoop out any surplus that spills over into the hole for the axle with the same pen top.

6 Screw the fixed cup into the chainside, tightening it anti-clockwise as hard as you can. Steady the axle with your fingers and thread the longer side of the axle, if there is one, into the fixed cup. The shorter side fits into the adjustable cup.

LOST YOUR BEARINGS ?
Look out for these basic faults when you are deciding whether to fit new parts. On the left-hand bearing cup above, the chrome has flaked off and the bearing track is covered in tiny pits. The right-hand cup is heavily worn and in some areas, the surface of the metal has been worn away. On the axles, the upper one has many small pits while on the lower one, the hardened surface is worn through and the soft metal underneath is crumbling fast.

3 Moving to the chainside now. The main problem is to find an adjustable spanner large enough for the flats on a fixed cup. Once you have found one, undo the fixed cup in a clockwise direction, but be careful not to chip the paint.

4 Clean everything up with solvent and inspect all the bearing surfaces. If they are OK, half fill the cups with waterproof grease and add eleven ball bearings per side. A pen top is fine for pressing the ball bearings into the grease.

WHEN YOU NEED TO DO THIS JOB:
◆ To stop a squeak.
◆ During a full overhaul.
◆ At least once a year.

TIME:
◆ Best part of 1 hour.

DIFFICULTY: 🔧🔧🔧🔧
◆ Getting the fixed cup in and out is a problem if you do not have exactly the right tools. In addition, the adjustment tends to loosen off the adjustment when you tighten the lock ring at the final stage of the job.

7 Screw in the adjustable cup until it tightens up. Turn the axle and if it feels tight, loosen the adjustable cup until the gravelly feeling goes away. Fit and tighten the lockring, check the axle turns smoothly and re-adjust if necessary.

C-SPANNER

PIN SPANNER

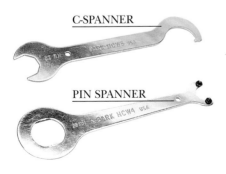

PITCH CIRCLE DIAMETER (PCD)
When you want to change the overall gearing on a bike, or the whole transmission is badly worn, you will have to change the chainrings. In that case, you need to know what the pitch circle diameter (or bolt circle diameter) of the chain ring is. So just unbolt the existing ones and measure the distance D, then check the table.

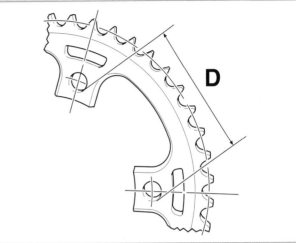

D (mm)	PCD diameter (mm)
34.1	58
43.5	74
50.6	86
55.3	94
67.7	110
71.7	122
76.5	130
79.4	135
84.7	144

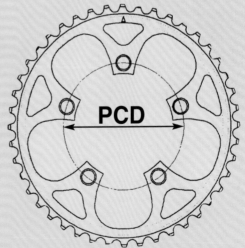

The pitch or bolt circle diameter is the diameter of the circle joining the centres of all the fixing holes. When ordering, you will also have to specify four bolts or five.

99

Cup and axle bottom bracket: 2

Specialised tools make it much easier to overhaul and adjust a cup and axle bottom bracket.

Fixed bottom bracket cups are a problem. Not only do you have to remember that they have a left-hand thread, so they tighten up anticlockwise. You also have to cope with the way they are a tight fit in the bracket shell to stop them coming loose.

You can tighten up a fixed cup with an adjustable spanner or a pair of Stillson's but either way, you are likely to chip the paint. A fixed cup bottom bracket spanner from Cyclo, Park or various other makers, will make it easier to fit and remove them. But you still have to be very careful to prevent the spanner slipping off the narrow rim of the bearing cup.

The adjustable cup often has two holes on the face so that you can screw it in or out with a pin spanner. Then, when doing the final adjustment, you can use the pin spanner to hold the bearing cup still while you tighten the lockring with a C-spanner. Remember, you have to hit the exact point where the axle turns freely but without any free play.

A C-spanner can also be used in conjunction with an open-ended spanner on bottom brackets with hexagon-shaped bearing cups.

1 The best fixed bottom bracket spanners fit right round the outside of the bearing cup. If you operate the spanner with one hand and push it onto the bearing cup with the other, you minimise the chances of it slipping and damaging the paintwork.

2 When adjusting a standard bracket, it is best to tighten the lockring with a C-spanner. Fit the dog on the spanner into a notch in the lockring and steady your hand on the frame. In this case, you can use an open-ended spanner on the adjusting cup.

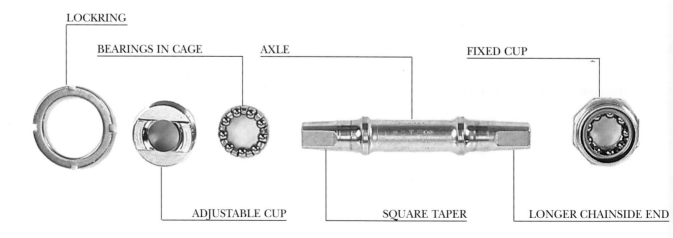

LOCKRING

BEARINGS IN CAGE   AXLE   FIXED CUP

ADJUSTABLE CUP   SQUARE TAPER   LONGER CHAINSIDE END

One piece cranks

This design is mainly used on kids' bikes but also on budget BMXs and adult utilities. Although designed to keep down the cost of building small bikes, one-piece cranks and the bottom bracket design that goes with them are surprisingly child-resistant. The cranks often get bent in a crash but they are made of steel. So if you have a big pair of Stillson's, you can usually straighten them up without too much difficulty. If the left-hand crank gets badly bent, consider taking the whole thing apart and straightening it in a vice.

The bottom bracket works well because it is a lot bigger in diameter than a standard one and so contains more ball bearings to share the load. The press-in bearing cups and the axle can get pitted but do not have to be replaced unless the cups are very badly damaged. Maintenance consists of removing the old grease, regreasing everything and fitting it back together with a full set of ball bearings.

It is worth going through this procedure as a precaution, if you have just bought a second-hand bike. And judging by the way kids' bikes are often thrown

1 First thing is to remove the pedals, then unscrew the lockring in a clockwise direction. The lockring is very thin, so steady the spanner to prevent it slipping off the flats. Once you have unscrewed it all the way, lift the lockring off the end of the crank.

2 Behind the lockring is a slotted bearing retainer. Position a cold chisel in the slot and tap it gently in a clockwise direction. As you unscrew the retainer, the crank assembly will tilt, so support it with one hand while you undo the retainer with the other.

3 Lift the bearing retainer off the end of the crank. If you then tilt the whole assembly until the plain crank is almost horizontal, you can draw it out of the opposite side of the bottom bracket shell. The crank assembly is made of steel and therefore heavy.

4 Finally, knock the bearing cups out of the frame. They are not threaded but are still a tight fit. When one side of the cup has moved a little, swap the cold chisel to the opposite side and hammer away until it also moves, otherwise the cups will jam in place.

together in the factory, it would not be a bad idea to strip and grease the bottom bracket on a brand-new bike as well.

It is not easy to get spares for this type of bike, so wait until you have got them in your hand before you strip the bike down. If your

local bike shop cannot help, search out a specialist in kids' bikes.

To refit the bottom bracket, follow the steps given here in reverse. But take care to tap the bearing cups back in straight, not at an angle, or you will never get them in.

WHEN YOU NEED TO DO THIS JOB:
◆ You have just bought a second-hand or new bike and want to check that the bottom bracket is OK.
◆ There is a grinding noise as you turn the cranks.
◆ The cranks have been bent in a crash.

TIME:
At least an hour to strip, clean and refit the whole assembly. Longer if you have to straighten the cranks as well.

DIFFICULTY: 〃〃
At first it is difficult to see how this assembly fits together. Once you have grasped that, you may also have problems driving out and refitting the bearing cups. The answer is to only drive one side out a little way first. Then go to the opposite side of the bearing cup and drive that out an equal amount so it stays straight.

SPECIAL TOOLS:
Large adjustable spanner, engineer's hammer and cold chisel.

BRAKING SYSTEMS

The brakes are one of the most safety-sensitive areas on your bike. So set up a working routine based on tightening up all the nuts and bolts firmly, checking alignment of the brake pads after every job and then double-checking everything, just in case.

Types of brakes

There are more variations in the design of brakes than of any other component. But they all need to be set up quite carefully to be fully effective.

Although there are many different designs, most braking systems work by pressing a pad against the braking surface on the wall of the wheel rim. How well this works depends on how hard the pad is forced against the rim, how flat the braking surface of the rim is and how well the pad material bites on it.

Brake pads wear fairly fast but do not forget that the braking surface of a wheel rim also wears. However, if the pad material is compatible with the rim, it wears very slowly. Only if the rim is allowed to become seriously worn is there a real danger of the wheel collapsing without warning.

To prevent this happening, check the condition of the braking surface when you fit new pads and occasionally during normal use. Get the wheel rebuilt with a new rim, as soon as the wear gets beyond the stage of shallow grooves. But remember, some rim walls now have a groove that acts as a wear indicator.

Disc brakes are the big exception to all this, but they are can only be fitted if the wheels and frame are suitable. Discs work much better than rim brakes in bad weather and deep mud, so they are ideal on MTBs. And they rule out any problems with worn wheel rims.

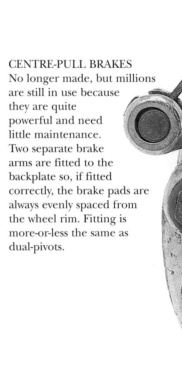

CANTILEVER BRAKES
Fitted to mountain bikes, hybrids, cyclocross and a few road machines. A sound design that has now been overtaken by vee brakes. Nevertheless, standard cantis combine low weight, powerful stopping and plenty of clearance for mud.

DUAL-PIVOT BRAKES
A big advance in brakes for road bikes. Each brake arm moves independently on a separate backplate. Once correctly set up, the brake pads stay at an equal distance from the wheel rim, without constant fiddling. Most dual-pivot calipers are 49mm deep but special deep calipers for use with mudguards are available.

CENTRE-PULL BRAKES
No longer made, but millions are still in use because they are quite powerful and need little maintenance. Two separate brake arms are fitted to the backplate so, if fitted correctly, the brake pads are always evenly spaced from the wheel rim. Fitting is more-or-less the same as dual-pivots.

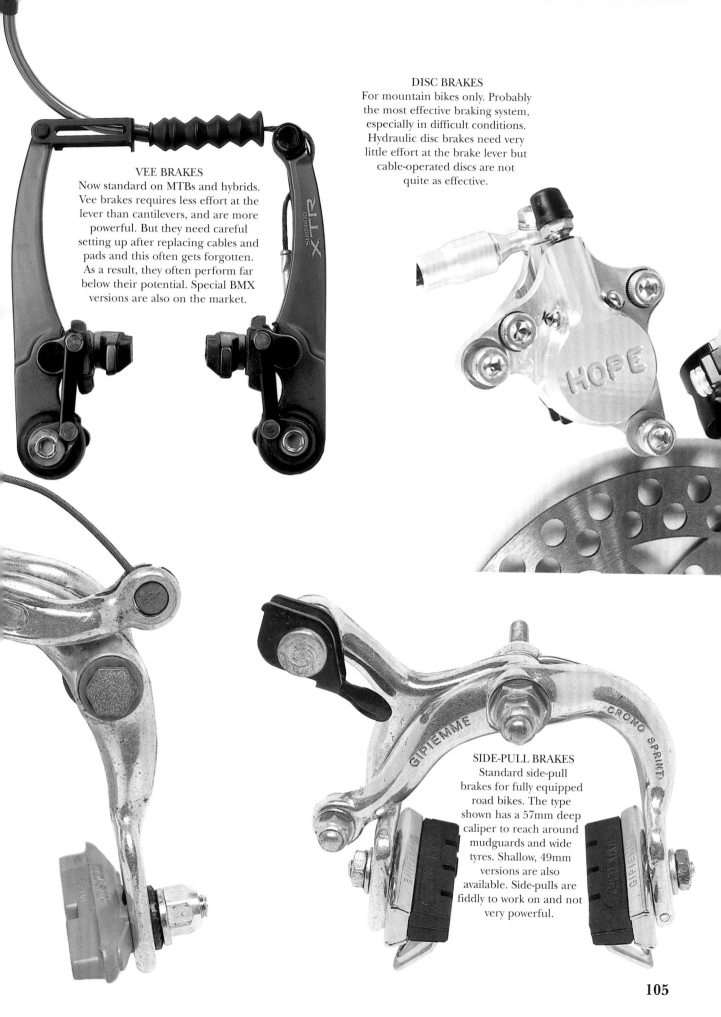

DISC BRAKES
For mountain bikes only. Probably the most effective braking system, especially in difficult conditions. Hydraulic disc brakes need very little effort at the brake lever but cable-operated discs are not quite as effective.

VEE BRAKES
Now standard on MTBs and hybrids. Vee brakes requires less effort at the lever than cantilevers, and are more powerful. But they need careful setting up after replacing cables and pads and this often gets forgotten. As a result, they often perform far below their potential. Special BMX versions are also on the market.

SIDE-PULL BRAKES
Standard side-pull brakes for fully equipped road bikes. The type shown has a 57mm deep caliper to reach around mudguards and wide tyres. Shallow, 49mm versions are also available. Side-pulls are fiddly to work on and not very powerful.

105

Brakes: inspection and lube

Pad wear causes a gradual fall in braking performance, so test your brakes frequently as you may not notice the slow deterioration.

There is nearly always a lot of give when you pull the brake lever. Some of it is cable stretch, the lever itself also flexes a little and so do the brake arms. However, brake arms should be quite stiff. If you notice they flex more than a few millimetres, consider upgrading to better quality brakes. If you have standard cantis, that usually means fitting vee brakes.

Road bike brake arms are longer and thinner than the ones fitted to MTBs, so they usually flex more. Side-pull brakes are particularly bad for this, and it is also very difficult to keep them centred correctly. Dual-pivot road brakes do not suffer from these problems, so they are much more effective.

If you notice that you pull the brake levers fairly close in to the handlebars when braking normally, cable stretch and pad wear has reached the point where servicing is well overdue.

QUICK-RELEASE
If the quick-release does not work or is missing, try screwing the cable adjuster in clockwise as far as possible. That should slacken off the cable enough to let you remove the wheel. If it is still not possible to remove the wheel, try letting the tyre down. When fitting new cables, it is a good idea to set the cable adjuster in the middle of its travel so that you can use it as a quick-release if necessary.

THE BRAKING SURFACE
The braking surface formed by wall of the wheel rim is the forgotten part of the braking system. First of all, the brake pad must be compatible with the material that the rim is made of. Most rims are made of aluminium alloy, and you should have no trouble buying pads to suit. But some utility bikes have chrome-plated steel rims and alloy-compatible pads just will not grip on them. At the other end of the scale, ceramic-coated rims and carbon rims both require their own special pads.

Test, inspect and adjust

1 Test the brakes by pulling the brake lever. It should not take much effort at first, then the pads will hit the rim. If you then pull harder, it will just stretch the cable a bit more. If the brake lever ends up close to the handlebar, adjustment is needed urgently.

2 Check for worn brake pads for contamination on the pad surface and wear ridges as well. If the slots are nearly worn away or the wear line has almost gone, fit new pads. Do the same if you cannot remove the contamination or the wear ridges go deep into the rubber.

Brake lubrication

1 If the frame has slotted cable stops, pull the outer cable out of the slot so you can fire lube down the outer cable. If not, just lube the inner cable. On standard cantilevers, aim one shot of lube at the back of each pivot, where it will protect the spring from rust.

2 Standard cantis need another shot for the front of the pivots (double arrow) and just a drip on the free end of the straddle cable. This is to prevent it getting stuck in its slot. Remember that the brake levers also need a drip of spray lube on the pivot.

In extreme cases, rims can be weakened to the point of danger by the pads. But if you go for a rim with a machined braking surface, the brakes will work better because the pads will make better contact with a flat surface. A machined rim also lasts longer because the wear is more evenly spread.

3 Now adjust the cables using the cable adjuster on the brake lever, on MTBs. Undo the thin locknut using pliers if it is stiff. Try tightening the adjuster two turns anti-clockwise but always leave three full threads in the lever for safety, to prevent it coming out.

4 Test and re-adjust the cable until total brake lever travel is about 20mm. On most road bikes, you again undo the locknut, then follow Step 3. On any type of bike, you may have to loosen the cable clamp and pull some cable through to tighten the cable enough.

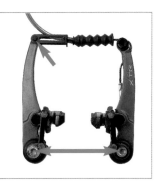

3 On vee brakes, the cables and brake levers need the same treatment as standard cantis. The pivots need a squirt of lube each side of the brake arm and so does the slotted link between pivot and pad, where fitted. Finally, give the cable holder a drip (arrow).

4 Side-pull brakes have a lot of internal friction, so lube the central pivot and spring. If the brakes feel heavy, unbolt them from the frame. If you find a lot of effort is then needed to squeeze the arms together, clean and lube the caliper, then fit a new cable.

Quick releases

Most braking systems have a quick-release device to increase the pad clearance when removing a wheel.

BRAKE RELEASE BUTTON

1 On Campag Ergopower brake levers, the quick-release button is on the brake lever. Push it in for more clearance. It re-sets automatically when you next use the brakes.

2 On cantilevers, squeeze the brake arms together with one hand while you unhook the loose end of the straddle wire with the other. If it will not budge, slacken the cable off with the adjuster, then use pliers.

3 Vee brakes have a fiddly quick-release. First grasp the top of the brake arms and squeeze them together. Then try to steady the cable holder with your thumb while you pull and lift the cable pipe and cable away from the cable holder. You have to lift the inner cable out of a narrow slot in the cable holder, so do not use force.

4 Most road bikes have a quick-release near the cable adjuster. You pull it upwards when changing the wheel and push it downwards to close the pads up against the rim. Sometimes, you turn the cable holder through 90°.

WHEN YOU NEED TO DO THIS JOB:
◆ Every 500 miles (800km) and whenever you do a minor service.
◆ You notice the brake lever travel when braking normally.

TIME:
◆ 5 minutes to adjust and lube the brakes.
◆ 5 minutes to tighten the cable.

DIFFICULTY: ✔✔
◆ Luckily it is very easy to keep your brakes up to scratch, so there is no excuse.

TAKE CARE WITH THE OIL CAN
When lubricating the braking system, take care not to drip oil or aerosol lube onto the rims or pads. It is OK to wipe oil off the braking surface, provided you do it thoroughly. But oil will sometimes contaminate the brake pads permanently.

Vee and Hub brakes

Vee brakes are standard on mountain bikes and hybrids. But many in daily use are ineffective because they are incorrectly fitted, so take a few minutes to do it properly.

Vee brakes are close relatives of the standard cantilever but pretty well all the problems of the ordinary canti are designed out. They are light enough to operate with two fingers, because the extended brake arms give more leverage. Fitting and adjustment is easier because there is only one cable. And they are more powerful, partly because of the extra leverage and partly because the brake cable works at 90º to the brake arms.

As a result, they have a very direct or linear effect, meaning that the amount of pull on the brake lever is translated directly into the same amount of pull on the brakes. That is why you must not use levers for canti brake with vee brakes. Canti levers are designed to create maximum braking power with a long, hard pull. If you apply the same amount of force to vee brakes, you will stop very fast and maybe find yourself diving over the handlebars. One other warning – you must use vee brakes very gently to start with. They stop you so fast, compared with ordinary bike brakes, that you must get used to them before using their full power.

If your bike has cantis, it is easy to upgrade to vee brakes. But your frame must be fitted with brake bosses 80mm from centre to centre. Check this measurement if the bosses look bent or you cannot get vee brakes to work well.

For fitting vee brake pads, see pages 122-123. Make sure you fit the cables correctly because the majority of vee brakes in daily use are incorrectly fitted. Many are even being used with the cable pipe or noodle missing, so they are almost useless. Luckily, spare cable noodles are now supplied separately by Fibrax and other firms selling brake pads and cables, so it is easy to put things right.

Strictly speaking, vee brakes are made by Shimano only. If another maker offers brakes made to a similar design, they are known as long arm cantilever brakes.

Hub brakes are staging a slight comeback on utility and city bikes because they are clean, very powerful and work equally well in all weathers. The drawbacks are that you have to have them regreased every six months, plus their weight.

Cable adjustment is very easy but if you have any problem getting hold of new cables, try a motor bike shop. Should you ever see grease leaking out of the brake, or hear odd squealing or grinding noises, take the bike back to the dealer without delay. The six-monthly regreasing is also a job for the dealer. However, this is almost the only maintenance required as the brake shoes are made of steel.

1 Most vee brakes are operated by combined gear and brake levers. There is a normal cable adjuster but Servo Wave brake levers also have a device to regulate the amount of pull needed. Do not alter this setting yourself.

6 Lube the cable noodle and pull the inner cable through until the slack is taken up. Fit the inner through the slot in the cable holder and position the end of the cable noodle in the cable holder as well. Pull the inner cable tight.

HUB BRAKES

To adjust a hub brake, try to prop the bike up so that the wheel is right off the ground. Then tighten the cable with the adjuster so that you can feel the brake binding when you spin the wheel. Next, back off the brake about half a turn clockwise of the cable adjuster. The back wheel should now spin without any drag at all. If there is still some drag, turn the cable adjuster clockwise a fraction. Finally, check that the brake comes on fully, well before the brake lever hits the handlebar.

2 First of all, test fit the brake arms on the pivots. If they seem tight, remove any paint or polish the metal with a light abrasive and test again. Once the brake arms move easily on the pivots but without any slop, apply a little grease.

3 Each brake arm has a small coil spring with a stopper pin on the end. Fit this pin into the middle hole of the boss – do not use the other two. Then push the brake arm onto the pivot and screw the fixing bolt into place.

4 Make sure that the long part of the spring is on the frame side of the brake arm, where it sits up against a metal pip. Next, tighten the fixing bolt, which presses the brake arm onto the pivot and then fit the other brake arm.

5 Flip open the cable cover (arrow in step 1) on the brake lever, push the plain end of the inner cable through the brake lever and adjuster, then the outer cable. Finally, feed the inner cable through the cable pipe or noodle.

7 Slide the cable bellows onto the inner cable and thread the end into the cable clamp. Rotate the brake arms into an upright position and check that there is 39mm or a bit more inner cable showing between the brake arms.

8 Tighten the cable clamp but not fully yet. Adjust the brake pads as explained on page 122, making sure that there is an equal gap between the pad and the rim each side. The pad to rim gap should only be about 2mm in total.

9 Fully tighten the cable clamp. Then use the cable adjuster on the brake lever to set the total pad-to-rim gap at around 2mm. Finally, adjust the tiny Phillips or socket head screws on the brake arms to equalise the pad-to-rim gap.

WHEN YOU NEED TO DO THIS JOB:
◆ When upgrading from standard cantis.
◆ The grease on the brake bosses has dried up.

TIME:
◆ Two hours to remove old brakes, clean up pivots and fit both new brakes.

DIFFICULTY: ///
◆ It can be tricky getting the brake arms as upright as possible, while keeping the 39mm between them. It sounds easy but some people find it awkward.

BRAKE MODULATION
Brake modulators are found on quite a few recent bikes. Some modulators are built into the brake lever, as on the Shimano Servo Wave brake lever for vee brakes. Others are fitted to the brake arm, yet others are part of the brake cable on some children's bikes. It is said that by adjusting the modulator, you can choose exactly the amount of power that the brake will produce and the length of pull needed on the lever. However, the real reason for fitting modulators is to enable bike manufacturers to buy only one type of lever and use it with various types of brake. Probably the best thing to do is leave the modulator alone unless you have very definite reasons for fiddling with it.

Cantilever brakes: strip and adjustment

When properly set up, cantilever brakes generate plenty of reliable stopping power. You only need to strip them down if they have seized up due to lack of use, or rust and mud has got into the pivots.

The original type of cantilever brake has a straddle wire that joins the two arms and which is connected to the main brake cable by a metal yoke. The set-up works well but this type of cantilever is not being made in large numbers any more as vee brakes are better.

Many Shimano cantilevers have a different arrangement. In this design, the main brake cable passes through a cable carrier. It is then sent to the left so that it can be connected directly to one of the brake arms. The other arm is connected to the cable carrier by a short link wire.

Some types of Shimano cantis have the pad mounted on the other side of the brake arm from the one in the drawing. This brings the pad closer to the pivot, reducing vibration and smoothing out the braking. There is no other difference.

Link wire types are harder to set up but give you better control over, and better modulation of, the amount of braking. However, when you are working on any type of cantilever brake, use the adjustment procedure given here together with the advice on fitting new cables on page 112.

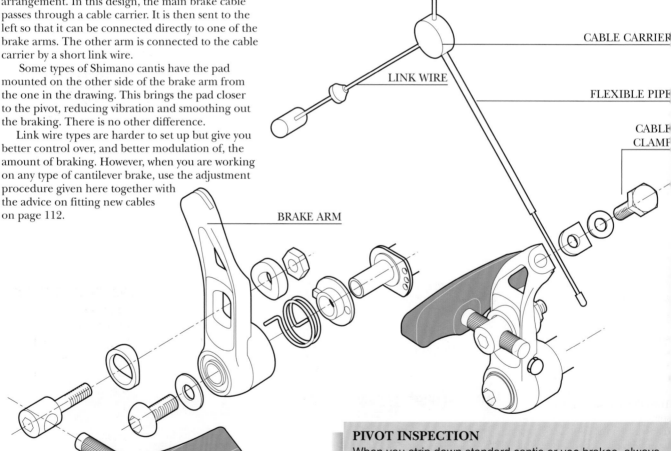

CABLE CARRIER

LINK WIRE

FLEXIBLE PIPE

CABLE CLAMP

BRAKE ARM

BRAKE PAD

PIVOT INSPECTION
When you strip down standard cantis or vee brakes, always inspect the frame pivots. If they are rusty, polish with emery cloth and reassemble with waterproof grease on the pivots. Check that the pivots are straight by measuring between their centres. If the distance is 80mm, they are probably OK. If not, or they look bent, get them looked at by a bike mechanic as you may have to get new pivots brazed on.

1 Screw in the cable adjuster to reduce the tension on the brake cable. If there is a straddle wire, unhook one end and lift it out of the yoke. On a link wire type of brake, undo the cable clamp with a hexagon key and pull the cable away from the brake arm.

2 Undo the pivot bolt, freeing the brake arm and allowing you to pull it off the pivot boss. Try to hold the spring and washer in place on the pivot bolt or they could fly anywhere. Clean up all the parts ready for reassembly.

3 Once you have cleaned and greased the pivots, fit the spring into the middle hole on the pivot boss and fit the brake arm followed by the pivot bolt. Turn the adjuster with a spanner until each pad is 2mm from the rim, then lock by tightening the pivot bolt again. It is important to set pads an equal distance from the rim at this point. On standard cantis, you can fit the spring in the other holes in the pivot boss, if you want to increase or decrease the power of the spring. On vee brakes, you must use the middle hole only.

4 To make fine adjustments to the pad-to-rim distance, there is often a small screw at the base of the cantilever arm. Adjust by turning the screw clockwise to move the pad away from the rim and anti-clockwise to bring the pad closer to it.

5 Aim at a situation where the pads are equally spaced, 2mm from the rim. Sometimes the pads are also toed-in about 1mm, but this varies with the type of brake and brake pad. Full brake pad adjustment is covered on page 122.

WHEN YOU NEED TO DO THIS JOB:
◆ Brakes feel stiff or jerky when you pull the brake lever and neither lubrication nor a new cable are any help.

TIME:
◆ 30 minutes.

DIFFICULTY: 🔧🔧🔧
◆ It is sometimes fiddly to fit the spring in the hole on the pivot and to adjust pad clearance.

Replacing cantilever cables

Setting up a cantilever brake is about getting the cable lengths right and centring the brake pads.

Though pretty rare now, the original type of cantilever brakes, using a triangular cable carrier and a short straddle wire, is still around. The brake cable is fitted to the cable carrier with a normal cable clamp, and the straddle wire sits in a channel at the back.

To set up a basic cantilever properly, first adjust the length of the straddle wire so that it roughly makes a right-angle with the brake arm when you lift it in the middle. Fit the straddle wire into the cable carrier next. Then try to gauge where the cable carrier should be fitted on the main brake cable. It must be high enough to pull the brakes on fully but not so high that it hits the outer cable or anything else that would prevent the brakes coming on fully.

On both other types of cantilever brake, the main brake cable clamps directly to one of the brake arms, with a short link wire joining the cable carrier to the other one. Early designs have a cable carrier with a bolt running through it, or two separate slots for the cable. The wide slot is for adjusting the cable, the narrow one for when the brake is in use.

The latest link wire brakes have a cable carrier with a diagonal line running across it, or a round window for the nipple of the link wire.

The first step when fitting a new brake cable is to slot it into the cable carrier. Then slide the flexible hose on to the brake cable and fit the cable into the cable clamp on the brake arm. Set the length of the brake cable so that the end of the flexible hose touches both the cable carrier and the brake arm, then tighten the cable clamp. Now hook the link wire into the other brake arm and check that the link wire roughly aligns with the diagonal line running across the cable carrier, as in the picture in Step 7.

Next, adjust the spring tension with the small Phillips screws on the brake arms. Spring tension is correct when the cable carrier sits directly below the point where the inner cable emerges from the outer. Now fit the brake pads but do not worry if they touch the rim at this stage.

Re-set the length of the main brake cable so there is a 2 to 3mm gap between the end of the flexible hose and the brake arm. When you have done so, the link wire should line up with the diagonal line across the cable carrier, as in the bottom picture on Step 7. Provided it does, centre the brake pads using the Phillips screws again. Finally, make sure there is at least 20mm free cable above the cable carrier.

On all types of cantilever brakes, the final stage is to adjust the pads properly - see page 122.

Link wire cantilevers

1 Screw in the cable adjuster and pull out the old cable. Check the new nipple fits, grease it lightly and insert the nipple into the hole. Slide the outer cable over the inner and slot both in to the adjuster.

2 On the early type, unhook the link wire from the brake arm next. Then, feed the new brake cable through the wider slot in the cable carrier and slide the flexible hose over the end of the cable

Straddle wire cantilevers

1 Feed the brake cable into the cable clamp on the cable carrier and tighten lightly. Squeeze the brake pads against the rims and see if you can now lift the straddle cable into the channel on the back of the cable carrier. If it is a tight fit, lengthen the main brake cable slightly. If it is too loose, reduce the length of the cable a little. Tighten the cable clamp.

2 With the brake off, the pads should now sit 2mm from the rim. If necessary, correct the clearance with the cable adjuster. For top braking power and control, the straddle wire should roughly form a right-angle with the brake arm. If it does not, loosen the cable clamp on the brake arm and adjust the length of the straddle wire until it does. Finally, check that there is enough free cable above the cable carrier for the brake to come on fully without fouling the outer cable.

3 Set the length of the brake cable so that the flexible hose touches both the cable carrier and the brake arm. Hook the link wire back into the other brake arm and adjust the spring tension.

4 The spring tension is right when the cable carrier hangs directly below the end of the outer cable. The pads should be an equal distance from the wheel rim. Lengthen the brake cable if necessary.

5 Finally, check there is enough free cable above the cable carrier to enable the brakes to come on fully. Then move the brake cable into the narrow slot in the cable carrier, the slot for normal braking.

WHICH BRAKE CABLE GOES WHERE?

In Great Britain, the right-hand brake lever must be connected to the front brake and the left-hand brake lever must be connected to the back. This is part of the British Standard governing bike construction, to prevent riders getting confused when riding a particular bike for the first time. Remember:

FRONT BRAKE – RIGHT, BACK BRAKE – LEFT.

6 On the later types of link wire cantilever, the cable fits into the brake lever and the cable carrier in roughly the same way. Once you have centred the brake pads with the adjusters, the brake cable must be lengthened to leave a gap of 2mm to 3mm between the end of the flexible hose and the brake arm.

CORRECT ANGLE FOR LINK AND STRADDLE WIRES

When setting up any standard cantilever brake, try to get something close to a right-angle between the link wire or straddle wire and the brake arm that it is attached to. In order to do this, you will have to experiment by lengthening or shortening the wire or the cable. When set up properly like this, all types of cantilever brake should feel smooth and powerful.

7 Again on the later types of link wire cantilevers, the wrong angle of the link wire shown in the top picture will cause brake judder and make it difficult to control the amount of braking. In the bottom picture, the link wire lines up correctly with the diagonal line on the cable carrier. The brakes should therefore work quite nicely.

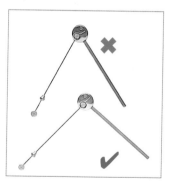

WHEN YOU NEED TO DO THIS JOB:
◆ Brakes tend to snatch or lock the wheel.
◆ The cable is frayed or broken.
◆ Lots of effort is needed to make emergency stops, suggesting the cable is sticking somewhere.

TIME:
◆ 10 minutes to fit a new cable to a straddle wire brake.
◆ 20 minutes for a link wire brake.

DIFFICULTY: 𝄇𝄇𝄇𝄇
◆ It is easy working on a straddle wire brake, but link wire brakes need careful adjustment to achieve a good balance between stopping power and delicate control.

SPECIAL TOOLS:
◆ A cable puller is very useful but not essential.

Side-pull brakes: strip and adjustment

It should not be necessary to strip down and rebuild side-pull brakes very often but if grit gets between the brake arms, it is the only way to get them working again smoothly.

1 Pull off the cable end cap and undo the cable clamp. Now pull gently on the outer cable – with luck the inner will come out without fraying. Once the cable is free, the nipple may drop out of the cable anchor in the brake lever.

All the moving parts of a side-pull brake caliper fit onto the central pivot bolt. This creates a lot of friction, although the nylon washers, brass washers and even ball bearings sometimes fitted between the brake arms help to keep it down.When you strip a caliper, lay all the parts out in order to help you keep track. If you find any washers are damaged or missing, make sure you replace them. They do not have to be an exact fit, so you may be able to use bits from another make or possibly second-hand bits if you find you cannot get hold of new ones.

If you find the brakes tend to stick on, it may be possible to increase the spring pressure by reversing both nylon pads where the spring touches the brake arms. Brake levers are often spring-loaded as well, to make sure that the brakes release as soon as you let go of the brake lever.

You will probably find that the caliper constantly moves to one side, sometimes allowing the brake pad to rub against the rim. If you slip a heavy washer on the pivot bolt so that it sits in between the brake and the fork, you may find it easier to centre the brakes and that they stay centred longer.

Campagnolo monoplanar calipers can be stripped in roughly the same way as a standard side-pull caliper. Do not strip dual-pivot calipers. If they seem to be sticky or notchy, clean the whole caliper in degreaser, paying special attention to the pivots. Then re-lubricate with heavy oil. On some dual-pivots, you may be able to increase the spring tension by reversing a nylon pad, as on side-pulls.

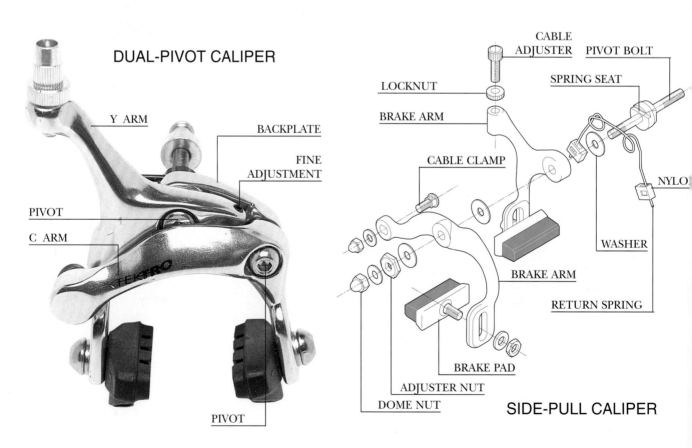

DUAL-PIVOT CALIPER

Y ARM

BACKPLATE

FINE ADJUSTMENT

PIVOT

C ARM

PIVOT

CABLE ADJUSTER

PIVOT BOLT

LOCKNUT

SPRING SEAT

BRAKE ARM

CABLE CLAMP

NYLO

WASHER

BRAKE ARM

RETURN SPRING

BRAKE PAD

ADJUSTER NUT

DOME NUT

SIDE-PULL CALIPER

2 Check how the brake is fixed to the forks next. Sometimes it is a self-locking nut or, more likely, a chromed socket-head sleeve bolt. Undo with a spanner or hexagon key but be careful, it is sometimes hard to get replacements.

3 Pull the brake away from the forks. Then undo the dome nut and adjuster nut holding everything in place on the pivot bolt at the front of the caliper. Hook the ends of the spring off the brake arms, then pull the brake arms off.

4 Clean and reassemble, coating all points where friction occurs with anti-seize. Adjust the nuts on the pivot bolt for minimum friction between the arms without any sideways movement. Bolt the caliper back in place.

5 If one of the pads is close to or even touches the rim, loosen the fixing bolt, then use a thin spanner to hold the pivot bolt so that the pads are evenly spaced from the rim. Retighten fixing bolt. You may find this part a bit difficult.

Dual-pivot brakes

1 Slip the fixing bolt of the caliper into the mounting hole. Then fit the socket head sleeve bolt onto the long end of a hexagon key and screw the sleeve bolt onto the end of the fixing bolt.

2 The end of the fixing bolt will not be visible inside the fork crown, so you will have to waggle the hexagon key a bit until you find the end of the fixing bolt. Then adjust the brake pads for the first time.

3 Fit the wheel back in the frame, centralising it carefully. Then slacken off the fixing bolt and adjust the position of the caliper so that the gap between the pad and the rim is equal on both sides.

4 Tighten the fixing bolt for the last time and re-adjust the brake pads (see page 122). Finally, use the tiny screw on the Y brake arm to set the pad-to-rim distances exactly equal both sides.

CENTRING A SINGLE-PIVOT CALIPER

If you have to keep on centring a caliper, only to find it keeps on moving to one side again, try this trick. Rest the end of a small cold chisel on the circular part of the return spring and hit the cold chisel sharply with an engineer's hammer. Hit the same side of the return spring as the brake pad that is too close to the rim. This should solve the problem permanently, but if you cannot get the knack, go to a bike shop and get it done there

TOE-IN ON SIDE-PULLS AND DUAL-PIVOTS

It is nearly always best to fit brake pads with about 1mm toe in – see page 122. There is no set way of doing this on a side-pull brake although you can use an adjustable spanner to bend the brake arms. But before going that far, try fitting a shaped washer behind the pad holder, as used on MTB brakes and sometimes supplied with new brake pads. You will have to fiddle with the shaped washer until you find exactly the right position for it.

WHEN YOU NEED TO DO THIS JOB:

◆ Brake action is still stiff after fitting a new cable.

◆ Braking action feels rough and perhaps snatchy.

TIME:

◆ Half-an-hour to strip, clean and reassemble. But maybe hours to centralise single pivot types.

DIFFICULTY: 𝄘𝄘𝄘𝄘

◆ It can be difficult to refit the return spring and centralise the brake pads.

New cables for side-pull brakes

If you fit them carefully and keep them lubed, brake cables will last for years. But if they are frayed or the brakes tend to stick on, fit new cables now.

Like gear cables, brake cables are now sold in sets or as individual cables. Nearly all pre-packed sets have Teflon-coated stainless steel inner cables to reduce friction, with high quality outer cables, or a Teflon lining for the outer. You can also buy separate Teflon-coated inner cables but check the Teflon trademark on the packet to make sure.

Brake cables come in 1.5mm and 2.0mm diameter but both types are much thicker than gear cables. That means you must only use sharp cable cutters – blunt ones will just crush the cable and it will immediately start to fray. Once you have cut the cable to length, fit a cable end cap to prevent unsightly fraying in future.

Brake outer cable is also thicker than the type intended for gears. It can be cut to any length and the the same type is used whether it is routed under the handlebar tape, comes out of the top of the brake lever or goes through the frame.

Mountain bike rear cables are shorter than road bike rear cables. In addition, there are several different shapes of nipple, so take the old cable with you as a pattern when buying. And clean the nipple up with a file if it is tight in its housing.

Remember carefully: European bikes have the front brake lever to the right of the handlebars and the rear brake lever to the left. Bikes in America have the brake levers the other way round.

DUAL-PIVOT BRAKES
Fit new cables to dual-pivot brakes using the method given here for ordinary side-pull brakes. Use the same type of cable as well, bearing in mind that low friction cable probably works even better with dual-pivots than with side-pulls.

1 Frayed cables tend to get stuck in the clamp. So cut the cable wherever convenient and extract the remains of the cable with pliers. It will be easier to pull the nipple end out of the brake lever if you slide the outer cable off first.

6 Spray aerosol lube into the outer cable until it bubbles out of the other end. Then thread the inner cable into the outer. If it comes out of the top of the brake lever, the outer cable often sits in a neat separate ferrule.

SPECIAL TOOLS
◆ A cable puller or third hand tool is desirable but not essential.

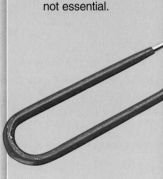

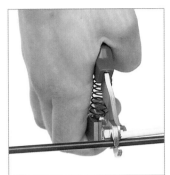

2 In a few cases, you have to peel back the rubber hood and prise out a plastic cover to get at the nipple. If the outer cable is concealed under the handlebar tape, undo that next, because that will make it easier to fit the cable later.

3 Working from the brake end of the outer cable, try pushing the inner cable out. The nipple should pop out of the brake lever, allowing you to pull the rest out with pliers. If the nipple will not move, lever it out with a screwdriver.

4 If the plastic covering of the outer cable is cut or damaged, or the cable is kinked, cut a new length of outer and smooth off the cut end if necessary. Use the old outer cable as a guide to the length of the new one.

5 In concealed cable brake levers, as here, the inner cable passes through a guide hole at the back, emerging by the inner curve of the handlebars. In the older type, the cable simply emerges from the top of the brake lever.

7 Bring the outer cable up to the brake lever, turn the round nipple housing in the lever until the slot faces you, then slip the inner cable into place and seat the nipple. Pull the cables tight and tape the outer to the handlebar.

8 Once the nipple is in place, keep the inner cable under slight tension to prevent it slipping out again. Pass the inner through the cable adjuster and the cable clamp, then pull it tight. Check that the nipple is still fully seated.

9 Screw the adjuster halfway in, then find a ring spanner to fit the cable clamp. Hold the brake pads with one hand and pull the cable tight with the other. Tighten cable clamp and adjust the pad-to-rim distance if necessary.

10 Alternatively, tighten the cable clamp a little and use a cable puller to tension the brake cable and pull the brake pads into the rim. Fully tighten the cable clamp, then use the cable adjuster to fine-tune clearance.

WHEN YOU NEED TO DO THIS JOB:
- ◆ Brake cable is frayed.
- ◆ Lubing the cable does not free it.

TIME:
- ◆ 20 minutes if the cable is routed under the handlebar.
- ◆ 15 minutes if it sprouts out of the top of the brake lever.

DIFFICULTY: ✔✔✔
- ◆ The only real problem is pulling the new cable tight enough to bring the pads close to the rim. A cable puller helps here.

TWO NIPPLES, ONE CABLE
Brake cables are sometimes supplied with a different nipple at each end. One is pear-shaped to fit the hooded brake levers usually fitted with drop handlebars. The other is a drum-shaped nipple to suit the various brake levers fitted to flat handlebars. This includes mountain bikes with cantilever brakes and utility bikes fitted with flat touring handlebars and side-pull brakes. You have to cut one or other of the nipples off before you can use the cable but make sure the cutters are sharp or it will probably fray immediately.

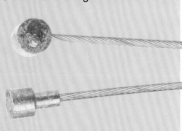

Cable disc brakes

Disc brakes are now being fitted to mountain bikes in all price ranges. Cable designs are effective but hydraulic disc brakes, shown on the next page, are even more powerful.

Disc brakes were developed for high-speed downhill mountain bike racing in the first place. But now that prices have dropped sharply, they are fitted to most new cross-country and free-ride bikes as well. The original designs used hydraulic pressure to apply the brakes, in a similar way to car braking systems. The simplified versions using cables, as shown here, are very popular as they are cheap enough to be fitted to budget bikes. But remember, the particular design shown here is just one example. If your bike is different, refer to the manufacturer's handbook or web site.

Cable or hydraulic, disc brakes can only be fitted to frames and forks equipped with disc brake mounts or tabs. Most types of caliper can be fitted to International Standard mounts but Hayes go their own way. As for the discs themselves, the International Standard six-hole hub fitting is almost universal, although there are a few bikes that still use the classic Hope five-hole fitting.

In wet and muddy conditions, rim brake pads just skid along the rim but do not grip. This is where discs really score, with powerful and consistent braking under all conditions, partly because the pads are larger and the caliper develops more power, but mainly because they are positioned away from the worst of the mud.

For instant braking, the gap between the pad and the disc is very small. So small that you can sometimes hear a light scraping noise when you spin the wheel. The small gap also means that when refitting wheels, after a puncture say, you must carefully slide the disc into position between the pads, before you fit the wheel to the frame.

The gap between the pad and the disc also makes it vital for the disc to run absolutely straight and true. Do not kick the disc, let it ground on a rock, or damage it in any other way. If the disc does go out of true, you will hear it rubbing on the pad and it must be replaced without delay.

As for maintenance, Fibrax say disc brake pads should be replaced every 1,200 to 1,600 miles (2,000 to 3,000km) or when they have worn down to 1mm in thickness, whichever comes first. Check in your bike handbook or with the seller for other makes. If the pads are not changed when specified, the steel backing will score the disc.

Whenever you fit new pads to cable disc brakes, or if you find that you have to pull the brake lever a long way to stop quickly, you must adjust the gap between the pad and the disc – see the Blue Box. The only other maintenance job is to apply a little anti-seize grease to the caliper mounting pins every so often. But check with your retailer immediately if the discs get scored or distorted, or you hear any unusual noises, especially screeching or grinding sounds.

1 To remove a front wheel with a disc brake, turn the quick release lever to the open position. Then let the wheel drop out. If it seems to stick, undo the friction nut a few turns. When refitting, lift it carefully into place and tighten up the quick-release again.

5 Now shake the pad out of the holder. For health reasons, you must not inhale the dust but it must be cleaned off, so use an aerosol lube to wet any dust inside the brake body or the pad holder. Check the thickness of the pad to see if it needs replacing.

HYDRAULIC DISC BRAKE MAINTENANCE

For downhill mountain bike racing and similarly tough applications, four piston calipers (top picture) are used to control the speeds of 50 mph 80 kph) plus. But two piston calipers (bottom) are far more suitable for cross country rides or everyday road use.

Nevertheless, even a two piston disc brake system needs more maintenance than any other braking system. If there are no leaks, the hydraulic fluid should never need topping up. But if a bike is given a lot of heavy use cross country, it is advisable to change the fluid once a year. When a bike is only used on the road, a change every three or four years is good enough.

As for the pads, they first need checking after about 500km on a road MTB. But the checks should become more frequent, the closer the pad gets to 1 mm of 'meat' left. In muddy conditions, you can halve those figures. And any mud on the caliper or rotor should be cleaned off between rides.

2 To fit a new cable, hold the back of the cable clamp with a spanner while you loosen the cable clamp with a hexagon key. You also have to do this when you have to strip down the caliper to free it off or when you want to fit new brake pads.

3 When changing the brake pads, you next have to free the inner pad holder from the caliper body. So locate all three socket head fixing bolts and undo each one half-a-turn at a time. This careful method of working is to prevent any distortion of the parts.

4 When you have removed all three socket-head bolts, gently lever the pad holder away from the caliper body. The brake pad is held in place by a tiny spring, so prise it away with a small screwdriver. Be careful as the spring could fly in any direction.

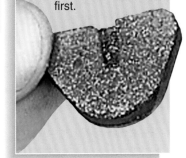

6 Fit the new pads into the pad holder and disc brake body, holding them in place with the springs. However, the springs do not hold the pads in place very firmly and the pins on the pad holder are a tight fit in the holes in the caliper body, so be careful.

7 When properly fitted in place, the pad holder is a snug fit on the face of the disc brake body and there should be an even gap all the way round. Re-fit all three fixing bolts next, but only tightening them a quarter or a half-turn at a time to prevent distortion.

8 The disc brake body sits on three sprung pins. If you press it, the whole assembly should move sideways a little. If it seems to be stuck, strip it down and take care to fit it back together again evenly. Finally, refit the wheel and adjust brake pad clearance.

DISC BRAKE PAD WEAR
Fit new brake pads every 1,200 to 1,600 miles (2,000 to 3,000km) or when the pad has worn down to a friction material thickness of less than 1mm, whichever comes first.

ADJUSTING BRAKE PADS
Rest the bike on the saddle and handlebars. Locate the adjuster at the fork end of the brake arm. Use a 2.5mm hexagon key to stop the central bolt moving while you undo the 8mm lock nut around it about one turn. Turn the hexagon key clockwise until the pads scrape the disc when you spin the wheel. Turn it half-a-turn anti-clockwise so that the pads scrape the disc very lightly. Hold the central bolt still with the hexagon key while you tighten the lock nut. Operate the brakes a few times and spin the wheel. There should still be a very light scraping noise. Re-adjust the pads if they bind (scrape) on the disc, or there is complete silence.

WHEN YOU NEED TO DO THIS JOB:
◆ Every six months to clean out dust and check pad wear.
◆ You hear squealing or grinding noises when you apply the brakes.

TIME:
◆ Half-an-hour to strip, clean and re-assemble a disc brake.

DIFFICULTY: 🔧🔧🔧🔧
◆ Most of the parts are small and are only too easy to lose. Adjusting the pads can be tricky.

Hydraulic disc brakes

Though more technical than most other bike components, hydraulic disc brakes are so effective they are worth the trouble.

When working on hydraulic brakes, think of the hydraulics as the perfect brake cable. There is no stretching or binding and no friction, so the brake lever should always feel light but highly effective in action. If it does not, or the brakes seem to be loosing their effectiveness, check for fluid leaks.

The best way to do this is to get a mate to pull the lever while you check the hoses and the area where the hoses are connected to the calipers. You will soon spot the leak if there is one.

On the other hand, if the lever feels spongy and the brakes do not pull you up hard, air could have got into the system.

If that has happened, when you pull the brake lever, the air just compresses and very little force reaches the pads. Once the air has been removed or bled out of the hydraulics, the pressure created by pulling the brake lever will once again push down the continuous column of fluid until it reaches the caliper. There it forces the pistons out of their bore in the caliper, and they press the pads against the disc.

As the pad wears, the piston moves out to compensate. So on most hydraulic discs, there is no adjustment for the pads. But they must be replaced before the friction material wears down to 1mm thickness. Keep an eye on the amount of wear because if you wear the pads down to the metal backplate, the resulting metal-to-metal contact will wreck the disc.

One method of bleeding the brakes is detailed here. But there are different procedures for the various makes, some requiring the use of a syringe, so you must always go by the manufacturer's instructions. Use the method given here only as a guide. The same applies when changing pads. Whatever the procedure, keep dirt, oil and other fluids away from the fluid reservoir. And be particularly careful when you are pouring fluid into the reservoir.

Bear in mind also that each maker specifies a particular type of hydraulic fluid. Some, like Shimano, use mineral oil, which must be kept away from the pads, discs and tyres but is fairly harmless otherwise. Other makers specify an automotive brake fluid. There are various grades and you must only use the correct one, but they will all strip your paint and mark plastics if you spill it on them. They will also do you a lot of harm if you swallow the brake fluid or get it in your eye. Just in case, always wear protective glasses when working with these types of fluid.

During manufacture and normal use, a pattern of wear builds up on the surface of the disc. So when you fit new pads, they have to bed in before they can generate anything like full braking power. Allow at least 50 miles riding for this process and keep on applying the brakes lightly to help the process along.

Be very careful with the brakes when the wheels are out. If you operate the brake lever, the pistons could just pop out. They can also pop out by themselves if shaken. So if you have to move the bike with the wheels out, put a wooden block between pads and tape it there to make sure it does not drop out.

Bleeding hydraulic brakes

1 First, check that the fluid reservoir is horizontal. If necessary, loosen the lever clamp so you can adjust the position. Then open up the reservoir to check the level and refill as required.

2 Sometimes the reservoir has a screw top but here, the lid is held on by two screws. If you do not have a bike stand, get a mate to hold the bike upright. Now find the bleed nipple on the caliper.

3 Clean the area with a rag, then open the nipple a quarter-turn to check it opens easily. Fit a plastic tube onto the nipple and put the end of the pipe into a glass or metal container to catch the fluid.

4 Open the bleed nipple at least half a turn and gently pull the brake lever. Fluid plus air will squirt down the pipe into the container. Shut the nipple and repeat until the fluid comes out free of air.

Changing the brake pads

1 You can maybe get some idea of pad wear by peering through the window at the back of the caliper. But to get an accurate check, it is best to remove the pads after 500km and more frequently after that.

2 Take out the front wheel. Locate the end of the split pin (or maybe two) and bend them straight with heavy pliers. Then pull it right out. You may have to turn it a few times with the pliers to free it.

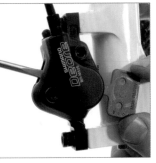

3 The pads should more-or-less fall out of the caliper. If they do not, push them out gently with a small screwdriver through the window in the back of the caliper. Do not inhale any of the dust.

4 There are two pads and sometimes a spring retainer as well. This will probably come out with the second pad. Check around the caliper for fluid leaks and wipe out the inside with a clean rag.

CHECKING BRAKE PADS AND DISCS FOR WEAR

Looking at a new brake pad, it consists of a metal back plate plus a layer of friction material 3 or 4 mm thick. The friction material is hard wearing, unless conditions are very muddy. Abrasive mud can accelerate the rate of wear enormously. If all the friction material gets worn away, the metal backplate will contact the disc and wreck it within a few miles.

The surface of the disc must be smooth and free of deep scoring marks. Even small defects will make the brakes snatch. If you ever have to change a disc, leave it to a bike shop because incorrect fitting could be very dangerous.

5 To refit old pads, sandwich the spring retainer, if there is one, between them. Then press them into place in the caliper. Check they are in the right place through the window in the caliper.

6 As the pads wear, the pistons move out slightly. So if you are fitting new pads and finding it difficult, very gently lever the pistons back into the caliper so there is room for the thicker new pads.

7 The holes in the spring retainer and the pads must line up, so push a small screwdriver though to check they do. Finally, fit the split pin and bend the ends over for safety. Always use a new split pin.

WHEN YOU NEED TO FIT NEW PADS:

◆ When the friction material as worn down to a thickness of 1mm or less.
◆ If the pads have been contaminated by oil or dirt

TIME:
◆ 30 minutes to fit new pads. Allow another 20 minutes for bleeding if necessary.

DIFFICULTY: 🔧🔧🔧🔧
Depends on make.

Fitting new brake pads

Safety is the number one factor when you inspect the brake pads or fit new ones. Check wear often and never let the pads touch the tyre - it could cause a sudden blow out.

Before changing pads, check the braking surface on the wheel rims. Light grooves in the braking surface are normal. On the other hand, if they go more than about 1mm deep, have new rims fitted without delay as there is a danger of the wheel collapsing. But some rim walls now carry a groove, to act as a wear indicator. Replace the rim when the wear reaches the bottom of the groove.

If the rims seem to have worn out in months rather than years, the chances are the brake pads do not suit the material that the rim is made of – see page 104. If you fit the correct pads, it will improve the braking because they will have more 'bite' on the braking surface.

Look also for pad material and dirt on the rims and check if they feel rubbery or slippery. If there is any sign, try cleaning the braking surface first with bike degreaser or, if that does not work, methylated spirit. Then scour the rims lightly with an 3M green abrasive pad. This will keep the new pads contamination free and give them a clean rim to bite on. And clean the rims and pads to prevent rapid wear after riding through mud.

Before starting work, check the instructions to see if toe-in is recommended. In some cases, pads are supplied with special spacers to set toe-in. By letting the front of the pad touch first, toe-in takes up the natural spring in the brake arms, preventing judder and noise when the brakes are used gently.

There may also be a particular way round to fit the pads. This may be indicated by an arrow, which should be fitted so that it points in the direction of rotation of the wheel. Pads may also be marked left and right. But if the drain slots on the pad are arrow shaped, they should point in the opposite direction. Alternatively, fit the closed end (if there is one) of the pad holder at the front.

Worn cartridge pads are usually removed from the pad holder by undoing a short screw or bolt to release them. The new pads then slip in but do not forget to retighten the screw.

Dual-pivot and most centre-pull brakes are fitted with new pads in the same way as side-pulls, but Mafac centre-pulls have two-way adjustable pad clamps similar to some cantilevers. When fitting a new brake cable to any centre-pull brake, use the method given for straddle wire cantilevers.

Standard cantilevers

1 Slacken off the cable adjuster at the brake lever and then unhook the link or straddle wire from the brake arm. Loosen the pad clamp by undoing the nut behind the brake arm, holding the pad holder to stop it moving.

BEDDING-IN PERIOD
Do not expect your brakes to generate top braking power with brand-new pads. The surface of most brake pads is slightly glazed and the braking surface of the wheel rim is never perfectly flat. So allow 10 or 20 miles (16 or 32km) of gentle riding to bed the new pads in. You can help this process along by applying the brakes lightly when freewheeling down hill.

Vee

Side-pulls

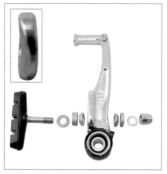

2 Pull the pad holder out of the clamp and check the condition of the pad. If there is a wear ridge either top or bottom, do not misalign the new pad in the same way. Take great care to keep the washers in the right order.

1 On some vee brakes, the pads are removed as on standard cantis. But on others, the pad fits in a slot as on side pulls. If so, there will be washers and spacers to set the toe-in. But some have one shaped washer – picture top left – to adjust the toe-in.

1 Screw the cable adjuster in and operate the quick-release to give you enough room, then undo the brake pad fixing. Sometimes it is a socket-head bolt, sometimes a domed nut. Slip the pad out between brake and rim.

2 When fitting a new pad, turn the pad holder to one side if necessary, so you can squeeze it between the caliper and the rim. Leave a gap of about 2mm between the pad and the rim each side, in case the wheels are slightly wavy.

BRAKE PAD ADJUSTMENT

Brake pad adjustment must be checked as in Steps 1 to 3 whenever you adjust the brakes, remove the brake pads or fit new ones. If brake pads are fitted parallel with the rim or – even worse – toe-out, it can cause judder or a squeak when the brakes are applied. On cantilevers and vee brakes, this can be prevented by adjusting the position of the spacers and shaped washers that you should fit between the brake arm and pad holder.

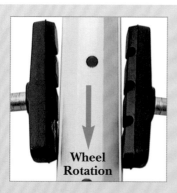

Wheel Rotation

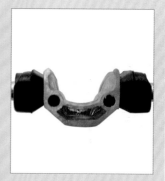

1 Check that the pads are the right way round and tighten the pad securing nut a little. Fit the wedge-shaped washer so that there is a 1mm pad-to-rim gap at the front and a 2mm gap at the back. Use a piece of card to gauge this.

2 Now pull the brake lever gently and check that the top edge of the brake pad is between 1mm and 2mm below the top of the wheel rim. It is permissible to overlap the base of the rim a little but try to avoid this if at all possible.

3 Next, pull the brake lever again to see if the whole surface of the pad contacts the braking surface. If not, adjust the angle of the pad holder, check Steps 1 and 2 again and finally, tighten up the pad fixing nut.

MOULDED ONE-PIECE BRAKE PADS

Most cantilever brakes have an adjustable pad clamp. You fit the post through the clamp, and can then adjust the pad in any direction. On the pads themselves, the wheel direction arrow and the wear line are usually moulded into the pad material. The gap between pad and rim is set by moving the post towards or away from the rim. As the pad wears, you can move the post closer to keep the 1mm or 2mm clearance. Finally, check that the rim hits the rim squarely, at least 1mm below the top edge.

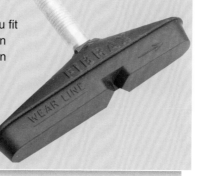

Brake levers

When a brake lever is correctly positioned, you should be able to use the brakes hard, without moving your hands from the bars and in full control of the steering.

Mountain bike brake levers all follow roughly the same design. The handlebar clamp fits round the handlebar and is held in postion by the clamp bolt. It is easy enough to alter the position of the brake lever, if you do not find it comfortable. But if the brake levers are integrated with trigger-type gear changers, this will limit where you can position the brake levers very substantially.

The main difference between budget and more expensive levers is the quality of the materials used and the provision of reach adjustment. Do not forget about this point as a comfortable hand position on the brake lever helps prevent you locking up the brakes on a loose surface. But people with really small hands should fit proper short-reach brake levers.

Utility, hybrid and Fast Road bikes also use a flat style of brake lever. They do not really have enough travel or leverage for side-pulls or dual-pivots, so make sure you keep the brakes well up to scratch if your bike has this type of brakes.

Hooded racing bike brake levers are all very similar to each other. So you can mix one make of brake lever with a different make of caliper, without any problem. The main variation is that the cable springs out of the top of the lever on ancient types. On later designs, the brake cable comes out of the side, allowing you to tape it to the handlebars for a much tidier look.

On the other hand, STI and Ergopower combined brake and gear levers are very different from each other. On STis, there is a groove on the outside edge of the lever body down which you fit a hexagon key to loosen or tighten them on the handlebar. With Ergopowers, the band-on fixing is in the same position as a normal brake lever. See pages 62-63 for both types.

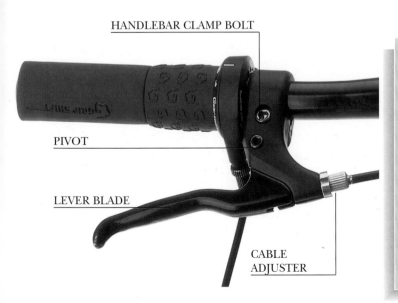

HANDLEBAR CLAMP BOLT

PIVOT

LEVER BLADE

CABLE ADJUSTER

VEE BRAKE DANGER
Vee brakes require special brake levers designed to be used with direct or linear-pull brakes. If vee brakes are used with brake levers intended for standard cantilevers, the brakes will come on hard almost as soon as you pull the lever and you will find it very difficult to apply the brakes lightly. Servo Wave vee brake levers are fitted with an adjuster button on the brake lever, others have a plastic modulator that is only visible when you pull the brake lever. Do not tamper with either type.

Road bikes

1 To reduce the effort needed for braking, lube the brake lever pivot in case it is sticky with old oil. Pull the brake lever next, so you can spray lube on the end of the cable – then work the lever so the lube spreads along it.

2 If the brake lever is loose or you want to adjust its position, remove the cable and, at the back of the hood, you will see the fixing screw. It may tighten with a big screwdriver, but if it is a hexagon key fitting, go for extra leverage.

3 To remove the brake lever without undoing the handlebar tape, loosen the fixing screw and pull the complete brake lever away from the handlebars. That is useful if you ever need to fit a new rubber lever hood.

COMBINED BRAKE LEVERS AND SHIFTERS ON MTBs
To remove the shifter, take off both cable adjusters and undo the Phillips screws that hold the indicator in place. Pull off and undo the hexagon socket-head screw holding the shifter to the brake lever. To refit, select bottom gear on the shifter and line up the needle with the vertical line, then refit the socket-head screw.

Mountain bikes and hybrids

1 Mountain bike and hybrid brake levers are exposed to the wet, so lube the pivots frequently. Pull the brake lever so that you can lube the cable as well. And give the cable adjuster a squirt of lube so it does not stick or corrode.

2 To adjust position or take off the brake lever, loosen the clamp bolt. Where the gear shifter is fitted to the brake lever, the fixing screw is usually tucked away under the shifter lever. Push it forwards to get at the fixing screw.

3 On good-quality MTB brake levers, there is a small Phillips screw just behind the cable adjuster. This allows you to alter the reach. With cantilevers, you should be able to do an emergency stop using the middle three fingers only.

4 On the other hand, if you have vee brakes, you should be able to do an emergency stop using your forefinger and middle finger only. Be careful the first time you do this, as vee brakes feel very powerful if you are not used to them.

WHEN YOU NEED TO DO THIS JOB:
◆ Brakes feel heavy but not gritty, so the cables need lubricating.
◆ The position of your hands when applying the brakes or resting on the brake levers is uncomfortable.

TIME:
◆ 2 minutes to lube the levers and cables.
◆ 5 minutes to tighten loose brake levers.
◆15 minutes to remove both levers.

DIFFICULTY: 𝄖𝄖𝄖
With racing bike brake levers, it can be difficult to reach the fixing screw at the back of the lever or refit the brake lever to the fixing band on the handlebars.

SPECIAL TOOLS:
◆ Long workshop hexagon keys or T-shaped hexagon keys are extremely useful when working on road bike brake levers.

CHAPTER 7

WHEELS
&TYRES

Bikes have to plough on through potholes, punctures and pile-ups.
They are more likely to come through unscathed if you look after the tyres
and wheels, the most important components on any bike.

Wheel care and inspection

Spare yourself a long walk home with a punctured tyre or a buckled wheel by following the care routine laid down here.

Whether you ride tough mountain bike 'knobblies' or lean-as-a-greyhound road bike wheels, they need very much the same sort of care. Point one is always to check the braking surface on the walls of the rim. See page 104 for more details.

Even on budget bikes, the axle bearings should run pretty smoothly. But on quality bikes, they should feel as smooth as silk. If they do not, strip, clean and regrease the hub bearings immediately or they may be permanently damaged.

Nearly all hubs are now fitted with a seal to keep the water out, so once you have got the bearings running right, they should be OK for quite a while. But make sure the seals are installed correctly or they may introduce a lot of drag.

The only maintenance hubs need is a drop or two of bike oil occasionally, if you do not have time to strip and regrease. Some hubs have an oil port in the body, others have a tiny hole near the axle. But even if there is no oil port, you can always pull the rubber seals on the axle away, then drip some oil round the cones.

Leave it there a while so that it finds its way past the seals and into the hub. Clean the area around the axle before you oil, wiping the dirt away from the cones so that you do not push it into the hub.

Punctures can be a problem but most can be prevented with a little timely maintenance. Plus the willingness to buy good quality tyres and change them before they are on their last legs.

WHEN YOU NEED TO DO THIS JOB:
◆ After every serious ride off road.
◆ Every couple of months on a road bike.
◆ If you ride through a patch of fresh road grit.

TIME:
◆ Takes 5 minutes as part of a general inspection.

DIFFICULTY:
◆ Be vigilant on tyres.

NEW WHEEL FORMATS

During heavy use, it is not unknown for spokes to break at the bend close to the hub. And the 32 or 36 holes in the rim also introduce a weakness there. So there are now many different wheel formats to get around these problems. Shimano's concept (right) has fewer spokes and these are paired to cancel out the tension. The spoke nipples locate in the hub, so they can be trued with a special spanner, if ever necessary, in a similar way to a normal wheel.

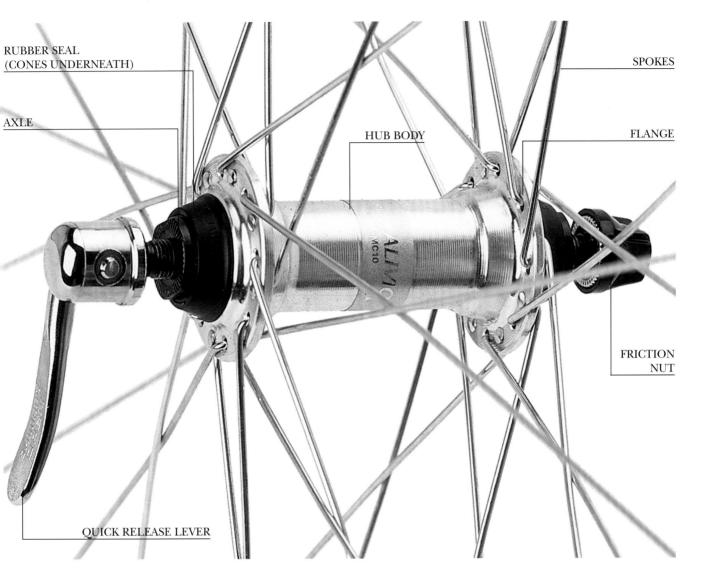

RUBBER SEAL
(CONES UNDERNEATH)

AXLE

HUB BODY

SPOKES

FLANGE

FRICTION
NUT

QUICK RELEASE LEVER

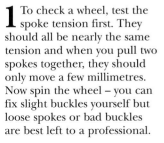

1 To check a wheel, test the spoke tension first. They should all be nearly the same tension and when you pull two spokes together, they should only move a few millimetres. Now spin the wheel – you can fix slight buckles yourself but loose spokes or bad buckles are best left to a professional.

2 Lift the front wheel off the ground and try to move the rim from side to side. Any movement here indicates that the bearings need adjusting. Next, rotate the wheel slowly with one hand. If you can feel or hear any traces of grittiness in the bearing, the hub needs stripping down and greasing.

3 Even if there is apparently nothing wrong with the hub bearings, you should give them a few drops of bike oil occasionally. If there is no oil port, spray one side of the hub with aerosol lube to clean it, then lay it flat and apply a few drops of oil around the edge of the bearing cone.

4 Examine the tyre for cuts, gently dig out any flints and flex the sidewalls to check for damage and to make sure the rubber coating is OK. Then spin the wheel slowly to check for bulges in the tread and the tyre walls. Replace any tyres that fail these checks or are just badly worn.

Removing wheels

It sounds easy enough to undo the wheels and pull them out, but you really need three hands.

When removing or refitting wheels, first operate the quick release on the brakes so there is room for the tyre to fit between the brake pads – see page 107. This is particularly important on mountain bikes with their massive tyres. Then select top gear so that the chain is running on the smallest sprocket. If you have a workstand, you can remove the wheels with the bike the normal way up. If not, or you are fixing it by the roadside, turn the bike upside down.

Quick-release hubs are easy to work with, but if you do not do them up tight enough, they can come loose and cause an accident. You have to develop an instinct about how hard you have to turn the quick release lever to lock it. If the lever leaves a slight mark on your palm when you have closed it, that is probably tight enough.

Remember that most recent bikes have a safety device on the forks that prevents the front wheel dropping out, even if the quick-release lever is not closed. On these, you have to undo the friction nut several turns before the wheel can be removed.

When re-fitting a wheel with hub nuts, the problem is to keep it centralised between the chain stays while you do up the nuts at the same time. Try steadying the axle with one hand and holding the spanner with the other, then swap round. Although it is usually easier if you use two spanners. Then give the wheels nuts a final tighten, using three fingers on the spanner and lots of force.

Wheels fitted with brake discs need extra care. And if they are hydraulic discs, do not touch the brake levers when the wheels are out or you may push the pistons right out of the caliper.

WHEN YOU NEED TO DO THIS JOB:
◆ Tyre has punctured.
◆ Hub bearings need maintenance.
◆ Back wheel has pulled over to one side.

TIME:
◆ 10 seconds to remove and re-fit front wheel.
◆ 20 seconds to remove a back wheel.
◆ 60 seconds to re-fit back wheel with nuts.

DIFFICULTY:
◆ There is a bit of a knack getting the chain on the sprockets and getting it past the rear mech.
◆ Doing up the back wheel nuts alternately, half-a-turn at a time each, while keeping the wheel centralised, is also a knack. You may find it easier using a spanner in each hand.

BACK WHEEL SAFETY SYSTEMS

Watch out for the wheel safety retention system on the back wheel of some bikes with hub nuts. One system uses a pear-shaped washer that fits between the hub nut and the drop-out. The tab on the pear-shaped washer has to be fitted into a slot in the fork end, before you fit the hub nut. Both hub nuts are then tightened in the normal way. However, the wheel cannot fall out, even if you have not tightened up the hub nuts enough.

An alternative system is based on dished or conical washers. One washer is fitted under each hub nut, with the serrated side A next to the nuts. A third washer is fitted on the chain side only, between the dropout and the axle. This time the dogged side B sits next to the frame. Tighten the hub nuts in the usual way.

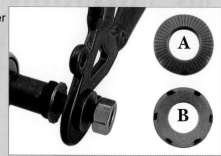

Bolt-in wheels

1 First select the smallest sprocket, then undo both hub nuts three or four turns. Good-quality hub nuts – usually known as track nuts – have a built-in toothed washer to grip the frame and help prevent the wheel being pulled to one side. Change to this type if your bike only has plain wheel nuts with a separate washer.

2 Pull the rear mech backwards so that the chain cage pivots right out of the way. That will allow the wheel to slide forward out of the drop-outs, although it will be tight. Give the tyre a hefty push with your free hand if it sticks.

3 As the wheel drops out of the frame, it will bring the chain with it. So let the rear mech return to normal position and try to lift the wheel away. If it will not come, you will have to lift the chain off the sprocket with your fingers.

4 When you are ready to re-fit the wheel, pivot the rear mech backwards again and pick up the top run of the chain with the top sprocket. Lift the wheel into the mouth of the drop-out, taking care to bring the chain with it.

5 Pull the wheel back into the drop-out and let the rear mech spring back. Next, check that the wheel is centred and fit any safety washers. Do the nuts up finger tight, check the rim is centred again and then tighten the nuts finally.

Quick-release wheels

1 For safety reasons, the front fork drop-out on recent bikes has a lip that prevents the front wheel falling out, even if the quick-release is undone. On older bikes, the front wheel usually drops out as soon as you operate the quick-release.

2 To remove a wheel, operate the quick-release. Then hold the friction nut still with one hand while you unscrew the quick-release lever with the other. After a few turns, there will be enough room for you to guide the wheel past the lip.

3 When re-fitting the wheel, you may have to spread the forks a little to fit the axle into the drop-outs. Then hold the friction nut again and turn the lever clockwise until you have taken nearly all the play out of the quick-release.

4 The first movement of the quick-release lever requires very little pressure. By halfway, it should need noticeably more force and the final locking stage should take quite a push with your palm. If not, tighten the friction nut a little more.

WHEELS WITH DISCS
When re-fitting the wheel, take great care to fit the disc between the brake pads held in the caliper. If you do not, it will simply be impossible to get the wheel back in again. If you have problems, try gently levering the pads apart using a medium-size screwdriver, so there is enough room between them for the disc.

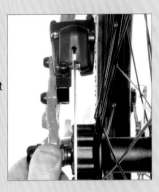

Tyres and tubes

When fixing a puncture by the side of the road, you will have to know how to remove and refit the tyres quickly.

PLASTIC RIM TAPE

Some riders get a lot of punctures. Others go for months without a problem, so regular puncture sufferers must be doing something wrong. The most common fault is not pumping the tyres up to the right pressure. That is between 30 and 50psi for MTBs and between 90 and 120psi for 700C tyres on road bikes.

Correct pressure makes it harder for flints to cut into the tyre - they bounce off instead. It also reduces the amount of energy loss caused by the tyre distorting as the wheels go round, and extends tyre life. Top up the pressure about once a fortnight and all will be well.

Low tyre pressure is the particular cause of snakebite punctures, when the tube gets nipped between the sharp edge of the wheel rim and a pothole. This usually results in two similar punctures some way apart. Snakebites are very common on MTB's and city bikes.

The next big cause of punctures is worn out tyres. If there are more than half a dozen serious cuts in the tread or the sidewall is deteriorating, fit new tyres. Similarly, if a tube has more than a couple of patches, throw it out. Many riders replace the tube every time they get a puncture, in case the patch lifts.

Remember, also, that tread rubber starts to deteriorate after three or four years. So if you are bringing a bike back into use after a while, it is usually worth fitting new tyres.

When buying new tyres, consider paying extra for Kevlar reinforcing. Kevlar is a strong composite fibre woven into a tape and placed under the tread. Only the sharpest bits of glass and gravel can get through the Kevlar strip and puncture the tube. It can be used in tread rubber as well. Kevlar also extends the life of a tyre and so does the silica compound used in tread rubber.

As for the tubes, butyl ones are best for everyday cycling. They resist punctures, are easy to repair and reduce the need to pump up the tyres. Latex tubes are best for racing as they are much lighter.

If you ever get a puncture on the inside edge of the tube, the rim tape is probably damaged or missing altogether, allowing the spoke heads to poke into the tube. So check the rim tape every time you take off a tyre and fit a new one if it is damaged or looks well past its best.

CLOTH RIM TAPE

Removing the tube

1 Most tubes have these Presta valves. Undo the brass valve nut with your fingers. Then go to the opposite side of the wheel and push the sidewall away from the rim with your thumb. You will see the ridge of the tyre bead on the side wall.

2 Push the rounded end of the tyre lever under the bead and pull the lever down hard to lift the bead over the rim. Hook the end of the tyre lever onto a spoke and move round the rim about four inches. Repeat the process.

3 Insert the third tyre lever in the same way as the other two. You will probably need a bit less force to lift the tyre bead over the rim. As you pull the tyre lever down, the second tyre lever will fall out now that the tyre is getting looser

4 Go right round the tyre now, pushing the sidewall away from the rim with your thumbs in case it is stuck. Then take one of the tyre levers and run it round between rim and tyre, lifting the rest of the tyre over the rim wall.

5 If using a Speedlever, press the sidewall away from the rim all round the wheel. Then hook the working end under the bead at the base of the sidewall, clip the other end on the axle and pull it gently but firmly right round the wheel.

6 With one side of the tyre now free from the rim, reach inside and start pulling the tube out. When you reach the valve, push the tyre bead back over the rim and pull the valve out of the hole. Be careful not to damage it.

TYPES OF TYRE VALVE

When working with old bikes, you may come across the Woods tyre valve. These have a rubber sleeve which fits tightly round a tube with a hole in one side. When you pump the tyre up, the air pressure makes the rubber balloon out slightly, allowing the air to enter the tube. If a bike with these valves seems to have a mystery puncture, the chances are that the rubber sleeve has perished and air is escaping back through the valve. Either fit a new length of valve rubber or fit the modern insert shown here.

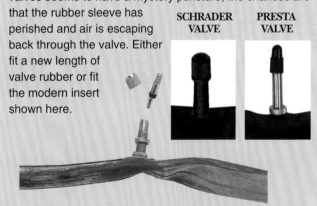

SCHRADER VALVE   PRESTA VALVE

FINDING A PUNCTURE

The easiest way to find a puncture is to pump the tyre up before removing it, then listen for the hiss of escaping air. You may well be able to see whatever caused the puncture stuck in the tread as well. If this does not work, take the tube out, pump it up a little and dunk it in a bowl of water or a handy puddle. A stream of bubbles will indicate where the puncture is. But it is only too easy to lose the puncture again when you take the tube out of the water, so wrap the punctured portion of the tube round your finger or mark it with the crayon usually supplied in puncture outfits.

PREVENTING PUNCTURES

To prevent punctures, install a sealant in the tubes. You just connect the bottle to the valve with a short length of tubing and pump some in. The material flows round the tube as the wheel revolves. If a puncture occurs, the escaping air forces some of the material into the hole, where it goes solid and seals the puncture. This does not work on serious gashes but it seals flint and thorn punctures without any problem. Dispensers for use with Schrader valves and pre-treated tubes are also available.

Puncture repairs

It is easy to repair a puncture but you must keep everything clean and do not expect patches or glue that have been around for years to work effectively.

Once you have got the tyre off the rim, feel round the inside of the tyre for flints, thorns and damage to the carcase. Then look round the tread for cuts and the sidewalls for any cuts or deterioration of the carcase. Buy a new tyre if in doubt about whether there is any useful life left.

Most cyclists on a long run or a serious cross-country ride carry a spare new tube and some even carry a spare folding tyre. These have flexible beads, usually made of Kevlar, and will fit in a bottle cage or under the saddle.

You may have trouble pumping up a tyre with a Presta valve, particularly when using a push-on adaptor. If so, undo the knurled brass valve nut two thirds of the way, then push in the valve stalk for a second, just in case it is stuck. Push the adaptor onto the valve, check it is straight and hold the pump horizontal. Finally, wrap your index finger round the valve to hold the pump in the correct position.

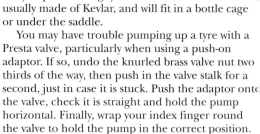

Repairing punctures

1 Even if you spot the puncture right away, it is easy to lose sight of it. So draw a circle round the spot with the yellow crayon found in most puncture outfits. Do not mark the actual area of the puncture.

2 Lightly roughen the area round the puncture with abrasive paper, again supplied in most puncture outfits. This makes a key for the adhesive and removes any dirt or rubber dust from the surface.

3 When you are satisfied that the tube is clean, dry and free of dust, select a suitable patch. Apply a thin, even coat of rubber solution around the puncture, then put the tube out of the wind to dry.

4 If you are using standard rubber patches, wait until the rubber solution is dry. Then lift a corner of the white backing with your finger nail, pull the rest off and press the patch into position.

Refitting the tyre and tube

3 Make sure the tube is sitting evenly inside the rim and is not twisted. Settle the tyre on the rim evenly all the way round. Then, starting at the valve, push the tyre bead over the edge of the rim with your thumbs.

1 Position the valve hole at the top. Then lift the sidewall so that you can insert the valve in the hole in the rim. Do not screw on the rim nut yet but try to keep the valve at right angles to the rim. Coat the tube with French chalk to make it easier to fit.

2 Work your way round the wheel, tucking the tube into the deepest part of the rim. Try to avoid twisting or creasing it as you do so. This bit is easier if you pump the tube up a a little, so that it does not get pinched between the tyre lever and the rim..

TYRE CHOICE

When a tyre has taken a beating, the casing will start to bulge, indicating that puncture resistance is getting low. New tyres are needed without delay but there is an enormous variety to choose from. Puncture resistance is covered on page 132. As for wear, tyres with silica in the tread not only last longer, they are also faster for a given energy input, especially the types that use two different tread compounds. For MTBs in daily use on the road, the full knobbly is no fun. It is hard work and best kept for serious off-road work. That leaves a choice of the multi-purpose tyre capable of mild cross-country work but with reasonable road performance, or the fast semi-slick, available right down to a width of 1.5in, with only a light tread.

Top road tyres also have dual compound silica-filled treads with a Kevlar layer. But there is not much point in going narrower than 700 x 23 as that sacrifices both comfort and performance.

TOP: Semi-slick tyre for road use and commuting on a mountain bike.
MIDDLE: A full-out cross-country tyre with a Kevlar casing.
BOTTOM: Directional multi-purpose tyre. Good for the mud but also OK on the road.

 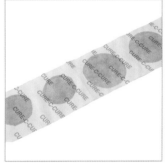  

5 Try to position the centre of the patch right on top of the puncture and smooth it out from there to avoid trapping any air. Then use the end of a tyre lever to press the patch down, especially the edges.

6 The best patches come on a strip of foil. With these 'feather-edge patches', you wait until the glue is dry, then peel one off the foil. Position in the way already described. Then press the patch into place.

7 Press hard from the centre outwards using a tyre lever. After 20 seconds, fold the patch in half. The paper cover should split - then peel it off from the centre. These patches should blend into the tube.

8 Some feather-edge patches have a transparent backing. But they work in a similar way. Glueless patches are seldom as effective as glued ones. They often shift, causing a slow puncture. Emergencies only.

4 Continue this process all round the tyre, pushing the other side of the tyre down well into the rim with your fingers and forcing the tyre wall over the rim with your thumbs. Do not use the tyre levers until right at the end. Make sure you seat them on the rim, not the tube, to avoid pinching it.

5 Check the tyre is fitted evenly, then pump it up a bit more to straighten out the tube inside the tyre. Check the valve is upright, screw on the rim nut finger tight and spin the wheel to check again that the tyre is fitted evenly. If not, remove the tyre and refit more carefully, before pumping up to normal pressure - page 41.

Strip down hubs

Water, dirt and grit are the enemies of all hub bearings. So strip and re-grease them if you can feel the bearings dragging.

You have probably decided to strip the hubs down because of problems revealed during an inspection. But if you have been out in a downpour, especially when riding cross-country, it is worth checking the hub bearings in the next few days, just in case water has got in.

But serious off-roaders should reckon on a routine strip down every three months or so. Road riders can stretch that to a year or even two if inspection reveals the bearings are running smoothly.

Most hubs have some sort of rubber seal to keep out the wet stuff but they are not designed to keep out water under pressure. So do not ever point a hose at the hubs, let alone a pressure washer, no matter how dirty your bike.

Some seals are external to the hub and fit around the axle, locknut and cone, pressing on the flange of the hub. In other cases, a rubber or labyrinth seal is positioned in the flange itself and presses on the outside edge of the cone. In this case, it may be necessary to carefully prise the seal out in order to get at the cones and ball bearings.

This second type can be backed up with additional seals made by various accessory manufacturers. They are designed for MTBs but there is no reason why they cannot be fitted to city or touring bikes that might benefit from better bearing protection.

A front hub is shown in the picture below to keep things simple but rear hubs come apart in more or less the same way.

Some top-quality hubs have sealed ball bearings, not the loose bearings shown here. The bearings have to be drifted out for cleaning and re-packing with grease, then tapped back in again.

1 Remove the quick-release skewer by holding the friction nut and twisting the q/r lever until it comes to the end of the thread. Watch for the conical springs on the skewer, each side of the hub.

2 On mountain bikes, there is sometimes a separate rubber seal around the cones which helps to prevent water entering the hub bearings – they just pull off. But internal seals are also common.

5 When you have removed the cone and locknut on one side of the axle, you can pull the axle out the other side. Be careful as some of the ball bearings might come with it and drop onto the floor.

6 Almost certainly some ball bearings will be left in the hub, stuck there in the grease. Dig them out with a small screwdriver or a pen top and scrape out as much of the old grease as you can.

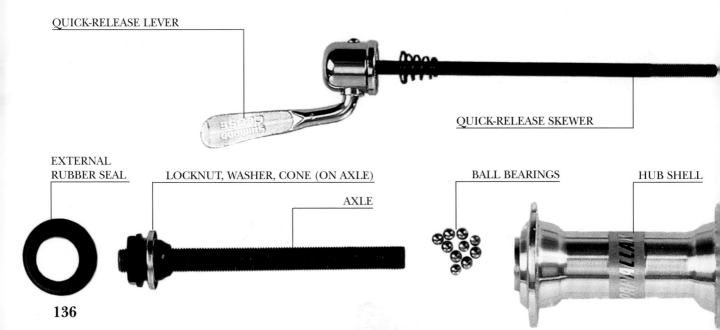

QUICK-RELEASE LEVER

QUICK-RELEASE SKEWER

EXTERNAL RUBBER SEAL

LOCKNUT, WASHER, CONE (ON AXLE)

AXLE

BALL BEARINGS

HUB SHELL

3 Use a cone spanner to hold the axle while you undo one of the locknuts. It will take quite a lot of force to start with. If you are working on the back wheel, it is usually best to work on the non-chain side.

4 Undo the lock nut and pull off the lock washer. This sometimes has a tag which fits into a groove in the axle, so you may have to prise it off with a screwdriver. Finally, undo the cone itself.

WHEN YOU NEED TO DO THIS JOB:
◆ When the bearings feel rough or seem to drag a bit when you turn the axle with your fingers.
◆ During a big overhaul.

TIME:
◆ 5 minutes to remove the axle.

DIFFICULTY: 🔧🔧
◆ This is the easy bit, provided that you have a proper cone spanner.

SPECIAL TOOLS:
◆ At least one cone spanner, preferably a pair of them.

GREASE FOR HUB BEARINGS

That old tin of grease in the corner of the shed is probably intended for cars. Do not use it on your bike as it has three big drawbacks. One is that it is too heavy, so it causes a lot of drag in the bearings. Two is that it ceases to work if water gets in. Three is that it can thicken up badly and so lose most of its lubricating properties. Use grease specially formulated for bike bearings instead. It is thinner, tolerates water better and does not thicken up as much. Up to now, nobody has come up with a miracle grease for bikes but a Teflon-based grease is probably the best, although any branded waterproof bike grease will be OK for packing bearings.

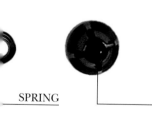

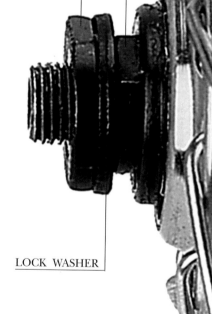

CONE

LOCKNUT

LOCK WASHER

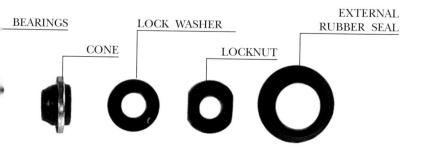

SPRING   FRICTION NUT

BEARINGS   LOCK WASHER   EXTERNAL RUBBER SEAL

CONE   LOCKNUT

Grease and adjust hubs

If a hub needs fresh grease, follow all the steps here. If you can feel play in the bearings but they run OK, the hubs only need adjusting.

The first thing to do after stripping the hubs down is check the cones for damage. If there is any sign of pitting or a track has been worn into the cone, it is best to fit new ones. Check also that the axle is straight – if one or other end of the axle appears to move up and down when you roll it along a flat surface, fit a new axle too.

Most cones have the same thread and shape, so there is usually no problem finding new ones. But if you are dealing with budget hubs, you may have to buy a complete new axle.

The core part of this job is adjusting the cones so that they apply the right amount of pressure to the bearings. Aim for the point where you cannot feel any movement at all at the end of the axle but it turns without any sign of dragging or grittiness.

Finding this exact point is mostly a process of trial and error. Even professional mechanics do not expect to hit it first time, so do not worry if you have to re-adjust the cones a few times.

One problem is that when you finally tighten the locknut, it increases the pressure on the cones and through them on the bearings. So to get the cone adjustment right, you have to leave just enough slack to make up for this.

When you think you have got the adjustment right and the axle turns really smoothly, pop the wheel back into the bike and see if you can detect any movement at the wheel rim. The distance of the rim from the hub magnifies any play, so it is OK if you can detect a tiny amount of movement. Re-check the adjustment after your next ride.

If the rim is not buckled but nevertheless rubs on the brake blocks, perhaps when you are out of the saddle climbing a hill, the cones probably need tightening a fraction.

Hubs for use with disc brakes have a special mount, usually six holes, built into the left-hand flange.

THEY ARE THE PITS
Once you have stripped the hub bearings down, you must inspect the inner surface of the cones for damage and wear. The cone above left is a brand-new, high-quality item which has a completely smooth unpitted surface. The middle one has a track worn into the metal and is pitted. Do not re-use. The right-hand cone has some wear which will probably accelerate from now on. Re-use only to stay mobile if necessary, while you track down a replacement.

1 Having cleaned away all traces of old lubricant, coat both bearing tracks with a thin layer of waterproof grease. Do not be tempted to fill the barrel of the hub with grease or it will be forced out later and make a horrible mess.

4 If you are re-using the old cones, screw the loose one back onto the axle and tighten it down until there is just a little play left in the bearings. Spin the wheel slowly now – it should already turn much more smoothly than before.

5 When fitting new cones, adjust their position on the axle so that the axle is central in the hub. This is particularly important on quick-release hubs. Fit the lockwashers and locknuts and screw down on to the cones finger tight.

2 Now fill the bearing tracks with new ball bearings. They have to be pushed down into the grease to make them stick and to ensure that you fit the correct number. Slim fingers can be used for this job but a pen top works very well.

3 Now spread a little more grease on top of the bearings. If the old cones are OK, there is no need to undo the one still in place on the axle. But clean everything up carefully before threading the axle back into the hub.

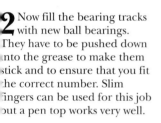

6 If you are re-using the old cones, the axle should already be centralised and one locknut fully tightenend. When fitting new cones, again check the axle is centred, then tighten one of the locknuts hard against the cone on one side.

7 Turning to the other cone, screw it in or out until there is a tiny amount of play left, then tighten the locknut against the cone. If you judge it right, this final tightening will eliminate that last little bit of movement in the axle.

WHEN YOU NEED TO DO THIS JOB:
◆ During an inspection, you have found that the hub bearings do not run very smoothly or you can feel a significant amount of play at the rim.
◆ As part of a major overhaul.

TIME:
◆ 40 minutes including stripping down and de-greasing.

DIFFICULTY: ✔✔✔✔
◆ Provided you have got proper cone spanners, the only real problem is adjusting the cones just right. Do not forget that the grease is quite thick to start with, so the bearings will loosen off a bit later.

SPECIAL TOOLS:
◆ You really need two cone spanners. These are long spanners slim enough to fit the narrow flats on the cones and locknuts. But if you use too much force, the jaws will distort and so become almost useless.

Wheel truing and spoke replacement

Do not be afraid to tweak the spokes a little if your wheels are out of true. But it is a job for the professional when the wheel is really out of shape.

If a wheel has very loose spokes and the rim is bent, your local bike shop will sell you a replacement. They will probably offer you a choice between off-the-shelf wheels and wheels hand-built to your own specification. If you decide on a hand-built wheel, it can be carefully tailored to suit your weight, the way you use your bike and, of course, your budget.

The spokes are usually retained in the rim by square-sided nipples, which are tightened with a nipple key. However, the square end is tiny so you must use a tightly fitting nipple key. If you use a badly fitting key, you will round off all the nipples and the wheel will be useless.

Occasionally you will find that the nipples have seized and will not move. Try loosening them off with spray lube. If that does not work, the wheel will have to be rebuilt.

Any time that you tighten a nipple, the end of the spoke pokes a little further through the rim and could puncture the tube. To prevent this, file the spoke end flush with the nipple.

When replacing spokes, the crucial thing is to follow the pattern exactly, crossing the same number of spokes and alternating sides where they fit into the hub.

Truing a wheel is a matter of increasing the spoke tension on one side to pull the rim straight and slackening it the opposite side to make up for this. Treat each bend separately and work from the edges to the middle, a quarter-turn at a time at the edges and half-a-turn in the middle.

Fitting a new spoke

1 Spokes usually break just below the nipple or near the bend close to the hub. It is normally easy to extract the remains but if the spoke has broken on the chain side of the back wheel, you will have to remove the sprockets.

2 Thread the new spoke into the empty spoke hole and wiggle it around so that the head seats nicely. Look at the next spoke-but-one to see if the new spoke goes over or under the spoke that it crosses and follow this pattern.

Truing a lightly buckled wheel

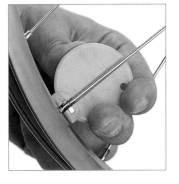

1 Unless you are doing a roadside repair, it is best to take off the tyre and tube first. Then fit the wheel in the frame and spin it slowly, noting where exactly it wanders and how far it is out of true.

2 If the rim bends to the left, loosen the left-hand spokes a little and tighten the opposite, right-hand ones. Work from the ends of the bend towards the middle. True each bend before moving on.

3 Do not try to get it right in one go but work little by little, checking that you are doing it right by spinning the wheel frequently. When the wheel is true, twang the spokes to settle them in place.

The truth machine

It is OK to tighten up a loose spoke or iron out a slight bend in the rim for yourself. However, all the spokes in a wheel should be kept at a high but even tension. Once you have slackened off some and tightened up others, you may have weakened the wheel quite considerably. The answer is to let a bike mechanic true up your wheels as soon as they start leaving the straight and narrow. Professionals use a special jig which allows them to correct side-to-side and also up-and-down defects. They will also re-tension the spokes so that the wheel stays true.

WHEN YOU NEED TO DO THIS JOB:
- ◆ As a roadside repair.
- ◆ When the wheel wanders a bit but you just have not got the time to take it to a bike shop.

TIME:
- ◆ 20 minutes to true a slightly wavy wheel.
- ◆ 30 minutes to remove a tyre and fit a new spoke.

DIFFICULTY:
- ◆ Quite difficult because you have to balance loosening and tightening spokes. Take it slowly and check frequently that you are reducing the buckle, not making it worse.

SPECIAL TOOLS:
Nipple key. The most common spoke sizes are 14, 15 and 16 but check before you buy. Do not use a combination spoke key as they are difficult to use and far more likely to damage the nipples.

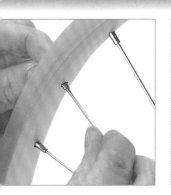

3 Remove the rim tape and pull out the rest of the old spoke. Unscrew the nipple on the new spoke and bend it gently so that you can poke the end through the spoke hole. Check that the spoke head is still seated correctly.

4 Do the nipple up finger tight and check that the new spoke is following exactly the same route as the previous one. If the rim has eyelets with angled seats, make sure you tighten the nipple right down into the base of the eyelet.

5 Twang the spokes with your fingers to get an idea of how tight they are. Then progressively tighten the new spoke until it is under the same tension as the rest. File off the end of the spoke if necessary and true up the wheel.

CHAPTER 8

BARS & SADDLES

On a bike, most of your weight is taken by your hands and your bottom. For maximum comfort, tailor your handlebars and saddle so that your weight falls fairly equally on them both.

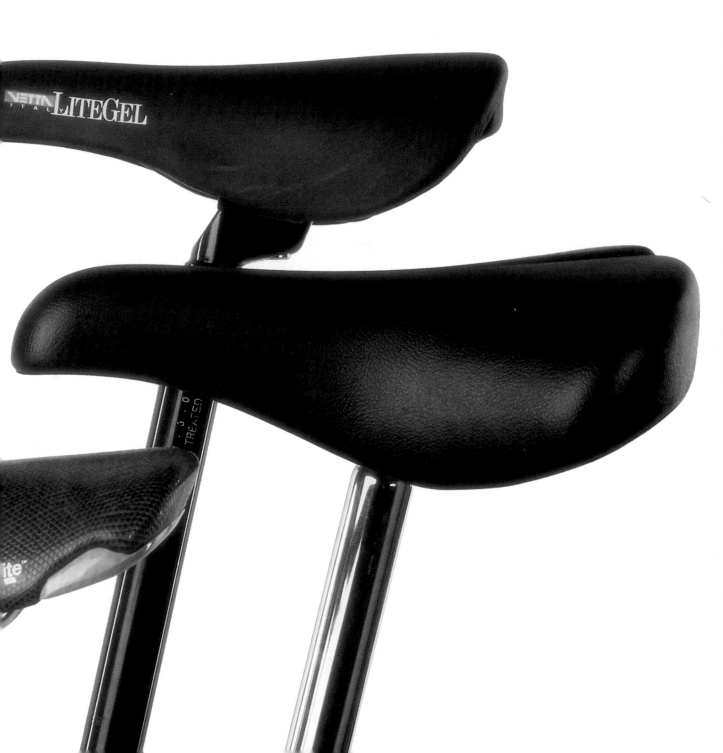

Component check

The handlebars, stem and saddle take a lot of weight, so check occasionally that all the bolts are tight. Inspect for cracks as well.

Rust on steel is easy enough to spot, but it seldom becomes a problem for cyclists because steel frames and other components have plenty of strength in reserve. It is just about possible that a steel frame could be fatally weakened by rust, but it seldom happens in the real world.

Aluminium alloy also corrodes but is much harder to spot because the white flecks of oxide blend in with the silver colour of the metal. Anyway, under normal conditions, corrosion stops at the surface. But handlebar stems and seat posts are a very tight fit in the frame, bringing aluminium and steel into close contact. If water gets into this area, it forms an electrical connection between the two metals, and this can speed up corrosion enormously.

You can combat this effect by using anti-seize grease wherever different metals come into contact. But even if you do so, it is worth occasionally checking highly stressed alloy components like seat posts, handlebars and stems. If you find any signs of abrasion, pitting, minor cracking or just an indentation on the surface of any aluminium component, stop using it immediately.

The welding on alloy frames and components can also fail, although most of these are now put together using automated Tungsten Inert Gas (TIG) welding. In this process, the area being welded is surrounded by inert gas, so the molten metal cannot be attacked by the air.

Thanks to this shrouding of the weld, the experience of welded alloy frames and other components is that, so far, they are very reliable. Nevertheless, it is still worth taking an occasional look at the welds, particularly when the items are more than three years old, and even more so when they are more than five years old.

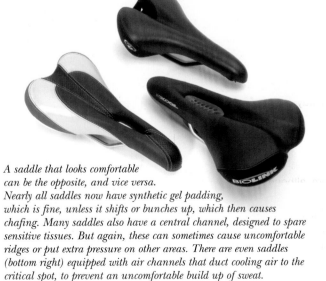

A saddle that looks comfortable can be the opposite, and vice versa. Nearly all saddles now have synthetic gel padding, which is fine, unless it shifts or bunches up, which then causes chafing. Many saddles also have a central channel, designed to spare sensitive tissues. But again, these can sometimes cause uncomfortable ridges or put extra pressure on other areas. There are even saddles (bottom right) equipped with air channels that duct cooling air to the critical spot, to prevent an uncomfortable build up of sweat.

1 Problem number one is corrosion. Second, a saddle clip can cut into the seat post and so weaken it. Third is overtightening of the seat post clamp or saddle clip. Replace one or both if necessary.

2 So it is OK to check that the seat post clamp is tight, but do not overtighten. If you do, it will cause cracking if the seat post clamp is a separate alloy component, or distortion if it is part of the frame.

3 Handlebars can crack close to the stem in heavy use, so consider fitting handlebars with a built-in brace. But keep an eye on the mounting bolts and handlebar clamp bolts as they are also highly stressed.

4 With Aheadset systems, the stem clamp bolts need checking. On triple-clamp forks, the socket-head bolts holding the legs into each clamp also need a tweak. Tighten the bolts to the manufacturer's torque settings.

5 Traditional-style stems only need a check on the main bolt, which must be tight enough to stop the handlebars from moving in the frame. On all types of stem, check they line up exactly with the front wheel.

6 Handlebars are usually made of thin alloy tubing. If the handlebar clamp or brake lever band cuts into the metal, cracks may fan out from there. Check when you remove the handlebar tape, just in case.

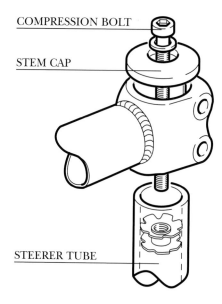

COMPRESSION BOLT

STEM CAP

STEERER TUBE

The star nut inside the steerer tube is the most vital part of the Aheadset system. It must be fitted perfectly evenly inside the steerer tube, 12 to 15 mm below the top edge. There are various special tools for inserting a star nut but it can be done by hand, with care. When the compression bolt is tightened, the 'petals' spread slightly and grip the inside of the steerer tube.

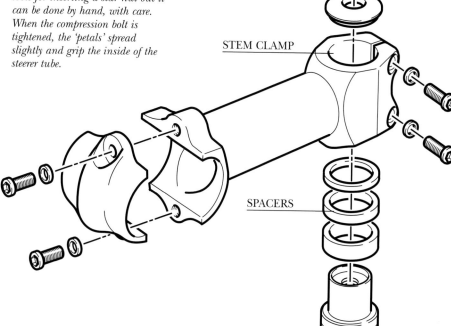

STEM CLAMP

SPACERS

The standard star nut fixing for Aheadset compression bolts is not a particularly good design. For tough conditions, there are a variety of alternatives that get a better grip on the inside of the steerer tube, without damaging it.

The Aheadset system is lighter but more rigid than the traditional set up. But the components are all more highly stressed, so take care you tighten all the bolts evenly. That way you will avoid distorting the clamps, or causing problems out on a ride.

The top of the steerer tube must be at least 3 mm below the top of the stem clamp so that the compression bolt can push the stem down onto the top bearing.

7 As welded stems get older, it is possible for corrosion to take a hold in the welds. So check the beads of the welds and the surrounding metal for pin holes and cracks. Replace soon if anything shows up.

SAFETY LIMIT LINE

When setting up your riding position or adjusting the height of the saddle or handlebars, you must check that the limit mark is not visible. If the handlebar stem or seat post are pulled out so far that the limit marks are visible, there is a strong possibility that they will either fall out of the frame, or break due to the additional stress placed on them.

If you need to set the saddle higher than permitted, just fit a longer seat post than standard. But now that there are many new ways of building a frame, you must be very careful that the new seat post is exactly the correct diameter for the frame.

You could also fit an angled stem, to raise the handlebars or even lower them, although you should avoid extreme riding positions, or you may be able to solve the problem by fitting a different style of handlebar. For example, replacing straight handlebars with risers, or drops with straights.

Handlebars and stems

Although they come in many shapes and sizes, there are only a few ways of fitting the handlebars and stem.

The stem and handlebars are the visible parts of the bicycle steering system, but the steerer tube is equally important, although you do not normally see it, because it is concealed inside the head tube. It is the steerer tube that carries the stem, connecting it to the forks.

Quill stems are held into the steerer tube by a long binder bolt. This screws into a wedge, which locks against the inside of the steerer tube. Quill stems are so called because the the stem is cut off at an angle, which makes it look like a quill pen.

There is also an older design in which an expander bolt screws into a cone, which fits inside the stem. As you tighten the expander bolt, the cone expands the stem tube and locks it to the inside of the steerer tube.

On both of these designs, the first step when changing the height of the handlebars is to loosen the binder or expander bolt. You then tap the binder bolt and that should dislodge the wedge or cone, allowing you to adjust the stem height, or remove it. Reverse this process after adjustment.

If a modern Aheadset-style headset is fitted, the stem clamps to the outside of the steerer tube. But this can only work with threadless forks, so it is not interchangeable with either of the older types.

To remove a clamp-on stem, first take off the stem cap by undoing the compression bolt. Then loosen the clamp bolts and lift off the stem. To re-fit, slide the stem into place on the top headset bearing, then fit the stem cap and tighten it down to remove any slack in the headset. Only then do you tighten the clamp bolts again. See pages 145 and 168 for more on the Aheadset system.

When you have finished work in this area, always check that you have tightened all the bolts and that the stem lines up with the front wheel.

HEIGHT ADJUSTMENT

The Aheadset system gives little height adjustment for the handlebars. If you need to raise them more, bolt a stem riser to the steerer, then fit the stem onto that. There is a similar-looking device that allows you to fit a clamp-on stem in place of a quill stem.

Removing the handlebar stem

1 On some quill stems, the top is neatly closed off with a large rubber plug. Pull out the plug and look for the socket-headed bolt a little way below. Do not confuse a quill stem with the Aheadset type. These have a smaller socket-head bolt on top of the stem.

2 The socket-head bolt is sometimes buried so deep that you can only reach it with the long end of a hexagon key. It should be done up tight, so slip a narrow piece of tubing over the short end of the hex key to give you enough leverage to undo the bolt.

Adjusting handlebars

1 To adjust the handlebars, start by removing the brake levers, gear levers, light brackets and so on. But do not bother if you are only altering the angle of the bars, just remember to adjust the position of the levers as well.

2 Now undo the handlebar clamp. You only need to loosen it a few turns to adjust the position of the bars, but remove the bolt if you are separating bars from the stem. See below for handlebar clamps with two or more bolts.

Front loading stems

1 To make it easier to swap handlebars, most stems are now front loading. Undo the clamp by loosening the clamp bolts half a turn at a time,

2 If you are trying to stop a creak, clean the mating surfaces with solvent. Then smooth out any minor damage with abrasive paper.

3 On older versions of the expander bolt stem; there is no rubber plug. In this case, it is much easier to undo the bolt with a hexagon key or spanner. Once you have undone it about four turns, give the head of the expander a sharp blow with a medium hammer.

4 If that does not dislodge the expander bolt, cushion it with a piece of wood and hit it harder. But the stem itself may be stuck in the steerer tube. If so, apply bike oil around the top of the headset, wait, then tap the top of the stem with a hammer to help loosen it off.

5 Aheadset stems clamp on to the outside of the steerer tube. They are removed by removing the stem cap, then loosening the clamp bolts and lifting. Adjust the height of the stem by varying the number of spacers beneath, but for safety reasons, the steerer tube must never be more than 10mm from the top of the stem.

3 You can now try to work the handlebars out of the clamp. Be careful as there may be a separate metal sleeve around the handlebars, inside the clamp. Do not hurry as it is only too easy to scratch the bars badly, especially drops.

4 If it is impossible to pull the handlebars out of the stem, try refitting the clamp bolt the opposite way round with a coin in the slot. As you tighten the bolt, it will open up the clamp, but this trick only works when the bolt hole is threaded.

MIXING AND MATCHING
In a perfect world, every handlebar would fit every stem, which is why the International Standards Organisation (ISO) specify that handlebars should measure 25.4mm at the centre bulge. Happily, most MTB components are made to this standard, but some makers work to their own sizes, with the idea of forcing you to stay with their products. Despite that, a lot of handlebars measure between 25mm and 26mm at the centre bulge.

Fortunately, if the stem clamp on a one-piece stem is only slightly smaller than the diameter of the handlebar centre, it is OK to gently open up the clamp with a large screwdriver. But do not use any force or you may crack the clamp.

Use only a minimum amount of force to tighten the handlebar clamp bolt(s), particularly on front loading stems. If you have to use more than that to stop the handlebar moving, change either the stem or handlebars for one that fits more closely.

3 When you re-fit them, apply anti-seize compound to the clamp bolts. Do them up finger tight, then half-a-turn at a time until the 'bars will not move.

4 Make sure that the gap around the clamp is even top and bottom. If not, re-fit the clamp as there is a danger of it cracking otherwise.

Grips and tap[

Nothing looks worse than a tattered set of handgrips or torn and dirty handlebar tape. Luckily, replacements cost very little.

Nearly all mountain bikes are sold with flat handlebars or risers. To make sure they fit most people, manufacturers sometimes fit ones that are too wide for many riders. This is OK on short journeys but forces you to use a tiring spread-arm riding position. If you are fitting new grips, consider whether you would be more comfortable with narrower handlebars or with bar ends that give you an alternative hand position.

The simplest way to reduce the width of the bars is to cut a couple of inches off the ends. But before you do this, check that it will leave enough room for the bar ends, brake levers and shifters. If you decide to go ahead, plumber's pipe cutters will do the job very neatly. You can get these at any DIY superstore but buy good ones – the cheap types are a pain. Do not remove more than a couple of inches of handlebar each side, otherwise it might be difficult to retain full control of the steering.

There are many different types and styles of bar end but the cheaper ones made of aluminium alloy suit most riders. When you are fitting them, do not overtighten the fixing bolts or the light aluminium handlebar tube might collapse under the pressure.

Handlebar tape is always used with drop handlebars, perhaps with extra padding to reduce the shock reaching the hands. Tape is available in various materials and lots of different colours and patterns. The most popular type is slightly padded plastic. But cork ribbon, which gives a cool sweat-free grip, is very pleasant to the feel and so is the ancient twill or cloth tape. This ages fast, but feels good. When you reach the brake levers, mould the tape neatly round the clip and the hood. But with STi and Ergopower levers, use a short length of tape to cover the fixing bands.

Drop handlebars often have a groove for the brake and gear cables. Use a few short lengths of insulation tape to retain each cable in the correct groove, before you apply the handlebar tape.

ADJUSTABLE STEMS

Many hybrid and leisure bikes now come with an adjustable stem to make it even easier to get the right riding position. To alter the angle of the stem and so lift the handlebars, loosen the clamp bolt that holds the stem to the steerer tube. Next, undo the socket head bolt on top of the stem until it is quite loose, lift the handlebar assembly and re-tighten the top bolt. Then re-tighten the clamp bolt in front of the stem, making sure that it is exactly in line with the front wheel.

If you are having trouble with your riding position, it is certainly worth fitting an adjustable stem to other types of bike as well. The type shown above right is suitable for use with an Aheadset-style set-up and threadless forks. The type shown bottom left can be used in place of a standard stem, with threaded forks, although few are in use so far.

Taping drop handlebars

1 Pull out the handlebar end plugs first. Some have a central screw which must be loosened first to ease off the pressure, but most just pull out or prise out with a screwdriver.

2 Undo all the old tape, cutting it with a utility knife if necessary. Then roll back the rubber brake hood and use a short length of tape to cover the edge of the lever.

New grips for flat bars

1 If the old grips are finished, just cut them off. But if you want to re-use them, open up the grip with a screwdriver, fire some spray lube into the gap and pull them off.

2 Remove the rest of the goo with methylated spirit, then spray the grip area with standard hairspray. Slide the new or re-used grip on before the hairspray dries.

3 If you do not have any hairspray, try aerosol paint. Use the palm of your hand to push the grip along the handlebar but move fast or it will stick in the wrong place.

WHEN YOU NEED TO DO THIS JOB:
◆ Grips and tape are old and tatty.
◆ Handlebars are too wide for comfort.
◆ You want to fit bar ends to give a better riding position when climbing hills.

TIME:
◆ 15 minutes to fit new grips.
◆ 30 minutes to cut down handlebars with pipe cutter and adjust the position of the brake levers.
◆ 15 minutes to remove old handlebar tape and fit new.

DIFFICULTY:
◆ Pretty easy, even if you decide to reduce the width of the handlebar.

SPECIAL TOOLS:
◆ Plumber's pipe cutter.

BAR END CLAMPS
Bar ends come in only one size and should fit any normal handlebar. But if you have problems getting the clamp onto the handlebars, try filing a slight chamfer on the end of the bar and lightly greasing the inside of the clamp. If that does not work, it may be possible to

cautiously open up the clamp with a screwdriver. But do not use any serious amount of force as you could crack the clamp and that is potentially very dangerous.

3 Start taping close to the centre of the handlebars, overlapping about one third and stretching it round the brake levers. When you get to the end, tuck it in neatly.

4 Fit new bar end plugs as a final touch. Sometimes they go in easily but you may have to use the palm of your hand to screw them round and round until they fit flush.

5 Cork handlebar tape often comes in a set. The tape itself has an open texture and feels cool and grippy but slightly rubberised. Short lengths are supplied to cover the brake/gear levers, plus end plugs. And if you start taping from the end of the handlebars, you can use the adhesive plastic tape to trap the ends of the cork tape to prevent it unwinding.

Saddles with clip fixing

Although they look simple enough, saddle clips can be pretty difficult to fit back once you have taken them off the saddle.

There is seldom any need to separate a saddle clip from the saddle, but if you have to do so for some reason, re-assemble all the bits in the correct order on the through bolt. Then hold the assembly together by tightening both nuts an equal amount. This keeps the through bolt in the centre of the clip. Do the nuts up finger tight.

Position the saddle rail retainers face outwards and slip them on to the saddle rails from the rear. Then slacken one of the nuts a little and rotate the curved outer retainer so that it closes off the saddle rail retainer. Repeat on the other side and tighten both nuts.

With the clip fitted to the saddle, push it onto the slimmer section of the seat post, then tighten both nuts equally.

Fit the circular part of the saddle clip above the point where the thin section of the seat post bulges out to the main part, otherwise it will eventually cut deep into the metal and the saddle will fall off.

To allow you to adjust the riding position, the saddle slides backwards and forwards on the rails. You can also change the angle of the saddle. This is best done by undoing both nuts a little at a time until they are loose enough to allow the ridges on the outer retainers and the saddle rail retainers to jump over each other. Retighten the nuts as soon as you have completed the adjustment.

SADDLE

SADDLE RAILS

SADDLE CLIP

SEAT POST

SEAT POST CLAMP

SEAT POST HEIGHT
Most seat posts are marked with a line showing the minimum length which should be inside the frame at any time. To put it another way, you should never see the line on the seat post when the bike is in use. As a rule of thumb, at least one third of the seat post length must stay inside the frame.

Final saddle adjustment

1 It is very important to get the angle of the saddle right, otherwise too much of your weight will rest on the most sensitive part of your anatomy. Undo the nut on one side of the saddle clip first.

2 Do not undo the nuts too far or it will be impossible to make fine adjustments to the saddle angle. To tilt the nose downwards, lean on the front of the saddle and lift the back with your hand.

3 A saddle clip also allows adjustment backwards and forwards. Loosen the nut slightly on one side and thump the back of the saddle with the heel of your hand to move it forwards and vice versa.

LEATHER SADDLES
Solid leather saddles must be allowed to dry out naturally, whenever they get wet. If the rain soaks right into the saddle, apply a dressing to feed the leather and build up water resistance. Tighten the nose bolt if the leather sags – the makers supply a special spanner.

Altering saddle height

1 Saddle height is adjusted by undoing the saddle clamp bolt until it is fairly loose. The seat post can sometimes be a tight fit in the frame, so it may not move easily. Turn it from side to side to get it to move. Then pull the seat post right out and coat with copper-based anti-seize grease to prevent it seizing in the frame.

2 Turn the saddle 2in or 3in each way and lean on it to adjust downwards. To raise the saddle, move it from side to side and lift at the same time. Then tighten the saddle clamp bolt fairly hard.

SEAT POST BINDER
Lots of mountain bikes have a seat post binder instead of a bolt. They are similar to the quick release on a hub so, when you tighten the binder, you must have to make a definite effort to lock it. If not, tighten the nut on the other side from the lever. Once you get used to whipping the seat post in and out, you can use it for security. Removing the saddle also makes it easier to load your bike into a car.

WHEN YOU NEED TO DO THIS JOB:
◆ Fitting a saddle to a standard seat pin, usually on an older type of bike.
◆ Swapping a saddle from a new bike to an old one.
◆ Adjusting the riding position.

TIME:
◆ Fitting a saddle clip can take 5 minutes or drive you mad and take 15 minutes.
◆ Adjusting saddle height is easy, unless the seat post is stuck in the frame.

DIFFICULTY: 🔧🔧🔧🔧
◆ Refitting a saddle clip is one of those jobs where you need three hands – one to hold the clip, one to hold the saddle and the other to use the spanner. It is best to assemble the clip away from the saddle and fit it back on all in one piece. If that does not work, get a bike mechanic to sort things out. Spray light lube or penetrating oil round the base of the seat post if it seems to be stuck in the frame. Wait a while, then try to move it from side to side to break the seal.

Saddles with micro-adjuster seat pin

Seat posts with a built-in clip are neat and light, but some have more fore-and-aft adjustment than others.

Seat posts with a built-in clip are far superior to those with a separate one. They look better, weigh less and are not so fiddly. Most have a good range of adjustment but this varies between different types and makes. So if you are unusually tall or short, you may have to change your seat post to get the correct riding position. Take a look at the 'layback' design pictured below if you want to get the saddle well back over the back wheel.

There are many variations on the basic design, some of which are not micro-adjusting because there maybe 2mm or 3mm difference between each possible saddle position; possibly a problem for the perfectionist, but not most riders. Other types have a two-bolt 'see-saw' design where you undo one bolt and tighten the other to adjust the saddle angle.

There are two important dimensions to watch – diameter and length. Diameter is more important because there are at least 14 sizes you could come across. These vary between 25.4mm and 31.8mm, so the differences in diameter are very small. Instead

of making all possible variations, manufacturers often supply shims so that one basic seat post covers a variety of seat tube sizes. But be careful - if you try to fit the wrong size seat post, it will either seize in place, or it will always be too loose unless you can find the correct size shim.

So when buying, either take the old seat post or, better still, the frame with you. Get the bike shop to check the correct size with callipers or a by using a micrometer, before buying.

Most road bikes have a seat post 220mm long, but most MTBs use a 300mm length because of the smaller frame sizes. Provided the diameter is correct, you can use an MTB-length seat post in a road frame, cutting it to length if necessary. BMX bikes use a steel seat post, 400mm long.

With all colours available, including lipstick red, saddles have become a fashion item. This one features a non-slip textured surface and Kevlar corners to prevent damage. Alternatively, some saddles are embroidered, also to create a non-slip

CREAKING NOISES
It is quite common for a saddle to make creaking noises, most often when you are climbing a hill or sprinting. If this annoys you, try a light coat of anti-seize grease on the clamp bolt as well as the cradle and clamp. Do not be tempted to overtighten the alloy clamp bolt as it will snap quite easily, or you could damge the thread.

WHEN YOU NEED TO DO THIS JOB:
◆ When fitting a new saddle or seat post.
◆ To adjust your riding position.

TIME:
◆ 10 minutes to fit a new saddle or seat pin.
◆ 2 minutes to make a change to the saddle position.

DIFFICULTY:
◆ You should find it very much easier with a micro-adjuster seat post than working on one with a separate clip, whether you are fitting a new seat post or adjusting the saddle position.

Fitting the saddle

1 On the standard-design single-bolt seat post, the saddle clamp is held in place by a bolt through the cradle. In the type shown, the cradle is part of the seat post, but it's usually separate. Always use anti-seize on the clamp bolt.

2 Fitting the saddle is usually easier if you take the seat post out of the frame. Turn the saddle upside down, support the top part of the cradle with two fingers and lay the square nut under the cut-out portion, supported by your fingers.

3 Now lay the other part of the cradle on the saddle rails. Then lower the saddle and clip onto a firm surface and check that the cut-outs in both parts of the cradle line up with the square nut. Do not worry about saddle position.

4 Finally, fit the clamp bolt through the hole in the seat post, through both parts of the clip and screw it into the square nut. Then tighten the clamp bolt until the cradle grips the rails, allowing you to remove your fingers at last.

Adjusting saddle position

1 When getting a new bike ready or bringing an old one back into action, coat the bottom of the seat post with anti-seize grease to prevent corrosion. Then set the saddle height using the guidelines way back on page 11.

2 For fore-and-aft adjustment, undo the clamp bolt one turn. But to adjust the angle, hold the cradle together with one hand while you undo the clamp bolt several turns. Lift and rock the saddle to change the angle and tighten.

3 Do not try to slide the saddle to a new position because there is too much friction in the cradle for you to do that accurately. Tap it with the palm of your hand instead, moving it by only a couple of millimetres or so at a time.

4 When you are satisfied with the new saddle position, check that the clamp bolt is tight – not overtight – and that the saddle is exactly aligned with the frame. Finally, do a short test ride to make sure you are comfortable.

SHOCK POSTS

For extra comfort, consider fitting a shock post. These fit in a similar way to a standard seat post but have 50mm of up-and-down movement to absorb bumps. The hexagon key adjuster allows you to alter the spring tension. The latest shock posts have elestomer springs, like a fork - page 163.

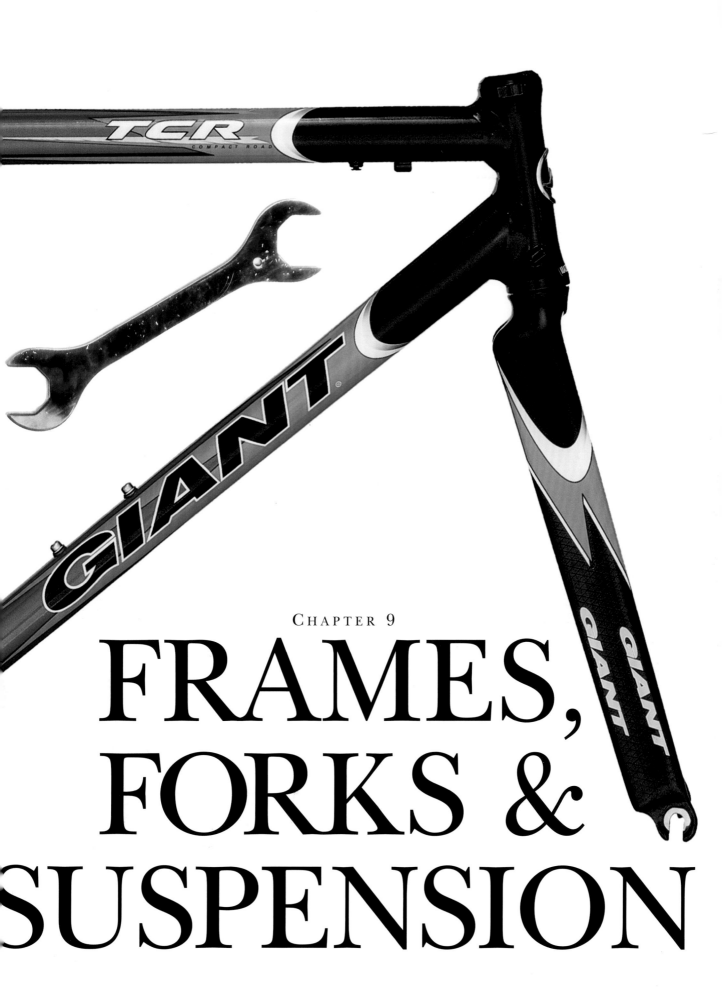

FRAMES, FORKS & SUSPENSION

Frame materials and design

Fully assembled bikes are such good value that you will seldom save money buying a frame and building up a bike yourself. But if you want a machine that is 100% yours, it is the best way to go.

Exotic materials like carbon fibre, titanium and magnesium have been used to build top-of-the-range frames for some years now. But these materials are getting cheaper all the time, so frames made of titanium and magnesium are now coming into Europe at fairly affordable prices for the first time.

On the other hand, when it comes to sensible money, welded aluminium frames have swept the board. It does not matter what type of bike, mountain bikes, hybrids or sports/racers, aluminium frames offer fantastic value for money. Mainly because they are made on a mass production basis in the far east, usually in Taiwan.

If you look at the welding on these frames, it is very even and neat, and experience so far indicates that it is completely reliable. This is due to the TIG (Tungsten Inert Gas) welding process, and the very close control over temperature exerted by the automated machinery. The quality of the finished product is also very consistent, for the same reason.

The aluminium tubes themselves usually come from an un-named supplier, so they are probably not top quality. Aluminium is not necessarily the best material for frames because the tubes have to be much thicker than steel ones. As a result, aluminium frames tend to feel dead and give an uncomfortable ride.

This is not important on MTBs because the tyres and suspension take care of the ride. But aluminium road frames are usually fitted with carbon fibre forks, to minimise vibration and improve ride comfort. Still at a budget price.

Aluminium frames are also made in Europe and America, in much smaller quantities. The standard of design and finish is much higher, as are prices. They are mostly built by the same firms that used to produce high-quality steel frames, and often still do so, in small numbers.

Steel frames are now around the same price as top quality, branded aluminium ones. But for touring and audax bikes, steel is still number one because it tends to give a better ride and is more durable. In the past, the steel tubes were joined together using lugs and molten brass. Now there are new types of steel tube that can take higher temperatures, allowing steel frames to be welded like aluminium ones, saving cost and weight and giving a neater joint.

Quality European frames and some American ones are built from tubes supplied by named manufacturers. This is partly because of the attraction of brand names, but also because it is an assurance of high quality and technical innovation.

As a matter of course, they are fitted with carbon forks, and recently, wishbone carbon seat and chain stays have become an integral part of the design.

Columbus and Dedacciai are the best-known makers of aluminium and steel tube sets, both of Italy. Reynolds of Britain, who make steel and titanium tubes, are also in the top league, and supply both ends of the market.

Apart from full-suspension MTBs, bike frames are all based on triangles, which concentrate the stresses where one tube is joined to the next. So good-quality frame tubing is thicker at the ends, where the stresses are concentrated, and thinner, in the middle, to save weight. The thick ends are called butts and the tubes are spoken of as double-butted if both ends are manufactured like this. Nearly all good-quality tube sets are double-butted but some are triple-butted, where they are amazingly thin in the middle.

Leisure or City Bikes

Even leisure bikes now have aluminium frames, replacing the heavy old utility bike that was never much fun to ride. Sometimes adjustable components are fitted, as above, giving you a multi-purpose all-rounder.

Mountain Bikes

Many full-suspension mountain bikes use variations of the Y-frame design. This design makes it easy to arrange the rear suspension but is only possible because the deep oval frame members can be reliably TIG-welded.

1 Carbon fibre frames have a slightly bulbous, seamless look. The joints are often reinforced with thickened sections and wishbone seat stays are also common. You can tell the tubes are not metal because they do not ring.

2 Larger compact frames usually have a shallow angle on the top tube and an extended seat tube. The high quality of the welding shows up in the regular ripples in the bead, the even bead thickness and the lack of pinholes.

3 Some top-quality welded frames are much better finished. The welds are so carefully sanded that one tube appears to blend seamlessly into the next. Fillet-brazed and silver-soldered frames have a similarly smooth look.

4 Any reasonable-quality MTB frame should have two sets of bottle mounts and a well-thought-out set of cable eyes along the top tube. There should also be a built-in gear hanger and the front mech cable should pull from the top.

5 Most high-quality road and MTB aluminium frames are fitted with keyhole seat stays and curved chain stays. The bend in the seat stays allow them to give a little, adding some much-needed resilience to an aluminium frame.

6 Built-in gear hangers indicate that you are looking at a reasonable-quality road bike frame. A chain peg (top arrow) is also a nice feature but most road frames now have short semi-vertical dropouts, instead of long horizontal ones.

7 Aluminium road frames are nearly always fitted with carbon fibre threadless forks for comfort, with an Aheadset-style stem and headset. Some have aero-dynamic straight fork blades, others are curved in the same way as steel.

8 Touring frames need more brazed-on bits than any other type. There should be rack-mounting eyes at the top of the chainstays, on the rear drop outs and on the forks. Chain stay pump pegs leave more room for bottle bosses.

Racing Bikes

Many sports and racing bikes have been influenced by the compact frame design. Budget versions as shown tend to have a sloped top tube but not the short head tube and extended seat tube of the full compact concept.

Touring Bikes

Traditional touring bikes are built with 531 steel tubing and look like racing bikes with mudguards. However, an MTB influence is creeping in with the use of vee brakes and very wide-range gearing.

Frame inspection and crash repair

Bike frames are strong but a crash can kink the tubes or put the whole thing out of kilter. So a quick check after a crash is a sensible precaution.

Luckily, most bike frames have plenty of reserve strength, but they can go out of alignment in a crash. When this happens, the wheels lie at an angle to each other and the bike will not steer straight.

Sometimes you will be able to spot this by eye, especially by checking the frame from different directions. Comparing the front and back view also helps. If you suspect that the alignment is out, have the frame checked professionally. It may well be possible to get the frame realigned.

Watch out also for damage to the forks, which take the brunt of many minor crashes. Luckily, it is now easy to find replacement forks for road bikes in steel and aluminium as well as carbon fibre.

As for suspension forks, you will probably have to strip them down and get a professional to assess any damage. But the simplest and cheapest solution might be replace the whole thing, if you know a suspension fork has been in a serious crash.

Carbon fibre components, especially forks, stems and handlebars, need special care. The problem is that the carbon fibres can separate from each other, without any sign of damage

on the surface, and once the fibres have separated or delaminated, much of their strength is lost.

So with no indication in the appearance of the component, and no other practical way to judge whether a particular component should be thrown away or nor, replacement is probably the best practice. Although it should be stated that so far there is no indication that carbon fibre bike components are any more vulnerable than metal ones.

Aluminium frames behave differently from steel frames. It is the welds that are most likely to go, especially if the tubes are well oversize. Alloy frames may also age more quickly than steel, so inspect them occasionally for cracks in the welds and for pinholes.

Ageing also shows up as a wobble when going down hill at high speed, on any type of frame. If you ever experience this sort of thing, regard the frame as scrap.

Most frames have brazed-on fittings. If you have trouble getting the rear mech mounting bolt (most likely) or the gear lever screw to enter the thread, have the threads cleaned out with a tap by a professional bike mechanic.

DESIGNER FRAME TUBING

REYNOLDS
500 Plain-gauge cro-mo (chrome-molybdenum alloy steel) tubes for budget mass-produced bikes.
525 – Butted cro-mo tubing, for brazed frames with lugs and for TIG welding. For good-quality mass-produced bikes.
531 – Famous since 1935. Alloyed with manganese and molybdenum so it can only be joined using brazing or silver soldering. No high temperatures so TIG welding is out. Tube sets now available for racing (531C) and touring (531ST).
631 – Upgraded version of 531. Air hardening, so it gets stronger after TIG welding or brazing. Strong, with a good ride.
725 – Cro-mo-butted tubeset for TIG welding and brazing, with lugs and without. Heat-treated for strength.
853 – Top-quality, air hardening, as strong as titanium. Used only by craftsmen frame builders.
X-100 – Top-quality aluminium-lithium alloy. Resilient like steel, stronger-than-normal aluminium alloys.
6-4TI and **3-25TI –** Titanium tubes that are light, very strong and extremely comfortable.

COLUMBUS
Aelle – Heavy, budget-priced cro-mo.
Gara – Still a budget product but butted.
SL and **SLX –** Roughly equivalent to 531. No longer used for new frames.
Thron – Quality tubes for mass production.
Foco – Top-quality steel tubing.
Columbus Altec – Drawn from 7005 aluminium, alloyed with zinc and magnesium.

DEDACCIAI
Scandium - Very advanced aluminium tubeset, maybe the best. Mostly used as oversize tubes.

ALUMINIUM ALLOY TUBE SETS
Easton – An American firm supplying various good-quality aluminium tubesets.
6000 – Aluminium alloyed with magnesium. Easy to extrude, so good for components like handlebars. Also used for frames.
7000 series – The most popular aluminium frame tubing, used for almost all budget aluminium bikes. Easy to weld but a bit prone to cracking near welds. Even if the tubes are butted, they have to be quite thick-walled. 7020 is probably the best grade.

Checking for crash damage

1 Position yourself at the front of the bike and look along the frame. You should be able to see if the short head tube and the seat tube that carries the saddle line up.

2 Stand over the bike looking down. You will be able to see if the horizontal top tube lines up with the diagonal down tube. Check also that the forks splay out an equal amount.

3 Now look along the frame from the back. The rear mech should hang straight down and the seat tube align with the head tube. Check also that the seat stays are straight.

4 Most important: run your fingers down the back and front of the forks, checking for ripples in the tubing. Next, take a look to make sure that the fork curves smoothly. Then take the front wheel out, so you can see if it fits back in easily and is centred exactly between the fork blades.

5 Finally, run your fingers along the underside of all the tubes, Damage like the tiny ripples in the tubes arrowed in the picture on the right often goes unnoticed during a purely visual inspection. Luckily, your sense of touch will often pick up defects that the eyes just skate over and miss.

Neither the tubes nor the welds have cracked on the crashed frame in the picture, showing the amazing strength of a really well-built frame.

WHEN YOU NEED TO DO THIS JOB:
◆ When buying second-hand.
◆ After a crash.
◆ If the bike is not running or steering straight.

TIME:
◆ 10 minutes is enough for a thorough inspection from several different angles. Always try to look along the frame against the light.

DIFFICULTY: 🔧🔧🔧
◆ When you first start, you will think you are going cross-eyed, but you will soon get the hang of it.

Suspension set up

**Full-suspension bikes and hardtails need careful setting-up.
Your height, weight and riding style all affect how they work.**

When setting up a full-suspension bike, you have to adjust the force needed to compress the springs. The idea is that when you put your weight on the bike, the suspension should sag by about 25% of the total travel. Total travel does not refer to the length of the springs themselves but the distance the front or rear wheel moves between the fully extended and the fully compressed position, within the limits of the design. If the forks or rear suspension reach the end of their travel when riding over rough ground, this is known as bottoming out. It should be avoided because it tends to shake your eyeballs out and can damage your bike, particularly the suspension itself. The opposite of bottoming out is called topping out and occurs when the suspension reaches its fully extended position, for instance when the wheels leave the ground. The 25% of spring travel allocated to sag is intended to allow the wheels to drop down into holes, allowing them to follow the shape of the ground more efficiently, particularly at the rear when braking hard going down a hill.

Hardtail mountain bikes with suspension forks only, as well as hybrids and leisure bikes with sprung forks, should also be set up for the same 25% sag.

When adjusting any kind of forks, try to adjust both legs evenly. If there is a difference between the springing of the legs, it will tend to produce uneven wear and possibly lead to distortion. Although many suspension forks now have the spring in one leg and the damping in the other, eliminating this problem.

Many of the suspension forks fitted to budget hardtails and full suspension bikes have steel coil springs but no form of damping. So the bike tends to bob up and down because there is nothing to control the springs or dissipate the energy of the bumps. When riding a suspension bike, try to develop a smooth pedalling style to stop the bike bobbing around. And on hills, change down to the lower gears early so that you do not have to get out of the saddle. This will help reduce the amount of bob, allowing the suspension to react more efficiently to the terrain instead of to rider-induced movement.

REBOUND DAMPING ADJUSTMENT

If you sit on the saddle and press down on the handlebars, the forks compress. When you take your weight off the 'bars, the forks extend once more. This is the rebound.

On many forks, the rebound is not controlled. So the forks compress and rebound a couple of times before they settle. If this happens when you are out riding, the forks will not be able to react properly to the next bump. They may be rebounding when they should be compressing, or the other way round.

Quality forks usually have oil damping to control the rebound. In addition to the pre-load dial, they usually have an extra control for the rebound at the bottom of one of the fork legs. Set this so that when you push the handlebars down, they only come back up once. Adjust it again, if you find the front of the bike still bobbles around when you are out on a ride.

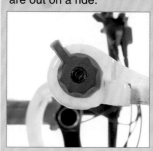

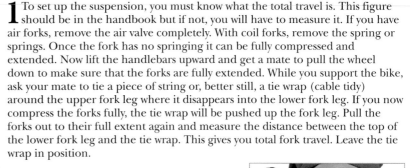

Front suspension

1 To set up the suspension, you must know what the total travel is. This figure should be in the handbook but if not, you will have to measure it. If you have air forks, remove the air valve completely. With coil forks, remove the spring or springs. Once the fork has no springing it can be fully compressed and extended. Now lift the handlebars upward and get a mate to pull the wheel down to make sure that the forks are fully extended. While you support the bike, ask your mate to tie a piece of string or, better still, a tie wrap (cable tidy) around the upper fork leg where it disappears into the lower fork leg. If you now compress the forks fully, the tie wrap will be pushed up the fork leg. Pull the forks out to their full extent again and measure the distance between the top of the lower fork leg and the tie wrap. This gives you total fork travel. Leave the tie wrap in position.

2 Refit the spring or the air valve and pump up the fork to the pressure given for your weight in the owners manual. Work out 25% of the total travel. Then sit on the bike in the normal way, with your feet on the pedals and bounce the fork up and down a few times, then get your mate to measure the distance between tie wrap and the top of the fork legs again. Subtracting this figure from the first measurement gives you the amount of sag. If that figure is less than 25% of total fork travel, the forks are too stiff. To correct that, turn the adjuster anti-clockwise one turn, or on an air sprung fork, reduce the air pressure. Turn the adjuster the other way if sag is over 25%, or increase the air pressure. Repeat until the amount of sag is correct. If you are unusually heavy or unusually light, you may have to change the coil spring to one of a higher or lower poundage (strength) to get the sag right.

Rear suspension

REAR SUSPENSION PIVOT

When buying a full-suspension bike, check that the pivots are large and meaty looking. They should also have some kind of built-in protection against water but you should still keep the area free of dust and mud. In normal circumstances, no maintenance is required.

1 Coil sprung rear suspension sag is adjusted by turning the spring seat on the suspension unit. If sag is less that 25%, turn the spring seat anti-clockwise to increase it and clockwise to decrease it. Keep adjusting the spring seat until you get around 25% of the total travel as sag.

2 If you are unusually heavy or light, adjusting the spring seat adjustment alone may not work. You can change the spring to one with a higher or lower poundage (strength). There are several specialist companies who stock springs of all shapes, sizes, and poundage.

3 Some bikes have two or more mountings for the rear shock unit. This changes the leverage between the rear wheel and the shock, and can increase or reduce the total travel. For example fitting in the lower position here increased travel by one inch at the rear wheel.

Suspension fork strip

Suspension forks must not be neglected. Inspect the gaiters regularly and be prepared to strip and regrease the forks several times a year.

Crashing up and down over rough ground, suspension forks take more of a beating than any other component on a bike. What is more, unless the sliding parts are protected by gaiters in sound condition, dirt will get between the moving parts and cause rapid wear. So day-to-day, keep an eye on the gaiters and do not ride cross-country if they are defective.

 If no gaiters are fitted, keep the sliders clean and give them a squirt of aerosol lube every time you go out on a ride. That will certainly lengthen the life of the working parts.

Every couple of months, the forks must be stripped so you can check the bushings and regrease the stanchions. The bushings are plastic tubes that fit in the tops of the fork legs. The fork stanchions are a close fit in the bushes, so they can slide up and down smoothly, without any judder.

When the bushings are regreased frequently, the stanchions will slide more smoothly and wear on the plastic bushing will be kept to a minimum. However, depending on how fast you ride and the terrain, the bushings will have to be replaced sooner or later.

You only apply a fairly thin smear of grease to the bushings, spring or elastomer stack, and upper stanchions. But you must use a synthetic type because mineral grease will attack the rubber parts. RST recommend Sylkolene Pro RG2, available from their dealers but any fully synthetic grease will do. Teflon-based grease is particularly suitable for the elastomers.

Upgrade kits are available for some forks, offering better quality gaiters and bushings. Soft rubber gaiters will always outlast hard plastic ones, but the bottom end of the gaiter must be held in place with a cable tie to stop dirt getting in.

You can usually get alternative springs to help you set up the suspension and you can change elastomers too. Cream ones are hard and blue ones soft. But fit the same stack of elastomers in each fork leg to avoid problems. The elastomers themselves damp down movement pretty well but many bikes are sold with spring forks but no damping at all. Consider upgrading to forks with oil or air damping if you find the front of the bike bobs around a lot or tends to act like a pogo stick.

SUSPENSION FORKS
The instructions on how to strip a suspension fork on this spread, and the next spread explaining how to change the oil, show these jobs being done on typical and popular examples. But there are many different designs , so check the manufacturer's instructions or their website for exact details before starting work. And remember, all these components are safety-critical, so it could affect your own safety if you get things wrong.

Sprung forks

1 Before starting the actual strip down, degrease the forks with solvent and water and dry them off. Then undo the countersunk Phillips screws or bolts holding the fork brace to the fork legs.

2 Check the brake pivots next to see if they are bent or cracked. Then unscrew them using a ring spanner right at the base of the pivot hexagon, in case the spanner slips. Lift the fork brace out of the way.

Triple-clamp forks

1 Strip the forks off the frame and degrease the whole fork assembly including the steerer tube and any rubber components. Then undo the top caps with the special spanner supplied.

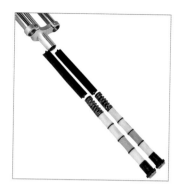

2 Once you have undone the top caps, withdraw the complete elastomer stack and wipe off any grease. Check that none of the elastomers are damaged in any way.

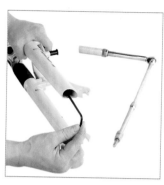

3 Lift the wheel end of the forks and undo the socket-head bolt buried in the end of each fork leg. You can then pull the lower legs off the stanchions and degrease them inside.

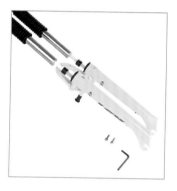

4 With the forks stripped and degreased, carefully inspect the plastic bushings at the top of the lower legs. If some areas of the bushing look shiny or scored, they need changing.

5 During a major overhaul, pull the compression rod out of the stanchions, degrease, and inspect for damage. Finally, reassemble by reversing the previous procedure.

3 Pull back the rubber gaiter and grasp the steerer tube with one hand. With the other, turn the lower leg anti-clockwise and pull it right off. Use Gillson's cushioned with rag to start it turning if necessary.

4 Wipe away any surplus grease and unscrew the spring using long-nosed pliers. Use your thumbs to push off the bush around the top of the fork legs, then clean and degrease this area as well.

5 Degrease inside the fork leg and all the bits. Place the new bush on a hard surface, sit the lip of the fork leg on the seal and lean on it with all your weight. Grease the springs and lower legs, then reassemble.

spension fork: oil change

Changing the oil in your suspension fork will keep it performing as intended. And stop it wearing out sooner than it should.

The oil in a suspension fork has two jobs. Firstly, it lubricates all the various parts as they slide past each other, which slows down wear. Secondly, it flows through the damper valves, absorbing the energy that each bump puts into the fork.

When acting as a lubricant, bits of metal and rubber worn off by use are carried in the oil. Changing the oil then flushes all these abrasive bits away, which substantially extends the life of the fork. But when acting as a shock absorber, the additives in the oil slowly get broken down by the action of the fork. Eventually, the oil will start to foam, which reduces the damping effect.

New forks do not become fully effective until they have been ridden for a couple of hundred miles or so. After that sort of time, you should notice that the fork move up and down much more smoothly. That is the signal that the period of 'breaking in' has finished, which is a good time to change the oil.

After that point, change the oil every 750 miles or 100 hours but more frequently in severe or very dusty conditions. If you are short of time, it is OK to just change the oil but a full service including regreasing the spring is worth the extra effort. In between services, keep the fork clean, especially the exposed chrome slider tubes. And every 250 miles or so, peel back the rubber seals and apply a squirt of the lubricant specified by the manufacturer at the top of the fork legs.

Bear in mind that the fork shown here is only one typical example among many. Check the manufacturer's instruction booklet or website for specific details about the forks on your own bike.

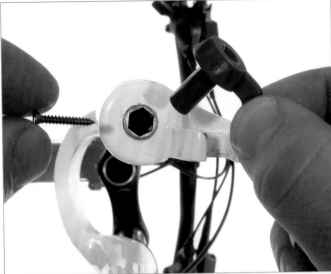

1 Remove the fork from the frame, as shown on pages 168-169. Brush off any loose dirt and mud, then degrease with a solvent cleaner. Rinse with warm water and dry. Then turn the fork upside down and rest the steerer tube on a bench or a Workmate. Undo the countersunk screw holding the rebound adjuster knob in place, then pull the knob away.

Oil for suspension forks is usually synthetic. The most important components are the anti–foam additives and lubrication properties. If they were left out, the churning of the oil would whip up a foam, making the oil thinner and providing too little damping. Various 'weights' of oil are available, to help you tailor the fork to your preferences. For example, if you change from 5 to 10 weight oil, the fork will have more damping.

9 Empty out the remaining oil in the fork tube, allow to drain for a couple of minutes, then wipe out. Check all the parts for wear, especially the fork leg seals, and inspect the fork legs themselves for cracks

2 Turn the forks the right way up, then loosen the plain top cap with a close-fitting ring spanner. You should be able to unscrew the top cap the rest of the way with just your fingers.

3 Pull the top cap away from the fork, waggling it slightly from side to side to prevent the damper assembly sticking in place. Lay it down on some clean rag so that the rest of the oil can drain off.

4 With a hexagon key, remove the adjuster knob on the other fork cap. Unscrew the adjuster assembly, then pull out the spring. It will probably be covered in old grease, so wipe it all off carefully.

5 Pour the old oil out of the other fork leg, catching it in a suitable container. Do not dispose of the old oil by pouring it into the drains or onto the ground as that will damage the environment.

6 Work the fork up and down several times to release the oil trapped at the bottom, then pour off into a container again. Repeat this process a few times until all the old oil is emptied out of the fork

7 Turn the fork upside down again and undo the small socket head screw at the bottom of the right fork leg. This holds the rest of the damper assembly in place in the middle of the fork leg.

8 You can now pull the fork crown assembly away from the fork legs. Lay the fork crown assembly on some clean rag to absorb the oil as it drain off. After a few minutes, wipe the rest of the oil away.

AIR FORKS

Most air sprung forks are very sensitive to the height of the oil. The air above the oil is used as a spring, and when air is compressed inside the fork it behaves in a manner known as "inversely proportional". This means that if you start with 50psi, and halve the fork travel, you will have 100psi. If you then halve the remaining travel you will have 200psi, and so on. The oil height is crucial to the performance of the fork throughout the whole range of travel of the fork. Raising the oil height makes the fork more progressive – stiffer towards the end of it's travel. Lowering it makes it softer at the end of it's travel. But always stick to the manufacturers instructions, otherwise you could damage the fork internals.

10 Replace any bits past their best, then slide the fork crown assembly back into the legs. Refit the adjuster and the socket head screw. Move the damper assembly around with a screwdriver if necessary.

11 Pour fresh oil into the fork until you can just see the surface when peering down into the fork leg. Work the fork up and down a few times so that the bottom of the fork fills up with fresh oil.

12 Fully compress the fork, then check the level with a tape measure. Adjust according to the maker's instructions. A lower oil level makes the fork softer at the end of it's travel, higher makes it stiffer.

Threaded headset

Stripping and greasing a headset is easy but fitting a new one requires special tools. This makes it a job for the bike shop.

When a bike is past its first youth, you may find the steering is not as smooth as it was. This could be because the headset needs stripping down and cleaning, although this should not be necessary more than once every couple of years, unless you ride the bike cross-country a lot.

But if the bike is a few years old, it is possible that the headset needs changing. Every time you go over a bump, the bearing race on top of the fork lifts and smashes the ball bearings into the bottom ball race. At the same time, the top bearing race is lifted away from the bearings, so it does not get battered in the same way. After this has happened many

thousands of times, tiny depressions form in the bottom races. The ball bearings then have to climb in and out of the depressions when you turn the steering, making it feel stiff and notchy. It can only be put right by fitting a new headset. It will also be difficult to wheel your bike straight.

Fitting a new headset is a job for your local bike shop because a special headset press is needed to remove and refit any type of headset.

Riding a bike with any amount of play in the headset increases the force with which the ball bearings smash into the top race. So if the front brakes start juddering or the bike 'knocks' over bumps, check for play and adjust immediately, otherwise the headset will wear out much faster.

LOCK NUT

TOP BEARING RACE

LOCK WASHER

HEAD TUBE

BOTTOM BEARING CUP

FORK CROWN RACE

FORK

CAGED BEARINGS

Most budget headsets are supplied with caged ball bearings instead of loose ones. Unless the cage is badly distorted, it is OK to re-use a caged bearing, although replacements are widely available.

Before refitting, clean the bearings with solvent, then rinse in water and carefully dry. Apply a little grease to the bearing race and press the caged bearing into it. The ball bearings must contact the bearing race, with the cage facing away from the bearing track. Finally, pack the space between the bearings, plus the cage itself, with grease

1 When stripping the headset on an MTB, disconnect the front brake. On a road bike, unbolt the front brake from the fork. Then undo the quill bolt, and lift the stem out of the frame. Let them hang down beside the bike.

2 Your next move is to undo the lock nut. A tight-fitting spanner is best but a pair of Stillson's or a big adjustable spanner will do. Most quality bikes have a soft alloy headset, which you will damage if you do not use the right spanner.

3 Below the lock nut is a tagged washer or spacer, or there may be a flat on one side of the steerer tube with a matching flat on the washer. Use a small screwdriver to prise the washer away from the top bearing race if necessary.

4 Unscrew the top race next. If the bike is standing on the floor, the steerer tube will stay in place. But if the bike is in a workstand, the forks will drop out as you undo the top race. Try to catch any loose bearings as they fall away.

5 If caged bearings are fitted, they will probably stay in place, so prise them out. Clean all the parts with solvent and a rag, then inspect all four bearing tracks for wear. Look very closely for dimpling on the bottom race and fork race.

6 Stick the bearings in the races with waterproof grease, and grease the crown race. Thread the steerer tube up through the head tube and then screw on the top race to hold it there. Adjust the top race to eliminate any play.

7 If the bearings cannot be removed from the races, flush the old grease and dirt out with solvent, then dry and grease. A grease injector is ideal because it will force the grease into the bearings better than your finger can.

8 Fit the washer and lock nut, then screw it right down. Turn the forks to check there is no friction. Adjust the top race to take out any movement in the forks. Then tighten the lock nut and check again for friction and play in the forks.

WHEN YOU NEED TO DO THIS JOB:
◆ The bike is due for a general overhaul.
◆ There is a judder when you turn a sharp corner or apply the brakes hard.
◆ Turning the handlebars requires effort or the steering is not smooth and accurate.

TIME:
◆ 30 minutes if you just lift the handlebars and let them hang down.
◆ 40 minutes if you decide to remove the handlebars completely.

DIFFICULTY: 🔧🔧🔧
◆ It is not too difficult to strip down, grease and adjust a headset, especially if you've got suitable spanners. Do not try fitting a new headset because you need a proper headset press to position the bearing races accurately in the frame.

SPECIAL TOOLS:
◆ Headset spanners.

O-RINGS AND SEALS
Watch out for very thin rubber O-rings in grooves around the bearing cups. These are very effective at keeping water out but must not be stretched or broken because you will not get replacements. Off-road and touring bikes should be fitted with the additional external seals available at bike shops.

Aheadset headsets

Aheadset and similar systems are very different from threaded headsets. The biggest difference is that they are held together by the handlebar stem, which clamps onto the unthreaded steerer tube and presses downwards onto the top bearing. See page 145 for a diagram.

To adjust the bearings on an Aheadset, you first loosen the compression bolt that holds the stem cap in place. Then loosen the clamp bolts on the stem and press it down onto the top bearing race. To get the pressure right, the bearing has to be 'pre-loaded'.

This is done by tightening the compression bolt, which forces the stem cap down onto the stem. The stem then presses down onto the bearing, applying the pre-load. Ideally, the amount of pre-load should be set with a torque wrench. But using two fingers only to apply a moderate force to the compression bolt works nearly as well. Anyway, you always have to balance between too much pre-load, making the steering feel tight, and not enough pre-load, causing the forks to knock over bumps.

After applying the pre-load, check that the forks turns easily, without any play or movement. Loosen the compression bolt and then re-apply the pre-load if there seems to be a problem. Finally, tighten the clamp bolts on the stem to lock in the pre-load.

Mountain bikes are usually fitted with $1^1/8$in Aheadset components, road bikes with 1in. But some road bikes also use $1^1/8$in headsets and there are a few bikes around with $1^1/{16}$in.

The only drawbacks of the Aheadset system are that the star washer in the steerer tube is not very strong, although better systems are available - see page 145. And it is impossible to adjust the handlebar height more than about $^1/2$in. For more adjustment, you have to fit an angled stem.

To keep out water and dirt, cartridge bearings are now supplied with good-quality Aheadsets. Fitting and adjustment is the same, but be careful to fit the cartridge the right way up.

Most new bikes are fitted with a stem, headset and forks designed as a single set of components.

STEM CAP

COMPRESSION BOLT

STAR NUT

Cartridge bearings

1 When stripping a headset, check the cartridge bearings are OK by turning the top and bottom halves in opposite directions with your thumb. If it feels gritty or sticky, prise out the seal using the blade of a utility knife and lift it away.

2 Then separate the two halves and wipe away the old grease. Clean all the parts with solvent, then check for indentations and severe wear in the bearing tracks. If all is well, re-assemble with fresh grease and press the seal back.

VARIATIONS ON THE BASIC DESIGN

Within the basic Aheadset design, there are many small differences. Sometimes the compression bolt is neatly hidden by a rubber plug, and there maybe a cover for the top race fastened to the steerer tube with three tiny socket-headed grub screws.

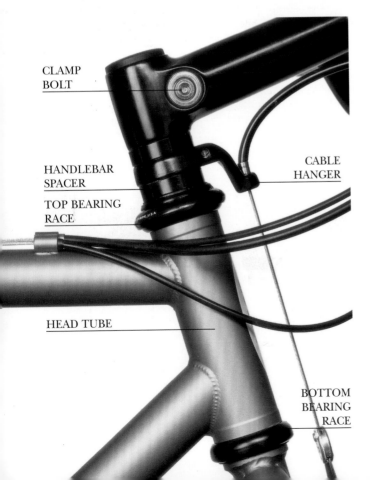

CLAMP BOLT

HANDLEBAR SPACER

TOP BEARING RACE

CABLE HANGER

HEAD TUBE

BOTTOM BEARING RACE

Stripping and refitting an Aheadset

1 Remove the stem cap, which is held in place with a compression bolt that screws into the star nut inside the steerer tube. Loosen off the clamp bolts, usually located at the back of the stem itself.

2 Lift the stem away and then take off any spacers and the top bearing cover, often fitted with cartridge bearings. The only thing stopping the forks dropping out now is the compression ring, so take care.

3 The compression ring is usually split. If it will not move, prise it out using the tip of a blade. Hold the fork in place as you do so, or the weight will make it difficult to shift the compression ring.

4 Push the compression ring up the steerer tube. This will give you enough room to lift away the cartridge bearing, or the top bearing race, whichever is fitted. There may also be a seal for the bearing.

5 Now let the forks drop down out of the frame. Remove the bottom bearings or cartridge and clean away the old grease so you can examine all the bearing races and bearings for pitting and wear.

6 Check that the cartridge bearings (if fitted) turn smoothly. But if caged bearings are fitted, pack them and the bearing races with fresh grease. Fit the bearings into the races, then grease the fork race.

7 Lift the forks back into position. Fit the top bearings or cartridge and hold the forks in the frame by pushing the compression ring back down into the angle of the bearing. See below for the final stages.

WHEN YOU NEED TO DO THIS JOB:
◆ During a major overhaul.
◆ If the steering is stiff.
◆ When the forks seem to judder in the frame.

TIME:
◆ 30 minutes. This type of headset is simpler to work on, so you probably will not need to take the brake levers and shifters off.

DIFFICULTY:
◆ The hardest thing about this job is grasping how it is all held together.

Fitting a clamp-on stem

1 You may find it easier to fit the stem if you tie the forks in place. Slip any spacers onto the steerer tube, then hold the forks with one hand and press the stem down onto the top bearing with the other.

2 Clean and grease the thread of the compression bolt, then screw it into the star nut. At this stage, leave the clamp bolts loose but check again that the stem is pressing evenly onto the top bearing.

3 Tighten up the compression bolt using two fingers. Check that the forks turn easily, and that you cannot feel any slack or play in the headset if you waggle the forks. Re-set the pre-load if necessary.

4 Do up the clamp bolts lightly, then line up the stem with the front wheel. Once you are sure that the steering is exactly aligned, tighten the clamp bolts fully. Check again, then road test.

Make yourself visible

Only a few new bikes have lights. That is a nuisance but a certain amount of preparation will turn any bike into a safe, 24-hour machine.

Legally, your bike must be equipped with one white front light and one red rear one, both marked to show they comply with British Standard 6102. It must also have a white reflector at the front and a red reflector at the rear. The rear reflector is allowed to be part of the rear light itself. According to current legislation, you can only attach a flashing light to a bike when a BS-marked light is also fitted. However, you only need to see a bike with a flashing light to realise how well they work, even in a street saturated with light.

Flashing lights do not have a conventional bulb. Instead, the light is generated electronically by means of a Light Emitting Diode (LED). These are vastly more efficient than a bulb with a filament so although tiny, the batteries have a long life. LED lights usually have a switch with three positions – off, steady and flashing. Theoretically therefore, they could pass the British Standard but most do not produce enough light to do so.

Battery-powered lights are the cheapest way of complying with the law, and, in conjunction with high-power halogen bulbs, they are quite bright until the batteries start to fade. Unfortunately, they fade fast and regular night riders often use rechargeable batteries to get around this problem. Batteries last longer with standard tungsten bulbs but are nowhere near as bright.

Various forms of dynamo use the rider's own energy to power the lighting. The commonest variety runs off the side of the tyre but there is an argument that the roller tends to slip. To prevent this happening, some dynamos are mounted under the bottom bracket. In this position it is possible to fit a much larger, slip-resistant roller.

Maybe the best solution for regular winter bike riders is the rechargeable battery which fits in a bottle cage. The lights are connected to this battery with electrical wire. When the lights dim or as part of a weekly routine, you recharge the battery as you would a car battery.

New batteries and bulbs

1 LED lights usually have a switch at the back, plus a clip for fixing the light to your clothing. That is legal, so long as a BS light is attached to the bike itself. The top left light is one of the few LED lights that meets the British Standard.

2 LED lights have a close-fitting plastic case. To fit new batteries, locate the notch where the red lens meets the black casing. Place the tip of a screwdriver in the notch and prise the case apart. Take care not to damage the rubber seal.

THE HIGHWAY CODE
The latest edition of the Highway Code has a lot of helpful advice for cyclists and cycling. So get a copy to bring yourself up to date, especially about cycle lanes and the areas being created in front of the other traffic for cyclists at busy traffic lights.

Fitting a dynamo

1 The best modern dynamos do not leave you in the dark when you stop. They have a capacitor that charges up as you ride and this keeps the light going. They also have a voltage regulator to stop bulbs burning out going downhill.

2 Fit the dynamo mounting round the fork blade so that the roller lines up with the file pattern on the tyre wall. Then loosen the angle bolt and adjust the position of the dynamo until the roller forms a right-angle with the spokes.

High-visibility clothing

3 Check frequently that your lights are working at full power. If not, change the batteries but when replacing bulbs. Do not touch the glass at all, especially if it is a halogen type. Keep spare bulbs and batteries at home.

1 Always dress in bright colours so that you get noticed when cycling, even during the day. But if you cycle a lot at night, go for a proper yellow cycling jersey with a reflective patch where it will show up best to motorists.

2 Foul-weather clothing is available in many colours but again, fluorescent yellow is best. Some of the latest waterproof jackets also have flecks of reflective material. They shimmer in headlights and cannot be ignored.

3 Track mitts padded with shock absorbent gel give you a more comfortable ride and protect hands from dirt and abrasions. If you go for ones with a reflective back, they make your hand signals stand out at night.

CLEANING THE CONTACTS

All bike lights start to give problems eventually. To get them working properly again, remove the batteries and check the contacts for greenish deposits. Remove these with a screwdriver and spray with aerosol lube. Give the switch a squirt as well, turning it on and off several times so that the aerosol lube gets to all parts.

A FEW REFLECTIONS

Plastic reflective material is one of the most cost-effective road safety precautions there is. Compared with the tiny light output of almost any bike light, reflective

materials are much more noticeable, throwing a large, unmissable patch of bright light back at other road users.

Among the most effective items are the arm and leg bands. These are almost always on the move, so they alert even the doziest driver to the fact that you are on the road and need room to manoeuvre. Sam Brown belts that go round the shoulders and waist are not quite as effective. You can also fix self-adhesive reflective material to frames, preferably to the back and the sides. However, pedal and wheel reflectors are more effective than anything else, although they do not fit all pedals.

3 Remove the paint on the frame under the grub screw on the mounting clip, coat with petroleum jelly and refit. Earth the lights in the same way. Then run the wires to the front and rear lights, keeping them as short as possible.

4 To prevent wiring problems, attach all wires neatly to the frame with zip ties. Apply spray lube to the connections and tighten lightly with a spanner if necessary. Road test to check that the lights work properly.

Frame-fitted equipment

You can fit almost anything on a bike frame, from a tool kit to panniers with enough luggage space for a world tour.

For winter riding, mudguards are more-or-less essential if you want to use your bike day in, day out. Especially if you count on getting home from work fairly dry. Luckily, the quality of mudguards and mudguard fittings has improved a lot in recent years. The best mudguards for road bikes are high grade plastic but even the thinnest stainless-steel mudguards are now strong enough to support the weight of a bike.

Nevertheless, mudguard stays are notorious for coming loose and getting caught in the wheel. If that happens, a nasty crash counts as coming off lightly, so tighten the frame and mudguard stay fixings frequently. Better still, go for the stays with a special fixing that allows them to be ripped away from the frame before the mudguard itself or debris from the road gets caught in the wheel and stops you dead.

If a frame has no mudguard or luggage rack mountings, there is a variety of kits available that will allow you to fit them neatly and securely.

Luggage racks and carriers often share mounting points with mudguards, although for enjoyable touring, separate mountings are a very big plus. Do not be tempted to compromise on the quality of racks or panniers because if they sway during cornering or threaten to burst open, they take away all the pleasure.

You can also fit bags to the handlebars. But low-mounted front panniers on a proper rack are a better solution because they keep the centre of gravity low, and that means better bike control.

On everyday bikes, a D-lock with a clip to mount it on the frame is the best security device. They are no problem to carry around, good quality ones are available at reasonable prices and are always there when you want them. But you must always lock your bike to an immovable object and put the lock shackle around the wheel rim and the frame for full security.

Bottle bosses

1 Bottle cages are designed to fit standard bottle bosses. Most bikes have one or two pairs. Just undo the socket head screw, position the cage and replace the screw.

2 Full-size bike pumps are fitted to the frame. But mini-pumps can be mounted on clips that screw onto the bottle bosses under the bottle cage, making room for both.

Fitting mudguards and racks

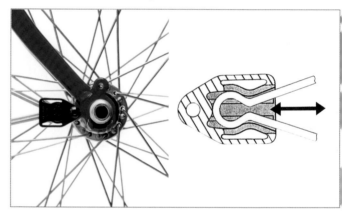

1 Secu Clip stainless steel mudguard stays are fitted to the frame through the hole at the back of the plastic fitting. If anything gets caught in the front wheel, the V-shaped stay just pulls out of the plastic fitting. These stay are available separately and can be fitted to most types of road bike mudguard.

5 Once you have fitted a rack, you can carry some things using an elastic luggage strap. But do not let the strap dangle or it will get caught in the back wheel. Pannier bags allow you to carry much more. Ideally, they should be tailored to fit the rack you are using.

TASTELESS
Aluminium drinking bottles are expensive, but they are far less likely to add a nasty taste to your drink than plastic ones. In winter, well-equipped riders use vacuum flasks tailored to fit the standard bottle cage.

Bicycle locks

1 Although heavy and ugly, the frame-mounted D-lock is one of the best ways of stopping thieves going off with your bike. However, some riders prefer to save weight by using a lock and chain.

2 The lock holder should be plastic-covered, so it does not damage your frame and does not squeak. Adjust the third screw so that when you operate the lever, the clip grips the lock securely.

3 When buying a D-lock, check that the shackle is large enough to go round a post, through your back wheel and frame and take in the front wheel rim, if you remove it from the forks.

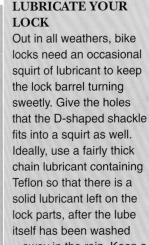

LUBRICATE YOUR LOCK

Out in all weathers, bike locks need an occasional squirt of lubricant to keep the lock barrel turning sweetly. Give the holes that the D-shaped shackle fits into a squirt as well. Ideally, use a fairly thick chain lubricant containing Teflon so that there is a solid lubricant left on the lock parts, after the lube itself has been washed away in the rain. Keep a spare key at home.

2 Slide the mudguard bridge so that the tab contacts the back of the brake bridge. Thread the brake fixing bolt through the tab and fit the nut and washer. Tighten up the tabs on the mudguard bridge with pliers, adjust the stay length and tighten everything.

3 If there are brazed-on eyes fitted to the chainstays, bolt the top carrier mountings to them. Otherwise use the brake fixing bolt. Then bolt the rack supports to the frame via the mudguard eyes. Use washers and self-locking nuts to prevent it coming loose.

4 If no luggage mountings are fitted, you can slip a neat clip onto the seat post instead. These clips are especially suitable for small bikes, where there is often not enough clearance for normal seat stay mountings.

CATCH CRUD

Crud catchers take only a few moments to fit onto the down tube of a normal style MTB. They are held in place either by strong elastic straps or with touch-and-close fastenings, so they can be fitted in moments if rain seems to threaten.

Crud catchers can be fitted to frames of almost any shape, including Y-frames. However, they can only cope with light rain and mud, not a deluge.

6 If you do not want to fit permanent mudguards, there is a large range of clip-on guards that will do the job OK. Some are for road bikes and clip on rapidly just for wet days. Others are for mountain bikes and fit around vee brakes, suspension forks and rear suspension. Most will cope with flying mud as well as rain.

WHAT DOES THAT MEAN?

This section explains the meaning of words often used by bike enthusiasts, including any technical words that the author has been forced to use in this book.

A

AHEADSET: *a design and brand of headset that has now largely taken over from the traditional threaded type. Can only be used with threadless forks and a clamp-on stem. Similar designs are produced by many other firms under licence.*

ALLEN KEY: *six-sided, l-shaped tool that fits into the socket of a socket-head bolt. Referred to as a hexagon key in this book.*

ALLOY: *usually short for aluminium alloy. A mixture of metals, often including copper*

and zinc, with better characteristics than a pure one.

ALLOY RIMS: *nearly all bikes have wheel rims made of aluminium alloy. Steel is the cheaper alternative material but the braking surface is so smooth that it is hard to stop quickly.*

ANTI-SEIZE GREASE: *a light grease often with powdered metal, usually copper. It is used to separate different metals, so preventing them seizing together.*

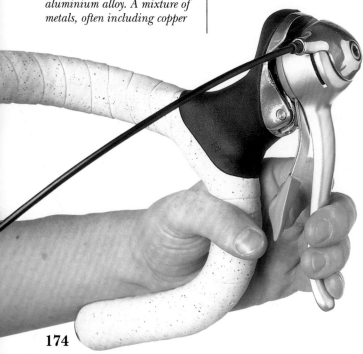

AXLE: *the central part of a hub or some other bearing assembly.*

B

BALL BEARING: *usually a hard-chromed, perfectly round, steel ball that fits between the cup and cone in bike bearings. Also means the complete assembly of inner and outer race plus ball bearings, as used in a cartridge bottom bracket and some hubs.*

BAR ENDS: *look like cow horns bolted to the ends of straight handlebars. Now mainly replaced by raised handlebars on cross-country MTBs.*

BEADS: *stiff inner edge of a tyre that engages with the hook on the inside edge of a clincher rim. Usually made of wire or Kevlar.*

BEARINGS: *any part designed to minimise the friction and wear in a rotating or sliding assembly. On a bike, the main bearings are the headset, bottom bracket and hub bearings.*

BOTTLE BOSS: *threaded insert used for attaching bottle cages and other items to the frame.*

BOTTOM BRACKET: *the bearings, bearing cups and axle that carry the chainset.*

BOTTOM BRACKET SHELL: *the housing at the bottom of the seat and down tubes into which the bottom bracket is fitted.*

BRAKE MODULATOR: *adjusts the amount of force needed to apply the brake. Not normally used.*

BRAZED-ON FITTING: *items like bottle bosses and lever bosses fixed to the frame.*

BUTT: *the thickened end of a tube. See double-butted.*

C

CABLE CAP: *a soft metal sleeve that is crimped on to the end of a cable to prevent it fraying.*

CABLE STOP: *a hollow tube or socket brazed on to the frame. The outer cable fits into one end, while the inner cable passes out of the other. Often slotted so that you can pull the outer cable out, without disconnecting the inner.*

CANTILEVER BRAKES: *attached to the frame via brazed-on pivots on the fork blades and chain stays. Fitted to many older mountain bikes because mud does not build up around them. Replaced by vee brakes.*

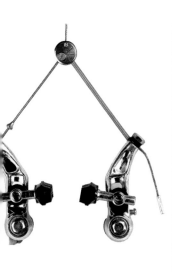

CARBON FIBRE: *high-strength, high-cost material mainly used for making forks for road bikes. Also used for complete frames, seat posts and many other high-end components.*

CARTRIDGE BOTTOM BRACKET: *bottom bracket bearing in which the axle runs on two or three sealed ball bearings, enclosed in a metal sleeve.*

CASSETTE: *a set of 7, 8, 9 or 10 sprockets which mount onto a freehub body. A freewheel mechanism fits inside the freehub body .*

CENTRE PULL BRAKES: *a brake with two separate arms independently mounted on a backplate. Powerful and reliable, but no longer made.*

CENTRE-TO-CENTRE: *usual way of measuring frame size. Distance from centre of the bottom bracket axle to centre of top tube. Given in either inches or centimetres.*

CENTRING: *usually refers to adjusting the position of a brake in such a way that the brake pads are equally spaced from the braking surface. Centring screws for this purpose are fitted to vee and dual pivot brakes. Can also refer to fitting a back wheel so that it is equally spaced between the chain stays.*

CHAIN CAGE: *on a rear mech, the chain cage consists of both jockey wheels and the side plates. Tensions and guides the chain.*

CHAIN STAY: *the small diameter tube that runs between the bottom bracket and the drop out. It is usually ovalised near the bottom bracket but some modern frames use square-section tubes. May be curved or S-shaped.*

CHAINRING: *the toothed part of the chainset which engages with the chain. Usually removable.*

CHAINSET: *together the chainrings and cranks are known as the chainset.*

CHROME MOLYBDENUM OR CRO-MOLY: *a steel alloy often used for frames and forks. Can be welded, so cro-moly tubing is ideal for budget bikes.*

CLINCHERS: *detachable tyres that are held on to the wheel rim by stiff beads that clinch under the raised edges of the rim.*

CLUSTER: *usually short for sprocket cluster. Cassette.*

COGS: *non-cyclists often speak of the chainring and sprockets as cogs because they are toothed.*

COLUMBUS: *Italian maker of high-quality frame tubing.*

COTTERLESS CRANKS: *cranks that bolt on to the shaped end of the bottom bracket axle.*

COTTER PINS: *slightly tapered steel pins with one flat side that holds the cranks on to the bottom bracket axle. Little used in modern times.*

CRANKS: *long arms that carry the pedals and transmit the rider's energy to the chainring.*

CUP AND CONE BEARING: *the standard bike bearing, which consists of loose or caged ball bearings between a semi-circular cup and a tapered cone. They are adjusted by moving the threaded part in or out until they turn freely, without play.*

D

DEGREASER: *any solvent that will dissolve grease. Includes paraffin, diesel fuel and various ecologically acceptable brand-name products.*

DERAILLEUR: *French word for gearing sytems that work by 'derailling' the chain from one sprocket to another.*

DIAMOND FRAME: *the standard shape for a bike frame since about 1890. Mountain bikes usually have a modified diamond frame.*

DISC BRAKE: *a brake using a flat rotor fitted to the hub and a caliper that carries the pads on the fork leg or chain stay.*

DOUBLE-BUTTED: *lightweight frame tubing which is thin in the middle for lightness, and thicker at the ends where maximum strength is required.*

DOWN TUBE: *usually the largest diameter part of the frame. Runs from the head tube to the bottom bracket.*

DROP OUT: *part of the frame that carries the front or back wheel.*

DUAL-PIVOT BRAKES: *a brake for road bikes using a Y arm and a C arm mounted on a backplate. More compact than centre pulls and more powerful than side pulls.*

E

EXPANDER BOLT: *long bolt carried by the upright part of the stem. Screws into the cone that expands the base of the stem and holds it into the steerer.*

F

FAST ROAD BIKE: *a bike with flat handlebars but buiilt like a sports bike in nearly every other way. Faster and more agile than a hybrid.*

FIXED WHEEL: *single sprocket on the rear hub, without a freewheel. Whenever the bike is moving, the rider has to pedal.*

FORK CROWN: *the top part of the forks, where they join the steerer tube. Often formed out of the fork blade itself.*

FORK END: *the part of the fork that carries the front wheel.*

FORKS: *the steerable part of the frame that holds the front wheel.*

FRAME ANGLES: *the angle between the top tube and seat tube; and between the top tube and head tube. Greatly influences how the bike behaves on the road.*

FREEHUB: *rear hub with the freewheel mechanism in the cassette body. Replaced hubs with separate freewheels to allow 7, 8, 9 and 10 sprockets without weakening the axle.*

FREEWHEEL: *most sprockets are mounted on a freewheel mechanism, which allows you to coast along without pedalling.*

FRONT MECH: *short for front-gear mechanism. Also called the front derailleur. Swaps the chain from one chainring to another. Two chainrings multiplies the number of gears by two. Three chainrings multiplies the number by three.*

G

GEAR HANGER: *part of the rear drop out that provides a mounting for the rear mech. Can be separate from, or part of, the frame.*

GEAR RANGE: *the gap between the lowest gear and the highest.*

GEAR RATIO: *the distance that a bike moves for each revolution of the cranks. In a low gear, this is about 1m (40in) per revolution and around 2.7m (110in) in a high one.*

H

HAMMER: *a tool of desperation and last resort.*

HEADSET: *the top and bottom bearings pressed into the head tube to support the forks and allow them to steer. The bottom bearing is subject to very heavy impact loads, so the races eventually become indented.*

HEAD TUBE: *the shortest frame tube. Fits between the top and down tubes. Can be almost non-existent on very small frames.*

HIGH GEAR: *a gear ratio in which you travel a long way for every revolution of the cranks. In high, the chain is on the largest chainring and one of the smaller sprockets.*

HUB GEARS: *alternative gearing system for city and leisure bikes. Contained within an enlarged rear hub. 3-, 5- and 7-speed versions are now available but they all tend to be heavy and absorb a lot of energy.*

HYBRID: *bike combining some mountain bike components and often sprung front forks with larger 700C or 650C wheels and a fairly upright design of frame. Faster than an MTB but purely for road use.*

I

INDEXED GEARS: *derailleur gears and changers designed together so that the changer has a definite position for each gear. Click stops usually indicate each gear position but STi and Ergopower levers work on strokes of the changer levers.*

J

JOCKEY WHEELS: *small wheels in the chain cage of the rear mech that guide the chain round the sprockets.*

K

KEVLAR: *high-strength artificial fibre used for reinforcing tyres, saddles and other components.*

KNOBBLIES: *deeply treaded MTB tyres for high grip in mud.*

L

LEISURE BIKE: *an often heavily styled bike for short distance use on hard surfaces. Can be fitted with hub gears. Also known as a cruiser bike or city bike.*

LOW GEAR: *a gear ratio in which you move a short distance for every revolution of the cranks. Used for climbing hills and off-road riding.*

LUBE: *short for lubricant, especially when packed in an aerosol can or grease gun.*

LUG: *a complex steel sleeve mostly used to join the main tubes of a steel frame.*

N

NIPPLE: *square metal nut that passes through the rim and screws on to the spoke, allowing the wheel to be tensioned by tightening up the nipple.*

P

PHILLIPS SCREWDRIVER: *screwdriver with cross-shaped tip. Sizes 1 and 2 are both used on bikes but not interchangeable.*

PLAY: *unwanted movement in a bearing due to wear or incorrect adjustment. Sometimes spoken of as 'a couple of millimetres play' or similar.*

PRESTA VALVE: *found mainly on sports and racing bike tyres. Has a knurled brass nut on the stalk to keep the valve shut.*

Q

QUICK-RELEASE: *a mechanism that allows you to remove a bike wheel by operating the quick-release lever. Also refers to other quick-release (q/r) items like seat post clamps and panniers.*

QUILL STEM: *handlebar stem with wedge fixing, only suitable for use with threaded forks.*

R

RACE: *the part of a bearing assembly in contact with the ball bearings. Can be fixed or not.*

REAR MECH: *short for rear gear mechanism or rear derailleur.*

ROADSTER: *old-fashioned sit-up-and-beg bike usually seen in the hands of old ladies and the police force.*

S

SCHRADER VALVE: *car-type tyre valve with a separate insert. Larger than a Presta valve.*

SEAT POST: *tube that fits into the seat tube and supports the saddle.*

SEAT STAY: *the small-diameter tube that runs between the seat lug and the drop out. Key-hole stays are S-curved for resiliance.*

SEAT TUBE: *the large-diameter frame tube which supports the saddle and bottom bracket.*

SHIFTER: *gear changer. Any mechanism for changing gear.*

SIDE-PULL BRAKE: *brake used on road bikes. The brake cable is connected to both brake arms at the side of the brake assembly.*

SLICKS: *smooth tyres used on mountain bikes for road riding.*

SPIDER: *the part of the chainset that the chainrings are bolted to.*

SPOKE: *round or flat wire that connects the hub to the rim.*

SPRINTS: *very light wheels and tyres used for road and track racing. The tube is sewn into the tyre and the whole thing is then stuck to the rim.*

SPRAY LUBE: *a silicon or Teflon-based aerosol lubricant. Types for general use and specialist bike lubes with a solid lubricant particularly for chains are both used on bikes.*

SPROCKET: *a toothed wheel or wheels that take drive from the chain to the hub.*

SPROCKET CLUSTER: *collective name for all the sprockets on a back wheel. Also cassette.*

STEERER TUBE: *tube connecting the handlebar stem to the fork crown, inside the head tube. Turns with the handlebars.*

STEM: *connects to the steerer tube, supports the handlebars. Various lengths are available to suit the build of the rider.*

STI: *combined brake and gear levers for sports and racing bikes, made by Shimano.*

STRADDLE CABLE: *short cable that joins two independent brake arms. Found on centre pull and cantilever brakes.*

SUSPENSION FORKS: *forks that allow the front wheel to move up and down to absorb bumps. Usually controlled by some sort of spring and a gas or fluid damper mechanism to minimise bounce and rebound.*

T

TOE-IN: *usually measured in millimetres. Refers to fitting brake pads closer to the rim at the front than at the back.*

TOP TUBE: *the tube joining the seat tube to the head tube. It is usually horizontal but compact road frames and most MTBs have a sloping top tube.*

TRANSMISSION: *all the components that deal with transmitting power from the rider's legs to the back wheel. Chainset, chain and sprockets, plus the front and rear mechs.*

TUBULARS: *a tyre where the tube is sewn inside the tread and carcase. Used with sprints only.*

TYRE VALVE: *device that holds*

air pressure in a tyre. Part of the tube unless tubeless tyres and wheels are fitted.

TYRE WALL: *also sidewall. The thinner part of a tyre between the tread and the bead. Often coloured to contrast with the black of the tread.*

TYRE – 700C: *the type of tyre normally fitted to sports/racers, and hybrids. Thin and light.*

V

VEE BRAKE: *standard design of cantilever brake for MTBs. The long brake arms bolt onto standard pivot bosses but are vertical, which increases leverage and allows the cable to pull directly on the brake arm.*

W

WHEEL RIM: *the outer part of a bike wheel that carries the tyre. Also the braking surfaces. Made of steel, alloy or carbon fibre.*

WISHBONE STAY: *design of chainstay in which the two tubes from the rear drop outs join above the back wheel. They are then connected to the seat tube by a larger single tube. Often made in carbon fibre in one piece with the chain stays.*

INDEX

FOR THE FOURTH EDITION, THE AUTHOR AND PUBLISHER WOULD LIKE TO THANK

◆ Alan Hewitt and Caroline Griffiths of Shimano (Madison)
◆ Graham Snodden and David Ward of SRAM
◆ Carole Armstrong and Dave Mayo of Specialised
◆ Peter Plummer of Venhill Engineering
◆ Lucy Raines of Scott Cycles
◆ Terry Bill of Reynolds Tubes
◆ Cedric Chicken, Chicken & Sons
◆ Andrew Willis of Select Cycle Components (Campagnolo)
◆ Neil Keen, Greyville Enterprises
◆ Hetty and David Bennett-Baggs of Weldtite
◆ John Phillips of Extra (UK) Ltd
◆ Andrew Ritchie of Brompton Cycles
◆ Joe O"Brien of Fibrax
◆ Martin Hall of Raleigh
◆ Zyro PLC
◆ Chris Compton, Compton Cycles
◆ Ian Young of Moore Large
◆ Ali and Chris Boon of Yeovil Cycle Centre/Tri UK

From the author, particular thanks to James Robertson and Louise McIntyre of Haynes, who made working on the Bike Book a very happy experience.

To Sally Mitchell, for a lot of support and tolerance.

To Paul Buckland and Peter Trott of the Haynes Project Workshop, for making me very welcome there.

And to Sandy and Sarah of York Cycle Works, 01904 626664, for advice on women's bikes.

Photographic credits
Key: t top, b bottom, l left, r right, m middle
Nick Pope: 36bl, bm, br; 37
Stockfile:4bl, br; 5; 17
Front Cover: Image Bank (Kenneth Redding); Tim Ridley, Steve Behr and Stockfile (Steve Behr, Bob Smith, Mark Gallup and Sue Darlow) Venhill Engineering, E.Reece/Univega, Dawes Cycles.